urteen Vagabond Fourteen Vagab

Things Written Randomly in Doubt

by
Allan Cameron

The work of a fool who has stumbled through life and, quite inexplicably, survived. Someone who can stumble that well should be listened to – not to evoke your consensus but your stupefaction at the random blows of fate that have allowed such a tiresome mischief-maker to continue with his rant.

Vagabond Voices
Glasgow

Published on 19 May by
Vagabond Voices Publishing Ltd.,
Glasgow,
Scotland.

ISBN: 978-1-908251-27-5

Printed and bound in Poland

Cover design by Mark Mechan

Typeset by Park Productions

The author acknowledges subsidy from Creative Scotland towards the writing of this book

For further information on Vagabond Voices, see the website,
www.vagabondvoices.co.uk

*In memory of Eric Hobsbawm whose friendship,
kindness and conversation I miss*

Things Written Randomly in Doubt

Contents

How Not to Be a Ruminant

I

Life is a serious affair that has to be treated light-heartedly.

To be light-hearted in the face of so much misery and remain human requires an effort of will.

Humour is a release, but not the purpose of life. Humour is an acceptance that not every wrong can be righted. The world should be turned upside down, but when it is the bottom floats to the top again.

Change is needed, but so is time. Hence the mix of gravity and levity we all must seek out in measures suited to our own natures.

The recurring problem with revolutions is that some mediocrity always wants to embody them.

To make a sensible decision a person must first be certain of the parameters involved. As no wise person can ever be certain of anything, we must infer that no wise person can ever make a sensible decision.

As decisions must be taken to govern the state and develop our parasitic corporations, it must also follow that our lives are at the mercy of knaves and chancers who have no mercy.

Why do men who chew gum throw their well-chewed gum in urinals? If we could quantify the mass of this sticky, piss-steeped matter, would we have a measure of male vacuity?

Why, in fact, does anyone chew gum? Is it to imbestialate a ruminant? If so, is that gentle satire of another being or solidarity across the species? Neither. It is the instinct to switch off and give up on the tedious task of being a *homo sapiens*.

The only way to love the abstraction that is this curious cosmos we inhabit is to love and experience fully its many particulars individually. On the whole, abstractions are unlovely.

A good understanding of literature leads to disdain for too many books. That is why an old practitioner nostalgically recalls the joy of her teenage years when she read indiscriminately and was excited by the unfamiliarity of ideas and forms. To understand is one of our virtues, but it can undermine another more innocent one: delight in the mysteries of this world.

The wisest man never destroys the child within him, but the child will abandon him nevertheless – perhaps in disgust.
The limitations of the written word are what make it the greatest art, and the greatest artist is the reader.

A powerful man at whatever level of society will always convince himself that his tyranny is benign and his intentions pure. Richard III's honesty and self-knowledge are peculiarly attractive solely because they could never exist.

Malignity is banal, because it lacks self-awareness. Pure malignity would lack it altogether and certainly would not strut the antechambers to the throne room listing its evil intentions and delighting in their cunning.

Our forbears were in awe of the immensity of our world, which is now remarkable for its lonely finitude in undistinguished orbit of a workaday star. We are crushed between claustrophobia and the immense diversity of the circumscribed – a universe in a postage stamp.

By instinct unaffected by education, the young believe in free will and the old in predestination or necessity. The young are dazzled by their liberty and potential, their ability to invent themselves; the old are impressed by the solidity of their past and disappointed by its meagre results. How could they not believe in its inevitability?

To live a full life is not to be perverse, but it is to appear so.

To live a full life is to follow the path of reason unflinchingly. People will think that you're perverse, but you are only being prosaically reasonable.

All violence should be condemned, but the violence of the powerful the more so, because it goes unpunished.

Violence in a good cause corrupts the cause it champions, and therefore destroys what it wishes to attain long before it attains it.

Those who fought for Irish independence and then divided over how and when to end the war were all in the right, but fated to another fratricidal bloodletting amongst themselves. That's the essence of tragedy. Courage and justice cannot avoid paying the tribute of violence: sparkling necessities and senseless brutalities mirrored in the sluggish waters of history.

The Scots, offered a peaceful route to independence, do not deserve it if, unconscious of their luck, they fail to vote for it.

To become an independent country and remain simply that would reveal a lack of vision. Every national independence must have a narrative that is both honest and moral. That the finger-waggers and finger-pointers will abuse it and exploit it for their own purposes does not remove the need to clarify the narrative.

The British Empire was an Anglo-Scottish empire, and Scotland – the junior partner as Britain is to America today – must compensate the world it injured by providing a new definition of what a nation is.

In politics and war, the most common tactical mistake is to use the tactic most successful in the past or elsewhere.

To love specific humans brings with all its joys the terror of loss.

To love the universality of humans is to be emboldened by the insignificance of the loss of oneself.

Beware of those who love the universality of humans without loving any specific ones. They are, at best, prophets of dull philosophies or, at worst, ferocious megalomaniacs of the left.

Admire and learn from those who love both the universality of humans and some specific ones. They are not so rare as we often think. It is the condition most of us would seek, if we weren't embarrassed by the idea of it.

Such a man was Jesus: not God dressed up in human form, but something less improbable and more divine: a man like any other, a complete man at ease with his God and unfrightened by his fate.

Admire the Christ-like, who may never have heard of Jesus, and shun bloodthirsty Christians, who would be considered oxymorons if they were not so numerous.

Some argue that nations do not exist, because they're abstractions that in reality lack uniformity and evolve, eventually dying. When they argue this, they explain the reasons for the existence of nations.

Nationalism as a solid state is a source of great cruelty. Its myths blind its peoples to reason. "Eternal" nations cannot last, and are outlived by more flexible neighbours.

A nation that does not belong to all humanity is a province.

A small nation can be less provincial than a large one, precisely because it cannot live wholly within itself.

Christianity is a pacifist religion in which all the major churches preach the concept of the just war, which goes back to pre-Christian times. Islam has the concept of the just war as part of its original credo but, excepting Wahhabism, it has been a slightly less bellicose religion in practice. Is a religion the better for not expecting too much of its believers? Or was the greatest misfortune to affect the followers of the dreamer of Gallilee that the religion he possibly did not intend to found became the state religion of an expansionist empire?

Did the universalist and egalitarian religion slightly improve the state that twisted it to its own political interests? Having become Christians, were the emperors slightly less afflicted by the madness of power? Good and evil mix in strange and unpredictable ways. Did the governors become better and did they benefit from the governed becoming more governable?

Distrust the pious, their masks disguise a mischievous desire to appear good.

Disdain the scoffers, they reduce existence to self-interest, a market and a jungle. They would have us and, perversely, themselves herded into a meadow of artificial grass.

To scoff at human nature is to build our prison walls.

Embrace the confused, their confusion expresses their loving intelligence.

Above all, beware the powerful, they perceive everyone as an instrument of their power.

If you're tired of my prescriptions, remember: you can always learn from a fool, and from a loser you can glimpse the advantages you lost through what little success you achieved in life.

To learn from a fool, you must first learn to distrust him.

II

Beware the powerful again: they can assist you and they can crush you. Better to be crushed than sell your soul.

Do we have any use for the idea of a free egalitarian society in which all can contribute and all can benefit in as equitable a fashion as possible without burdening that society with an over-inflated bureaucracy and installing a dismal rule by accountants? Of course we do. Hold it dear in your mind and learn to live in the society we have, whilst pinching your nose and keeping silent where silence is advised.

Silence is only an admission of your powerlessness. To support or, worse, to justify tyranny, however cleverly it dresses up its purposes, is an act of obeisance that will lead to others.

Happiness is elusive for those who seek after it.

Happiness passes unnoticed by those who achieve it, except in those moments of ecstasy.

Happiness is a product of love and creativity – both things that distract you from the self that undermines you from within.

Sometimes I have tired of London and sometimes, more seriously, I have tired of life, though not necessarily at the same time. But always life and London have revived my interest in them.

Is this surprising? Not at all, we all tire of our own lives and we tire of all places. Then we enthuse once again. Our condition is a cyclical one that fades in smaller and smaller circles, or is snuffed out.

If you fail, then fail spectacularly.

It takes as much work to fail spectacularly as it does to succeed spectacularly, and is more uncomfortable.

Discomfort keeps us alive – like a bed of nails.

To balance yourself unsteadily between success and failure produces a respectable and happy condition, which in the period of early capitalism was moderately achievable, but is now almost impossible – at least in the so-called "creative industries".

To succeed spectacularly in this field requires unscrupulousness and energy, assisted by a high degree of judicious mendacity, except a few who achieve it through a judicious mix of generous humanity and startling intellectual brilliance.

The high court of rumour and gossip is one in which the accused has no right to read the indictment and no right of appeal. Its sentence is final.

Jesus suffered on the cross because he unsettled the powerful with apparently innocuous truths. He did not die alone that day, nor did he in history.

The death of Jesus only has meaning if he was a man like you and I. He then comes to represent all the hundreds of millions of others – innocent and guilty – extinguished by power and hidden from history.

Even his message had and has been propogated by others, but that does not lessen its power. We should not turn our backs on the Christian ethic, just because we cannot believe in the Virgin Birth or the divinity of Christ.

His message and similar ones might have been argued by others, but churches have not been built in their names. He belongs to our history, and we speak the ethics of his stories as they have come down to us, battered and abused perhaps but still more vibrant than the sugared niceties of our materialistic *bien pensants*.

The pious are not necessarily those who believe in religion; they are those who believe in the moral rectitude of their own behaviour and wish to persuade everyone else of this act of faith.

The pious atheist is not the worst and most dangerous of the pious, but he is the most irritating and ridiculous – the most lacking in self-awareness.

The art of writing involves the avoidance of the sententious, except for the aphorism: brevity provides licence for the sweeping generalisation.

III

Tolerance is the oxygen of society.

To argue for tolerance is the primary task of any writer or intellectual. But is there anything new that can be said? The Italian philosopher Norberto Bobbio wondered about how tolerant we should be of the intolerant. We could also ask how tolerant we should be of those who are intolerant of the intolerant, because the intolerant will always be with us.

The intolerant are fractured human beings, and are therefore to be pitied. But in particular historical circumstances they are as dangerous as rabid dogs. Our tolerance should be contingent.

In his desire to conjure up an original thought an intellectual will twist a thought one more time and in so doing become a mere conjurer who produces not truths but entertaining tricks.

The truth is often banal, but occasionally miraculous.

Few truths have been uncovered outside science, where every discovery reveals our ignorance and increases our bewilderment.

Perhaps not: this impetuous technological advance that undermines our humanity and deskills us provides an opportunity to generate new ideas on our demise.

It is an opportunity to grumble our way out of existence. There will be some slight splenetic pleasure in that.

A programmer will eventually write the software to produce novels mechanically. It won't change things much: writers are already programmed by accountancy and market research.

IV

The peoples of Tasmania were visited by a plague of particularly virulent parasites that wiped them from the face of the earth: the parasites were called the British and came in the name of sweet religion and the wealth of nations, concepts unknown to the Tasmanians and we will never know what useful concepts they may have developed.

"Why do you always belittle our own potentates?" you ask. "They are not the only ones in the world." You're right, of course, but so what? A gadfly must act the gadfly, and a horse must act the horse. Would a gadfly go up to a horse's ear and whisper, "My dear horse, I promise not to bite you or torment you. I will only afflict the other horses. All I ask in return is that you allow me to make my home in your hair and appoint me king of the gadflies." A gadfly is an ugly little creature that quickly populates the air, but it has its purpose.

Satirists are the most effective gadflies, because they only have to ridicule the status quo; they do not have to propose any alternatives.

To improve society, we must first ask the right questions.
In choosing the right questions, we are guided by our moral priorities.

There are many of these, but only two fundamental ones. Some of us are guided by the sanctity of property, and others by the sanctity of humans, by which we mean the right to a voice and to a creative and useful life.

By revealing the absurdities of our regimes and leaders, satirists pose important questions.

Satire, like charity, starts at home.

An intellectual who denounces crimes and abuses of power abroad, but ignores them at home, is no more than a pen for sale, a cultural mercenary. Now they are legion, and how thoroughly they chew their cud.

Abel Tasman gave his sponsor's name to the island, and others, much later, gave it his. He discovered it, because the Tasmanians were incapable of discovering anything, including the malignity of discoverers.

Lucky is the land that becomes a nation after the age of nationalism.

Lucky is the nation that, at its birth, does not cry, "We must go out bearing our precious civilisation and spread it round this unhappy world," but pleads instead, "Come to us, we have a nation yet to build."

Lucky is the land that does not wish to replicate itself.

Lucky is the land that, uncertain of who it is, explores its own interior.

The modern nation must blind itself to nationality. Its citizenship must be based on residency alone.

If you breathe our air, you belong.

V

Revolutionaries treat society as a surgeon treats his patient; they ruthlessly sever limbs they consider to be diseased. In other words, a revolutionary perceives a living human collectivity as an entity on which he can operate without reference to its own views. Society is objectified.

That ideas are held by impatient revolutionaries intent upon forcing the pace of history does not mean that their ideas are bad.

A revolutionary movement rarely wins if it has no constituency of support, although that constituency may not fully understand its intentions.

Advocates of the "free market" perceive society as an inert entity subject to natural laws, over which no one can exert any control or influence. The freedom they speak of would be like freedom for the weather. Society is objectified.

A true liberal believes that society is made by its human components, who are in constant dialogue with each other. No individual can make the weather, as everyone must be free to express their will.

A liberal-socialist adds two essential ideas to that of the liberal: justice is as important as freedom, and there can be no freedom where there are huge inequalities.

Revolutionaries often start as liberals but are militarised by the warfare that almost always follows a revolution. They become generals and think like generals, forgetting their original motives for the struggle.

Revolutionaries abolish the death penalty and then restore it.

Revolutionaries come to despise the people they wanted to liberate, and secretly yearn for a normalisation of relations with the reactionary states that surround them.

Revolutionaries are all different, but end up the same if their revolution is violent. That is a tragedy within a tragedy.

The rich and propertied always rise to the top, even in revolutionary organisations intent upon the abolition of property. Property provides confidence and leisure to improve one's skills.

Only non-violent revolution can retain the integrity of its participants. This is the age of non-violent revolution and it will last for as long as we can defend our hard-won human rights, which are currently being dismantled.

VI

There never was an absolute free market, a fully socialist nation or a genuinely sovereign state. Today the sovereign state is an increasingly distant reality. The era of mutually interdependent peoples – a nineteenth-century dream – may yet begin.

The age of "ethnicity" is over and the age of culture has begun.

Without biodiversity, humanity cannot survive. Without cultural diversity, human culture cannot survive.

The essence of global capitalism is uniformity, not diversity.

The essence of Taylorism, once beloved of both the United States and the Soviet Union, is productivity and not creativity.

All production can be done creatively, and only through creative production can we maintain diversity and our species and cultures.

Humanity is now god of this planet, and holds the destinies of living things in its hands. To govern it properly it must rediscover the gods to guide it.

Not the god of the market, not the god of pleasure, but the god of altruism and the god of duty. Ultimately it must rediscover the God of Love and Bewilderment.

Individuals create their essence after their existence, as Sartre claimed, but he failed to admit that society gives them the tools to do this.

Of the tools a society bequeaths an individual, its language is the most important one, closely followed by its culture and its religion.

A good society has a plurality of languages and a plurality of religions, which will enrich it with complexities.

An oppressive society may desire pluralities for a different reason: to create divisions and exploit them for the furtherance of oppressive behaviour. It is not diversity that undermines society; it is the way it is used by the powerful.

A religion allows an individual to reject it, accept it, mutate it or place it amongst the unknowable things that teach us most.

A language empowers individuals to express whatever they want and to depict in words the meanders of their imaginations.

A child that is brought up without a rich linguistic environment is a child deprived.

A child that is brought up without a religion or a substitute like humanism, or at least a political morality, is a child deprived of something to reject.

We learn to think up new ideas by rejecting others and observing the evolving reality around us. Deprived of the ability to do the first, the second becomes an exercise in vacuity.

VII

Belief in God does not presuppose belief in an afterlife.

God concerns our relationship with others, the truth and ourselves.

God requires closeness to others and distance from the self.

Forget about the next life, pie in the sky and greenshield stamps for being good! The next life, if it exists, will look after itself.

We make our own decisions and act upon them, and are the happier when we take responsibility for them too. The reward for virtuous behaviour, when it comes, comes in this world.

Whatever your religion or non-religion, never be certain of anything – not even your own god, lest you kill him with your own fanatic will. Not knowing is not the terror you thought it was.

The infinite possibilities of our human existence are an ocean on which you can navigate for a lifetime, and when you die not that much the wiser for your efforts, you will have experienced life to the full.

A life lived in faith would be a life diminished, even were your one true faith the one true faith.

We know nothing of heaven, but we do know that, should it exist, entrance will not be restricted to those with the right membership card, nor will there be an entrance exam in theology.

We know nothing of hell, but we do know that, should it exist, it will not have been designed as an eternal Auschwitz.

When I observe the religious, I often feel more of an atheist, and when I observe atheists I feel more religious. This is not because any of them are bad people; it is just my irritation at their perennial certitudes.

A contrarian is a useless person who has at last found a role in society. It's my job to irritate those who irritate me, and it's their job to be certain of how the world is made, because without their certainties the world would cease to turn on its axis.

VIII

The Americans haven't understood yet that post-imperialism is more fun than imperialism.

With post-imperialism you no longer fear that the satellite and tributary states will refuse to do what they're told, because they already have.

The less well-off in imperialist countries have a miserable time and are fed on dreams of greatness.

The less well-off in imperialist countries are denied the dignity and authenticity of the less well-off elsewhere.

The English lost their imperial identity, but Thatcher resurrected it by invading a couple of islands whose sovereignty she had, six months earlier, been trying to transfer to Argentina on a fifty-year leaseback. The break-up of Britain within the EU will not be Balkanisation, but it will be a break with imperial discourse and the last few untidy imperial hankerings.

By losing Scotland, its former junior partner in a successful but now defunct imperial project, England will be free to choose between a future in Europe or a future as the current junior partner with the United States in a once successful imperial project now on the wane.

The only good thing about mercantile empires is the brevity of their reign. A scattered empire built on economic advantage cannot be held together for long by military might, once the economic advantage has disappeared.

Will America be the new Europe and become politically awake? We can only hope.

Will Europe, as we unlearn the hard-learnt lessons of the past, revert to xenophobia and internecine strife? We can only despair.

The great thing about history is that, if studied correctly, no nation can boast moral superiority, and each should look to its own crimes.

The current fashion for apologies over centuries-old crimes while ignoring current crimes is a perfidy worthy of our past. To weep over the clearances whilst assisting in the plan to flood the homes of another minority people, the Kurds of Turkey, is a fine example.

Clearance by water is even more effective than clearance by sheep.

It's pointless to decry the horrors of slavery in America while remaining silent about the horrors that continue to be inflicted on African Americans to this day: principally kangaroo courts, solitary confinement for endless periods of time, and a gulag of prison labourers. History is important because it teaches us about the present: its exploitation for moral posturing and inaction is an insult to those who suffered in the past.

Jean Cocteau wrote, "I've always preferred mythology to history. History is truth that becomes an illusion. Mythology is an illusion that becomes reality." How very wrong: history's contribution to civilisation has been to undermine and occasionally destroy myths. Mythology is a lie that more often than not becomes a brutal reality. Mythology interferes with rational thought.

Cocteau should have been wary of the chiastic attraction of his statement. A lesson to all of us who adapt our thoughts to rhetorical templates.

Real history is as elusive as it is fascinating. A historian who does not admit to its elusiveness and cannot exploit its fascination is not a historian of any worth.

IX

Each generation has its own culture, which is transnational. It crosses not only borders, but also ideologies. It has an individuality that will never be repeated, but will be resembled.

Each generation has its genius, each its terrible lacunae, for which the previous generation is in part responsible. One generation may have generosity and open-mindedness as a reaction against the lack of these in their parents, or a lack of formal education because their parents were too lazy, too self-obsessed and, above all, too mean as a society to provide them with one.

When people tut-tut over the misuse of the apostrophe and inability to calculate simple additions, they think that this is a permanent change. Probably not: it is quite possible that in fifteen years young people will be as obsessed about the health of their brains as they have been about their bodies for the past fifteen years. Perhaps they have already started to take them for regular exercise.

Jogging the brain is less visible than jogging the body.

It's true what they say: "Get an education. It weighs nothing when you have to move around." If, however, you hold your education too grandly, your body may be light and your nose lifted to the heavens, but your soul will fall to your feet and look like a sack of potatoes. Occasionally it will trip you up.

I knew a old man in Turin. Erudite and unassuming, he was held to that city by his weight of his and his family's memories. He was as hard on his birthplace as he was on himself. As a rootless individual, I admire those who are rooted in their own place but cosmopolitan in their thoughts and hopes. They belong to the few and they belong to us all.

Social goods – cultural, moral and political – have to be fought hard for unceasingly.

Social goods are hard to maintain from one generation to another. In each the battle has to be repeated, but by people who have never been without those particular social goods and therefore do not value them as much as they should.

Is it the case that it takes a degree of authoritarianism to maintain a social good over the long term? Probably yes, but authoritarian regimes maintain social goods by ossifying them. Then they become brittle and collapse.

The only way to maintain social goods is through an unending process of participation and reinvention. This is an exhausting idea for an old man like me who yearns for the return of ideas now dead. But how exhilarating!

If the meagre intellects of Reagan and Thatcher could reverse all the gains of a century of working-class movements and start running the nineteenth century backwards, there is hope for us to regain our past just as easily without violence and without the demonisation of any class or social group.

Reagan and Thatcher unintentionally weakened the West and remind us of the shabby restrictiveness of nineteenth-century economic theories. The dismal science may have started to rebalance wealth globally. In a hundred years, this may be what is remembered, rather than the devastation inflicted by their economic theories.

Only an idiot or a banker would think that capitalist consumption could not only continue but expand to cover all the globe without harming it irreparably.

Will we only start to dismantle capitalism when it is too late? Will we commission an army of consultants and spivs to dismantle the capitalism that spawned them? Will G4 police regulatory changes to the stock exchange, whilst launching another share issue to celebrate the new contract?

Are we a foolish species? There is great goodness and intelligence in the human race. The problem is that we quite rightly expend our goodness and intelligence on the crucial little things of life: our families, our friends and our work. We have never invented a political system – a public thing or common wealth – that works satisfactorily and creates a collective equal to our needs and worthy of our potential.

But every state, however vile, works better than no state, because amongst the goodness and intelligence there is a powerful minority of viciousness, greed and the will to power.

Where nominally there is no power, power is recreated in its crudest form.

So-called democratic politicians only see the worst in their electorates, and we despise them because they reflect back the baseness stored within us.

The class of politicians who go from privileged school to parliamentary "research" posts and then to parliament as members have ushered in the rule of automatons.

The rule of automatons is the perfect system for the capitalist elite. The automatons are even weaker than we are.

The automatons look pleased with themselves, because they think they are in charge, and there is a massive industrial-cultural apparatus whose principal task is to convince them and us of this delusion.

Gordon Brown says that the intrinsically British values are tolerance and fair play. Given the intolerance and lack of fair play intrinsic to that statement, we can marvel at its splendid incongruity.

And leaving aside the incongruity of arguing that foreigners are relatively intolerant and unfair compared with the British and not perceiving the statement's self-subversion, we can marvel at a former British prime minister being so ignorant of the history of the state he served.

Nations have cultural traits; they don't have moral ones.

More or less all states are immoral, particularly in their international relations. Some are more immoral than others. The British state has always been one of the most immoral precisely because it has been an imperialist one with an unquenchable global ambition and a far-reaching network of relations. Old habits failed to pass away with the passing of its empire.

If you are powerful, beware your friends, particularly your best and dearest friends – the ones on whom you showered your greatest favours. They will never forgive you.

X

Good music unites; good literature divides and unsettles – not humanity but the self.

Music speaks to everyone and everyone can hear; literature speaks to the literate and not all the literate can hear.

A good society requires both music and literature.

We are entering the post-literate society in which the image is all. We do not know where we're going, and the post-literate society doesn't care.

Literature requires as much effort from the reader as it does from the writer. Without a large community of skilled readers, literature as we have known it over the last three hundred years will die.

For both writer and reader, literature is a solitary activity that, unseen, builds society because it increases the collective intelligence by questioning easy myths and sharing ideas amongst those who never meet.

It is more difficult to find the solution than to ask the question: a country could not be run by satirists, but without satirists a country could not be run.

Literature abhors sameness. If all books become the same, it would be better not to read.

To write is to become another person or other people. That is the writer's true salary, worth more than all the royalties.

"No man but a blockhead ever wrote, except for money," said Samuel Johnson. Didn't he know that writing is for blockheads and madmen? Was he not a sublimely talented and bumbling example of both?

To be guided exclusively by pecuniary advancement is to mistake the purpose not only of writing but also of life.

The greatest acts of kindness come from the poor.

Money in this society is necessary for survival, but above a certain level it is like keeping rotten fruit.

Penury deprives us of our humanity, but so does excessive wealth.

A writer can receive no greater compliment than to be dismissed as a fool by those who have never read her words.

A writer should leave his rancours outside his study door.

A good writer should only remember his readership when it comes to the second or third draft. No great work of literature came out of a focus group.

A good writer should trust her readers to adapt to different voices and to enjoy them.

An elitist writer disregards his readers altogether. He would do better to stop writing and invite them to supper.

Good writing is produced by compulsives who can do nothing else. Professional writers find writing a chore, complain about meagre royalties and do other more remunerative jobs.

Thank God for arts council grants. Without them the compulsives wouldn't eat and the professionals couldn't buy their suits.

Life begins when you relinquish ambition.

You can move beyond ambition at twenty-eight or eighty-two,

but most do so around forty, when they have either failed or succeeded. Hence the wisdom in that apparently banal adage on when life begins.

Those who perversely become ambitious in old age, put their lives on hold and spoil their years of close relationships and reflection.

Putting ambition aside can be the second step towards creativity – paradoxically, because ambition may well have been the first step.

Ambition is both an obstacle to creativity and the drive towards it.

The flaw in ambition is that it cares too much about how creativity is assessed publicly. Hence it is a mixture of confidence and a lack of it.

Too much confidence undermines the self-critical approach required of writing or any other creative activity. Too little confidence deprives writers of their ability to write at all.

A mix of or, better, an alternation between supreme confidence and a complete lack of it can be extremely productive. Creativity is a manic, unstable condition – a form of controlled madness.

Write for the present and you'll be forgotten. Write for the future and you'll be forgotten too, most probably, and in the meantime you'll starve. Just get on and write. Fate favours the careless, in the arts as in all other fields.

If I could remember why I started to write, I might be able to stop.

There are some who would pay me for doing just that. An income at last!

XI

Printing and mass literacy gradually created nation states. The new media and the end of mass literacy will destroy the nation state. In their place may come either superstates or global fragmentation and anarchy.

To guess the future is only foolish; to forget about the future and live only in the present is criminal negligence.

The age of hope and progress that started with the French Revolution has now ended. If change for the better is to occur, it will be through the restless action of the many and not the grand ideas of the few.

But the grand ideas are still grand, and survive like broken treasures.

While land is owned privately, there can be no social freedom.

Real freedom today can only be in the mind.

An act of kindness is a powerful argument against our current economic model. It reminds us of the future we envisaged in the past.

A conceptual artist said that she would leave the country if they put the top tax rate up to 50 per cent. They did (clearly not having heard her threat), and she didn't leave of course. Where else would she find people willing to pay for her tedious self-obsessions?

Go, go! Fly to your tax haven and finish your days grumpily drinking gin and vermouth, while a red sun sets on a perfect sea and the locals clean the interminable detritus of your lurid bohemianism.

Another conceptual artist worked away less noisily turning commonplace rooms inside out, making concrete of the air and air of solid things. We saw that the common place is intricate and good, and understood our blindness. She will be one of the few such artists remembered in the future.

Every artistic movement produces dross. Do not judge it by the dross.

XII

The neo-conservatives scream about freedom, which demonstrates that they have no understanding of it. If they did, they would whisper.

By freedom, neo-conservatives mean not the freedom of human beings but the freedom of an abstract thing they worship like a god: the market or, more precisely, the market under the political control of America and lesser Western powers.

The unnatural stentorian advocates of the free market are quick to impose import controls when their own interests are affected – controls they would allow no one else to introduce.

Freedom is in the mind, and one person can be freer in prison than another addictively trading on the Stock Exchange.

Freedom is noticing that your car has been vandalised and not caring in the slightest. Even smiling at someone's pointless expenditure of energy and feeling mildly sorry for them.

Freedom is both earned and learnt. It requires a special kind of passivity: one that retains compassion while it relinquishes the desire to control.

Social and political freedom is an elusive concept – constantly abused and tethered to the carriage of state so that it can occasionally be drawn around town and displayed for the strange but imposing creature that it is.

One person's freedom not only excludes another's; it doesn't even perceive it.

Wealth is liquid freedom that can overwhelm by presenting too many choices.

Having too many choices is like having no choice at all.

Lucky are the thinkers of the left who work in a time when the right is dominant. Their companions are sincere, and no flesh-and-blood corrupters come close: this is a time for thought, and the principal question – how do we rebuild? – spins off in a myriad directions building not the left but complexities enough to provide for a lifetime.

But one abstract corrupter remains and fattens in this time of want: our ability to forget why we embarked on this troubled road, which comes and should come with small humiliations, and to think that it is, after all, little more than an intellectual game. Lucky are the thinkers of the left who retain their outrage and passion deep into their old age.

All understanding of the world requires categorisation. You can alter categorisation to achieve the analysis you originally sought.

After defeating the working class, the British establishment fragmented the concept, lest it should return.

The courtier intellectuals of modern Britain have renamed the lumpenproletariat as the precariat. Thus one callous label replaces another, and the least fortunate part of our society is dismissed as the undeserving, undisciplined and unthinking poor.

It is adversity that makes us think. Wealth and security merely seduce us into thinking we are thinkers – and splendidly entertaining ones at that.

Security means that you can make more mistakes without paying a high price.

True categories exist where there is little mobility between them. There has always been a high degree of mobility between the working class and the lumpen-precariat. Thus the two belong to each other. They are all working class.

Class is not about the kind of coffee you drink.

An important feature of modern society is not the fragmentation of class into eight castes with silly names like the "precariat" and the "emergent service workers"; it is the proletarianisation and casualisation of almost everyone except those in financial services, who once were risk-takers and freebooters.

The adventurous stage of capitalism is long gone, and its tragic contradictions are best expressed by Rudyard Kipling's narrative poem, "The Mary Gloster".

A certain brand of communist dismissed some fundamental freedoms as "bourgeois freedoms", although they were won by the working-class movement and the mass mobilisations of two world wars.

The proof of this is that with the defeat of the European working-class movement, those "bourgeois freedoms" are being eroded.

The revival of the left is inevitable, but will the same mistakes be made? The past is a lesson, not a golden age.

Even teenage rebellion and working-class history have been privatised and floated on the stock exchange.

Monetise is the word. I've heard it many a time on the mouths of those who live precariously, but only now have I used it for the first time.

Capitalism is secure when even the beggars think they are in business.

Capitalism is like yeast: its growth is phenomenal, but if another timely process does not act upon it to harden and secure its advances, it will render all the material around it barren and entirely useless.

Failure to understand is the surest route to success.

Failure, conversely, is the surest route to understanding.

Capitalism creates the spectacular success of the few, and therefore creates nothing.

A society that creates the mediocre wealth of the many will also be spectacularly creative.

Or will it only be smug and conformist?

Leisure allows creativity, but only in an educated society.

Without education we are restless and insatiable.

The main purpose of education should be to leave us dissatisfied with our education.

The main purpose of education as it is organised in our society is to convince children in one set of schools that they are highly educated when they aren't, and the children in the other set of schools that they aren't educated and never can be. The first set of schools equips children for power, and the second equips children for life in a consumer society.

XIII

What does it mean to say that there is life after death? If we drink the waters of the Lethe, forget our past life and clothe ourselves in a new body with new strengths and weaknesses, where is the continuity? We are no longer the same person.

If life is a moral test, isn't eternity too long to ponder our faults? Even for the saintly – especially for the saintly who will have little to do. Surely the universe cannot be organised like an everlasting boarding school run by a strict and joyless headmistress?

Goodness is more fragile than evil. All things beautiful and noble evolve and cannot endure, excepting the Ideal or God who is eternal and unchanging.

Humanity, lost and suspended between good and evil, has a short but intense life. For this it should be envied, even by God.

In a cold universe, the courage and emotional intensity of humanity is a quotidian work of art.

God loves humanity because only through its intensity does He find meaning to His timeless and spaceless existence.

God is a Form implanted in our souls by Himself, by Nature or by something else.

God is the realisation that the self and the will to power are a pit into which we can be drawn, and that only through the love of others do we achieve some contentment in this existence, but He does not tell us why.

God's message is an abstraction. Those who speak to Him engage in a mental exercise whose benefits may only be psychological. Those who believe that He has spoken back to them directly and individually are mad, and should be avoided where possible. There can be no dialogue with those who dialogue with divinity. They speak not just with certainty, but also with righteous fury.

God belongs not to the hundreds of one true religions that inhabit our societies, but to us all. He is the realisation that our souls are more important than our bodies, even though they too are very possibly mortal or precisely because they are.

We ruin our short contingent lives by seeking out a permanence and security that are not ours to have. We ruin the contingent by trying to fathom the immeasurable impossibilities of eternity.

There's so very little we can know with any certainty in this world; there's nothing we can know in the next (not even its existence).

The Epicureans were right: fear of the next world destroys our enjoyment of this one.

The Epicureans were wrong: the purpose of this life is not simply pleasure, not even their ascetic pleasure of secluded study and certainly not the obscene pleasure of unrestrained consumerism, which has no pleasure in it.

The purpose of life is to invent one's own purpose. Many have spent their lives in search of it, a noble and courageous purpose in itself. Others know their purpose from early childhood, but allow distractions to deny it.

To lay out a sentence whose reason for being is itself and not the representation of any thought would not delight the reader. Nor would it make them smile.

Subtlety is out of fashion. The age of the reassuringly predictable and the reassuringly shocking has come.

The purpose of our media is to titillate our baseness and leave uncultivated our finer and more humane nature.

The pen was mightier than the sword, but the gun and the television are each mightier than them both.

The television is mightier than the gun, as it hypnotises viewers and programmes them with simplicities. More dangerous than its manipulation for propaganda purposes is its inability to examine the complexities of our modern lives, reducing us to unconscious animals prey to an artificial and unnatural habitat.

Television is didactic and soporific at the same time. It therefore must also be mesmeric.

Television reveals our world with the same efficacy of the barred window of a prison cell.

XIV

Let humanity be everyone's religion, and religion everyone's personal philosophy.

Let the cathedral be the mosque and the mosque the cathedral – for a month in every year.

Let Friday be Sunday and Sunday be Saturday, and each moment one that we live.

Syncretism is obviously right, but once universal it might be a little dull.

Universal anything is dull, but universalism should be our passion.

We should all be universalists, but learn to do it differently.

Blessed are the Yezudis; I don't know what they do (except the constant baptism), but they do it differently.

The soul of capitalism is uniformity. The soul of humanity is human diversity. The soul of religion should be tolerance. That our societies are such a mess does not surprise us.

And yet our human desire for an unnatural order produces so much disorder and such a disorderly pile of ideas that I have to smile and congratulate myself on not being a hunter-gatherer, noble though he may have been.

Religions are ethical languages, taught to us in childhood and helpful in moral discussion. That people go to war or commit atrocities in their name is an obscenity to the gods of all religions.

Religions can be learnt like languages, and are the means to understanding a given society or community – not just the orthodox but also the more interesting heretics amongst them.

Heretics are not debunkers or non-believers, but people who hold a body of beliefs so dear that they take them seriously.

Heretics are subversive because naively they don't realise that they're being subversive.

Heretics are the most dangerous subversives of all. That is why Stalin filled the Gulag with devout communists.

Religions survive because of heretics, who only bring about partial reforms and unwittingly greater orthodoxy, because the religion or social movement defines itself more rigidly in the wake of the heresy and tries to police the new orthodoxy against any further change.

Judaism was a religion in constant radical evolution up to the time of the heretic Jesus, after which it changed more slowly. In its first three centuries, Christianity was a religion on the move, but after the heretic Arius the Empire set it in stone – created the monolith.

An atheist can be a better Christian than most Christians. George Eliot was a fine example.

It is true that every town, village or city has its poet, thief, fighter, maternal babushka, obsessive, dreamer, grump, the sexually promiscuous and the religious fanatic (the last one and the last but one are often one and the same), but they speak and comport themselves through the language and culture of their place.

Language and culture are important and formative but most fundamental is the individual. A European vase and a Chinese vase both hold water, but their appearance is very different. That difference provides us with the taste of life. However, both vases are more similar to each other than either is to a frying pan.

The free-market policies of Reagan and Thatcher laid the foundations for a global, post-nationalist consciousness they would have abhorred. This unintended consequence should be the platform for a fight-back from the left.

The uniformity of global capitalism is removing the taste of life, but it may be helping us to rid ourselves of ethnic mythologies. If we can rid ourselves of capitalism before it destroys our cultural diversity but late enough to destroy our ethnic identities (if indeed it is doing so), then global capitalism will have served a useful purpose to be balanced against the destruction it has caused.

Of one thing we can be certain, real existing socialism only temporarily submerged ethnic identities, and when it collapsed, they returned with a vengeance. Is there any reason to believe global capitalism has affected hearts more deeply, or has it temporarily submerged them too, creating unity around shared profits?

There are phenomenologies of urban life and rural life – so different between each other and yet that difference is constant around the world.

*

One change within urban life is its attitude to rural life: once it was utter contempt for what it considered to be bestial. Then it started to idealise the countryside – not in the bucolic sense – but a deep respect and desire to be amongst "nature". Very often this change of heart came after the disappearance of the alien people that once was nearly all humanity: the peasantry.

The peasantry is a courageous, moral, sociable and sometimes cruel or even brutal class. Its passing may cause more damage than we can imagine.

When the peasantry moves to the city, it brings with it many of the peasants' virtues and seizes the skills of the city with both hands. Recently urbanised peasants create the most radical, self-aware and unstable class in history.

The peasantry brings energy and solidarity to the city – a place that is both exciting and enervating.

The peasantry suffers when it arrives in the city, but then the peasantry knows how to suffer.

XV

George Eliot lost her belief in God, but managed to resurrect the meaning of Jesus's life in the modern world.

When she writes that fanatical, evangelical Christians "look on the rest of mankind as a doomed carcass which is to nourish them for heaven", she demonstrates that many Christians had lost their Christianity long before the advent of modern science and Darwinism. That kind of Christianity was invented in the Reformation, or perhaps as far back as Saint Augustine.

Christianity's great weakness in the Modern Era was its rootedness in power. Ultimately this led to the loss of its power, because it no longer had anything to give to power. It forgot that it has to keep a foot in both camps.

Better to serve egalitarian humanity than to reign through hell and hellish power games.

I don't say that we should fight for justice, but we should at least have the courage to speak up for it, and the bolder of us should place our cumbersome bodies in the road of injustice and the power behind it.

Awareness of injustice appears to be difficult to some people, but it is simplicity itself compared with finding a way to impose justice.

Imposing justice so often leads to greater injustices.

If you want your children to be happy, give them no toys. If you do this, you avoid stunting a child's imagination with an adult's one.

If you want your children to be educated, never underestimate their capacity to learn. They're much brighter than we are, unless we place our own limitations upon them.

Try to instruct your children in something. They need something to reject.

A true atheist needs a religious education. No one can reject what they simply cannot understand.

To say that your children need your love is to state an obvious but nevertheless essential truth. To say that they only need your love is to condemn them to lifelong imprisonment.

Having children teaches you the melancholy joy of closeness mixed with distance.

Your children live in another country whose values may be the only evidence of progress – tortuous progress but progress no less.

Those of us born in the late foties and early fifties belong to the last generation brought up to believe wholly in progress.

The religion of progress survived the horrors of the first half of the twentieth century, but floundered in the listlessness of "affluence", as the ghettoisation of poverty is often called.

From now on progress will have to justify itself with hard evidence of its existence. That perhaps is another shred of evidence.

Deskilled, we're increasingly dependent on technology and its autonomous progress. Isn't that regressive for our freedom, however we define it?

Early industrialisation empowered the powerless, and the powerful had to concede a little power and use their wits. Modern technology is not only a soporific; it allows the powerful to monitor everything.

The noble savage lived in the era of myth and is therefore as unknowable as God. To idealise him or despise him is an irrational act.

Running a business makes you dull, because it reduces creativity to economic gain – the dullest and most pointless good we can obtain, unless we are wise.

To be free in this society it is sometimes necessary to start a business. Thus Marxists fill in VAT returns and Thatcherites like Mario Monti act like commissars.

Beware those who feign self-disgust, who self-deprecate with panache and self-confidence, particularly when they're women, because women on the whole are better at subtlety and sophistication, and are therefore more convincing.

Literature is a continuation of religion and philosophy in the late modern era. It is religion without certainty and philosophy without system.

Has the late modern era come to an end? It is too early to know, but its cultural pillars appear to be cracking.

Anton Francesco Doni said in the sixteenth century that the fumes of the printing press drive people mad. He should have lived to see what our odourless mass-media can do.

Our mass-media rots, but its colours never fade.

The impossibility of understanding anything with *absolute* certainty is not an excuse for not wanting to understand.

Love and the desire to understand are the two elements that make life worthwhile. They detach us from our tyrannical selves.

Today the middle classes are only virtuous and empathetic within their own class. They have returned to their pre-war mindset and cannot perceive the "lower classes" – whatever strange names they invent for them – as anything except people without potential, and incapable of governing their own lives. In this sense, their social outlook is like primitive religion: enclosed within the group and fearful of those outside. The urban working class is more likely to be internationalist and classist or nationalist and xenophobic. Marx and other nineteenth-century radicals were not complete dreamers to place so many hopes in this virtuous and disciplined class when it tended to be more in the first category than in the second. Today in Europe, it is sadly tending towards the second.

Scotland has bucked the trend: it is internationalist and nationalist, because it wants to defend its "outdated" class analysis.

Unlike the middle class, the "traditional" working class was too disciplined and not insurrectionary enough to make a permanent difference, and the new middle class is too contemptuous to acknowledge that the labour movement created the freedoms it benefits the most from.

A riot is a beast, an insurrection is an artist, particularly if it has a good heart.

Do not confuse virtue with manners.

Manners are transversal to class, as they are more the product of family and culture. They depend on such things as honour and shame, or the lack of one or the other, or both.

A society with too much honour is stifling or often brutal when honour requires an absolute defence. A society in which there's no shame is unstable and will not last.

Manners vary from place to place, as do the subjects appropriate for discussion. Surely openness is best, as it makes for rational and honest debate. But isn't openness also likely to create cynicism and then shallowness: an endless jabbering of insatiable selves?

Perhaps the best society is neither a closed one nor an open one, but a closed one turning into an open one – possible only in transition.

This instability of a social good is the greatest social tragedy. There's no final utopia – a destination never reached. There are only heroic attempts and tragic failures.

When a problem is solved, another is created.

Good is built in the air and evil at the foot of the mountain. No wonder evil prevails, even though human beings are far more good than evil.

The powerful and wealthy should be called the "lower class" because they live at the foot of the mountain – secure and stable.

Those who live high above the mountains and subsist on air and their dreams are the "upper class" but maintaining their position is difficult. Gravity does not like to be defied for too long, and suddenly they fall down to the mountain tops, if they're lucky, or down to the soulless existence in the valley.

It is as asinine to say that everything must change as it is to say that nothing must change.

Ortega y Gasset was right to talk of the arrogance of the men of 1789 who thought they could knock together an entirely new society – complete with new language and religion – in a matter of years, but he failed to say that it was a more dramatic and heroic version of the arrogance of Louis XVI's court – the men of 1788.

If we defeat our enemies, they defeat us and our success by making us become their mirror image.

The smaller the project the greater our control over how it will develop.

Building socialism would be easier in a small country if it weren't for foreign intervention.

An island nation is more independent. That is why it fails to understand foreignness and to evolve through it. Its external strength creates its internal weakness.

The best relationships are across cultural divides, because they're not based on the language and manners of convention.

The most fragile relationships are across cultural divides, because the ways to misunderstanding are more numerous.

Fragility adds to experience.

XVI

Do not mention class if you want a stock conversation, just as in the sixties and seventies you would mention it to get one. Every age has its own prejudices and blindnesses.

The middle classes hate to be reminded of the working class: it makes them feel guilty – or perhaps only slightly uncomfortable.

When the working class are submissive, the middle class occasionally take a little time out to feel sorry for them. When they are active and conscious, the working class are almost universally feared and considered ungrateful and unreliable.

There are more or less the same proportions of well-mannered and ill-mannered people in every class, but each class is convinced that they're the well-mannered ones, because they mistake different manners to be bad manners without distinctions.

We want to believe that mankind is at least a potentially rational animal; as we get older, we experience the distressing sensation that we may always be an animal driven by the instincts of the pack, even when it comes to matters of high culture.

Bureaucrats and the politicians who promote reforms always believe in progress, because they're the ones who are introducing them – be they Soviet communists, American neocons or British New Labourites.

XVII

I was asked what I thought God was. "Uncertainty," I answered, with the intent of deflecting the question, but not without a kernel of truth: uncertainty reflects not so much the nature of God as our relationship with Him.

The desire to know is laudable. Knowing, or rather thinking that we know, is not.

Living with the possibility of God is beneficial. Living with the certainty of God's existence or non-existence is not, in most cases.

Some women and men live good and significant lives in spite of their faith in God or His absence from what becomes a wholly mechanical and material world. To do so they need absolute tolerance and a trinity of virtues: gentleness, loyalty and a clear morality they apply to themselves alone. I know these people exist because I have met them, and some I have loved. Those that I loved were all atheists. The first assertion is reliable, and the second is not, because it probably only reflects my natural social milieu.

The problem with believing in life after death is that it clouds our judgement in this world. It makes a patriarch of God and either sanctimonious conformists or terrified mice of us. We should either deny the possibility altogether or at least disregard the argument as irrelevant and unknowable.

There is the deists' God of creation and the theists' God of intervention. Surely they cannot be the same, and the theists' God must be as dependent on us as we are on Him. He exists because we are conscious enough to know good and evil. We are not made in his image, but He reflects an ideal that is within us all or He instils it in us.

God is a series of questions: "Do I really need this?" "Why be ambitious?" "What would I feel if I were this other person?" "Do I give back as much as I take?" He challenges the dominance of the self, which in consumer society has become a deranged ringmaster trained by the biggest ringmaster of them all: the mass media that attempt to manipulate our every action and want, and do so very successfully.

We need a God who takes us back to the earth, to the air, to the noise of argument and vitality, and above all to the meditative.

Taylorism did not improve our lives and led, a hundred years later, to our children being bombarded with ugly plastic toys made by exploited labour.

We need, God knows how, to build an economy of creativity in which we exploit our minds and imaginations more and our poor planet less.

The human being is a social animal and without society we could not survive, but to avoid becoming a pack animal (in both senses), she needs to get away from society and let her mind wander.

So God, you say, may only be a mental exercise. Possibly, but one that can do much good if done correctly.

Others might say, "Why do you blaspheme?" I would be blaspheming much more if I were to claim a revelation I have never experienced; I am working in the dark, as do we all, and reacting against the utilitarian certainties of enlightened self-interest. God leads us away from the demons of desire and into the land of possibilities generated by passivity and an active consciousness.

A friend said, "Your religious ideas are just a form of humanism." Maybe, but do I want to replace the sonorous name of God with that empty and cumbersome term, "the Voice of Ideal Humanity", just because theism implies an interdependence between God and Mankind.

Every week I am a theist for three days, a deist for another three and an atheist for a day – usually a Sunday. It's a state of utter confusion and I recommend it.

XVIII

Good writers must write in order to invent the language of the future. They will never succeed but they should try.

Good writers need to read the literature of the past in order to understand the character of the language they write in, and what it can and could do with a little pressure from writers themselves.

Writers should take pleasure in the achievements of other writers, and even if they are mediocre writers, this makes them good people, which for them is much more important. By working together and not competing, writers assist in building a literary culture – the essential environment for any good writer to become a great one.

XIX

Fanatical communists who cease to be communists become the most vicious anti-communists. They cannot live with uncertainty.

Cosmopolitan but anchored in a city – Moscow or Rome – and with very similar systems for reproducing power – Politburo or Conclave – Soviet communism and the Catholic Church had much in common: a powerful elite parasitically manoeuvring a committee of sacrifice and good intentions producing both good and bad effects, but representing something better than you would expect from the corrupt centre. The demise of the first, which I welcomed briefly at the time, turned out to be a tragedy for Russia and for humanity, and I suspect that the demise of the second would be similar.

Do not destroy something until you have something better to put in its place, and rely on a prolonged period of transition.

Before the collapse of the Soviet Union, the West used the Helsinki Agreement as a weapon against their Cold War enemy, then preoccupied with its own delicate transition. Since the disappearance of the Soviet Union, the West has, at best, shown little interest in human rights there and openly boasts of how it fixed the election of Yeltsin who had rehired the censors Gorbachev had sacked.

With the fall of the Soviet Union, the West started to dismantle all the advances in human rights achieved over centuries. Under the requirements of the so-called War on Terror, they have done away with Habeas Corpus and spy on us in a manner the KGB would have dearly wanted to, had it had the technology. Over the last thirty years, we have also fallen under the control of a state-financed private bureaucracy that regulates an ideological free market – a veritable army of lawyers, consultants, accountants and swindlers, no less malign and inefficient than the state-run bureaucracy of the Soviet Union was. Was 9/11 our Kirov moment? Is the worst yet to come?

If it hasn't become our Kirov moment yet, then we have a small group of courageous whistleblowers to thank for slowing down the progress of the right-authoritarian juggernaut. Can we rely on their assistance forever?

There is the left and the right, and there is the libertarian and the authoritarian, whatever our attitude to left and right, we must hold the libertarian dear, as without our stunted and fragile liberties there is little hope of honest political debate.

Social truth is manufactured by power structures, both locally and nationally.

Truth itself exists in an elusive realm, and all we can hope for is to snatch a few of its rays which, in their partiality, can create misleading images.

The many have intelligence and generosity, in spite of Nietzsche's misplaced contempt for what he called the herd, but they are badly misled by the few.

Being misled by the few requires a willingness to be misled, and that willingness derives from a desire for comfort and an existential sleep, particularly when we arrive at middle age tired by our wasted efforts and disillusioned by betrayals.

Another few maintain a "naive" belief in humanity and, having refused to believe the powerful few, they must pay a price for their naivety – a tax imposed by history and redeemed by later generations.

Nothing frees us more than a belief in our moral possibilities.

The deification of the crowd is the great deceit of modernity's so-called democracies.

The crowd at the stadium or the military parade has no purpose but to conform. In its bustle, it has no effect save that of shoring up the walls of power.

The active crowd is like a beast, and every member a potential god – if only they would leave the crowd and each go for their separate and appropriate paths.

The only crowd of any worth is the passive crowd that threatens no one and says, "I shall not budge, because you've gone too far. I do not hate you for it, but I will not move until you understand, or at least start to think." That is the crowd the powerful really fear: it moves them because it does not move, and it mobilises through its immobility.

"People power" is a term used by the BBC to describe demonstrations outside Britain and the United States.

People power should be judged by what it wishes to achieve and how it wants to achieve it.

People power often doesn't know what it wants to achieve, which is sensible but impractical.

People power sometimes wishes to do great harm to another part of the people – perhaps a minority.

People power occasionally desires the greatest human good – and then it is sublime. Its season will be short as spies and agents provocateur wriggle through the ranks of its naivety.

Come to my heart, the soul of humanity and warm it with your hope. It grew cold as I wrote those lines – lines that extinguish everything else I've written in this book.

XX

Community exists but a good community does not have a voice, as no single voice can represent it.

Community, like most social goods, is elusive.

When people talk of "the community", they actually mean an organised part of it. Themselves.

"Community", in the way the word is generally used, is something not just conformist but also stultifying and destructive to creative dialogue.

The task of democratic representatives is to represent the people's demands and best interests to the wealthy and powerful, and not to represent the demands and best interests of the wealthy and powerful to the people.

Which is more arbitrary: the market or a bureaucratic elite? There is little difference, although the market is always deaf to rational argument and yet, in its case, it *feels* to many that no one is to blame.

Some complain that democracy is the rule of mediocrity. They have a point, but aristocracy was the rule of stupidity. Progress, if it exists, is slight and always relative.

The fact that a perfectly functioning democracy is unattainable is no reason why we should cease to strive to get as close to one as possible.

If democracy involves a sense of involvement and ownership amongst the wider public, then democracy has never come to Britain, except perhaps in those first two post-war Labour governments. Even though it was an illusion. Because the establishment was temporarily buying off the people's post-war determination to obtain greater social justice, the people *felt* that they had more control and that was a wonderful gift to society. It would be even more wonderful if they had real control.

The principal elements of effective representative democracy were described by Marx in his comments on the civil war in France. They included the average workers' wage for representatives, short mandates and all elected officials recallable on demand. That less ambitious and more practical dream should be preferred to the utopian withering away of the state, which is a form more intangible than heaven or the lion lying down with the antelope.

Institutions are difficult to reform from within, because it is rare for someone to believe that a system which has promoted them to the top is in some way flawed.

XXI

Tomorrow always comes and brings along its burden of grime and crowded solitudes whose purpose we fail to comprehend, and glimpses of beauty, wonderment and love whose caress reveals the greatness of our lives and hopes.

Love is a proper concern for humanity and the world that sustains it. It is, in practical terms, the application of that concern in our relations with human individuals, animals and things, and the expression of it in our creative lives. By removing us from the tyranny of our selves, it is the balm that engenders a happiness incidental and unsought.

Hatred, so often an overreaction, is always a burden that brings no fruit but bitterness and further hate – a prickliness that obscures the real but elusive reason for our lives on earth, be they finite or, more unlikely, a shred of some infinite continuum. It adds nothing to our existence and binds us to our selves. It grates the skin and produces unnecessary wounds.

A theologian is someone who takes the wine of Jesus's words and turns it into acrid water.

A man who loves his enemies is not destined to live for long.

Jesus was not "God in disguise" but many of his thoughts were divine.

The Romans turned Jesus into a god in order to change his meaning. The Russians embalmed Lenin for the same reason.

Lenin was a man of hate who knew how to impose his will; Jesus was a man of love who probably did not. They were both motivated by outrage at human suffering. It may be that one led to the other and it took near two thousand years.

The communism of the future must be based on non-violence. It must not fight fire with fire, but fire with reckless passivity. It must not believe in class war but in the power of gentleness to overcome the fears of the powerful and the greedy.

All fear degrades. Lucky are the absent-minded because they forget what they should be fearful of.

To laugh disdainfully at others is to lose all understanding of your self. It is deadness of the soul.

Procrastination puts you back in control of time.

Frederick Taylor gave us affluence of unnecessary stuff, and took our souls in exchange.

Life is not for the extravagant expenditure of wealth on mere stuff; it is for the extravagant expenditure of time in purposeless wandering, loving encounters, endless inconclusive nattering, withdrawal to a book or a fishing rod, and the natural laughter of the unhurried (so different from the manic and coarse consumer's laugh).

Frederick Taylor turned production into slavery, and consumption into work.

XXII

The "wise man" will say such things as "We learn from suffering", which is only partly true, even in his case. An intelligent man will learn from suffering by observing – perhaps with great detachment – even as parts of his psyche are bruised, damaged or destroyed, but not everyone can do this. Some people – probably most – are simply crushed and destroyed by suffering, and never revive. Perhaps the imperatives amongst these confused thoughts may be the strictures of a wise man – so beware! I hope they're not a wise man's, as a wise man is rarely correct but merely persuasive, and his persuasiveness derives from his powerful self-belief. I would rather be a fool who, conscious of not only his ignorance but also of his lack of method (because no reliable method exists), rashly utters his wild, disjointed thoughts.

If you speak to a ghost, he ceases to haunt you.

The trouble with the sensitive is that they often consider sensitivity to be their exclusive preserve.

I believe (dangerous word) or I almost believe that every human being can develop sensitivity – excluding brain damage of some kind – as long as the inevitable mix of good and evil experienced is right for that person and not too extreme. But "sensitivity" itself should not be treated as a delicate flower, as it is forged in strife and adversity as much as it is in calm and security. The only sensitivity that matters is sensitivity to others and to art.

As for men who write about sensitivity, they are too busy analysing it to experience it. That is why I avoid mirrors.

Believe in nothing and your laughter is hollow. Believe in something too much and your laughter is too solid for it to contain any joy.

Laughter without joy is laughter that laughs at laughter – unkindly, for who would denigrate laughter, particularly when it comes from the heart?

Speak to a stranger and you will learn much. Speak to a friend and she will reassure you of your convictions. Speak to an enemy, and you will discover, if nothing else, that his resemblance to you is shockingly close. Speak to your fears, and you will travel continents of experience in peace.

If you order your physical environment, you disorder your mind.

In spite of all the fashionable comparisons with computers, your brain and your body are not machines.

XXIII

Every existing virtue is at least slightly diminished by awareness of itself, but self-awareness mitigates vices.

Self-knowledge destroys natural spontaneity and can lead to cynicism, but the ancients were right to prize it: it leads us away from the animals and closer to the gods, whoever they may be – the ideal perhaps.

Self-knowledge is accompanied on one side by heavenly Empathy and on the other by grotesque and tragic Self-Obsession.

If an independent thinker joins an organisation, he immediately becomes a heretic.

Be a heretic, if you want to be loyal to what you now belong to.

To disagree courageously is noble, but remember always that you may be wrong. Many a heretic has died in prison who, if he had escaped and prospered, would have imprisoned others.

Do not let the harshness and unkindness of others make you harsh and unkind. You came into the world to avoid these things, which destroy your pleasure and others'.

Better to be injured by your enemies than by your friends, who can be your covert rivals.

As friendship is your greatest balm, life takes many surprising turns. Accept them as you accept the power of the sea. No exhilarating voyage is without its dangers.

The greatest risk to a pleasant and meaningful life is your desire to live without risk. Do not over-insure yourself by rejecting unpredictable loves and friendships; the possible losses are not as great as they might appear.

XXIV

The uxorious man (who in modern times does not have to be married, in spite of the etymology) is happier than the man who believes that no woman is good enough for him.

Perhaps he is not happier but simply more attuned to his own emotional environment, for what is happiness and how fleeting that indefinable condition. More generally then, to love is to live and to desire is dependency – desire is to die in your consciousness.

The beauty of old age is that the brain is reconciled to its own limitations – imposed by the unknowability of the external world. The ugliness of old age is that the body refuses to accept its own limitations – imposed by its attrition with the external world.

No one can ever banish desire, nor should they completely: that is the road to the hermitage, monastery or, most extremely, the stylite's column – another form of desire perhaps.

The way to control desire and the troubles it brings is to busy yourself with exploring the world around you – especially the human world.

Distrust these few Epicurean ramblings – those of an old man as mildewed or dusty as the papers he reads or scribbles on. Take life for its joy, particularly when young. Learn from the saints and hermits who generally gave themselves body and soul to debauchery in youth and then became ascetics when body and soul were capable of nothing else (in Italian, *gaudente* describes someone who thoughtlessly and irresponsibly pursues physical pleasures, and *gaudioso* describes someone who follows a spiritual and ascetic lifestyle, and both derive from the same Latin word, *gaudere* – to pursue pleasure).

Follow your heart and you'll make a fool of yourself. Follow your head and you'll make an arse of yourself. Better to be a fool, but most people won't notice if you act the arse – they might even applaud you. Such are our times.

Think and occasionally utter your own wilful conclusions. Even if you embellish them with doubts and provisos, you will be disliked, not because you're smarter but because you're making people uncomfortable. The compensation is that you'll feel alive, heading into the wind and sensing its harsh coolness on your cheeks. And yet more rarely should you shout something from the rooftop just to see the crows and starlings leap into flight: the crows disorderly, cumbersome and angry like a group of indistinguishable men breaking up from an important meeting, and the starlings balletic in their dance of the masses. Give power a mildly bad afternoon; that's all you can achieve. Suddenly you feel that you understand the magnificent sweetness and beauty of life, and the air is like a gift from heaven. It's probably an illusion, but a sublime one. In other words, dear reader, be a garrulous failure, a fool like me. Ruminate but don't become a ruminant.

Weight and
Counterweights

Cats and Dogs, and Other Things
We Cannot Understand

Why *do* humans love their dogs? It appears that many enjoy the regular walks imposed by dog ownership, which no doubt is good for their health. As a walker myself – of the irregular and spontaneous kind – I am constantly aware that I am walking in a park without a dog. Not having a dog means that I am alone with my thoughts, a place of almost absolute freedom, even if, like all freedoms, it is not always well used. My dog-owning colleagues, however, cannot have a moment for their own thoughts, because a walk is not a walk but a constantly interrupted saunter in which the principal scope of the game is to avoid your dog getting enmeshed with another person's dog along the way. These encounters are accompanied by the ritual smiles generally used by indulgent parents in relation to wayward children. Amongst the tut-tutting and commands barked by the owners at their property, which occasionally barks back, couples make their acquaintance, discuss the weather and, above all, exchange their canine curricula vitae.

All this appears to be not only harmless, but positively beneficial to both man and beast. And unquestionably it is, but this doesn't answer our question. I want the answer because I cannot quite understand the attraction, although, quite bizarrely, dogs find me very interesting indeed. I don't know whether I'm unwittingly exuding some powerful pheromone that has more effect on these servile quadrupeds than it does on human beings or I'm attracting them precisely because I don't have another member of their species in' tow – they detect a perverse anti-canine disposition. Perhaps dogs are contrarians and keep this eccentricity secret from the human owners. Often their attentions to me are entirely amiable or even embarrassingly effusive. In these cases, the dog owners, immediately sensing that I'm not one of them, start to shout quite aggressively, "Here, come back here!" Just occasionally however, the dog in question displays marked homicidal tendencies, and then the dog-owners do exactly the opposite. Instead of coming to my aid, they affect insouciance and then surprise at my howling. "I realise that your dog finds my Achilles tendon and my various peronaei – the brevis, longus and, of course, tertius – particularly succulent, but could he or she – I haven't had a chance to check – please disengage his or her teeth from them, as I find them useful for the articulation of my ankle." Unlike the ones who want to spare me the discomfort of being slobbered over by a huge but over-friendly great Dane and continue to apologise for five minutes after their dog has run off for somebody else to lick, these calm and collected dog-owners greet my whimpering complaints as the ravings of a madman. "Are you sure that you feed your dog enough?" I ask in staccato as I try to shake my leg free of the beast. "If you're short of money, I'm sure your local butcher has some bones that are much more interesting than mine – and no longer attached to any sentient creature." A waste of breath: these owners use an SAS training manual on their dogs before the little pets are even housetrained.

But these dog-owners, both good and bad, must be only a tiny part of the entire tribe: they are the responsible ones perhaps. There is a whole city full of these creatures, of all shapes and sizes, and they are part of the city's economy. They employ trainers, behaviourists, psychologists, therapists, psychiatrists, stylists, beauticians, groomers, vets, canine toy manufacturers and surely many other human beings willing to provide for their increasing consumer needs. Dogs are not just consumers; they are also producers, working as sniffers and guards. They are, according to one advert, a "highly cost-effective, flexible and reliable indicator of contraband". If only they knew the nice things that are said about them! Particularly "cost-effective"; does our society have a greater accolade?

I fancy that in our city there are less energetic dogs belonging to less energetic owners. The dog, for instance, who enjoys watching daytime TV along with his kind-hearted owner who rarely leaves his one-bedroom flat. They spend their days in companionable indolence, and his owner eases the drudgery with an occasional can of beer. Then there's the dog that has to listen all day to the ramblings of an owner who labours under the delusion that dogs can eventually understand the English language and all the quirkiness of life in human society in the early twenty-first century. All in all the dogs I meet in the park are the lucky ones.

By now, you've realised that I'm an unpleasant curmudgeon and, if you're a dog-owner (which you most probably are), you're about to throw the book across the room. Don't, because there are cats to come, and you really need to know if it's going to get worse – especially if you're going to write that letter of complaint to the publisher.

Some dog-owners must surely be attracted to the dependency of their pets. Other domesticated animals quickly revert to their feral conditions when they escape or are manumitted by mankind, but dogs are only the fancy cousins of the permanently and irreducibly untameable wolf – they are so very needy. Dogs are not only obedient; they also never answer back or even question their owners. This is an animal that can become an extension to the human "I" – a part of the human owner, an extra limb that occasionally suffers a rebellious tic. But some of us find that answering back is exactly what makes company so exciting. We call it dialogue and we can have no idea of where it's going to go when we start it.

So what would the Israeli philosopher Martin Buber have thought of dog-lovers? Quite a bit, I think, as his principal theory concerned every relationship and how they can become dialogic. This was the subject of his most famous work, *I and Thou*. But first we need to take a step back. Schopenhauer, a cantankerous misogynist, said that human beings are divided between those who on encountering someone say "there goes another 'I'" and those who say "there goes a 'not-I'". He did not say which he belonged to, and you didn't have to be Schopenhauer to come up with this fairly obvious observation. Buber analysed the phenomenon in much greater detail, and extended it beyond relationships between human beings to those between human individuals and all things – not just living things.

In spite of my caricature, dog-owners could and do have what Buber called "I-thou" relationships with their dogs. These would be the ideal dog-lovers who acknowledge their pet's autonomy and, most importantly, what it actually is – its essence. They enter into a relationship with an animal, accepting its difference, its limitations and its abilities. Not only do they accept it for what it is; they also love it for what it is. In other words, they don't anthropomorphise it and they don't turn it into a human substitute. Those who do such things, on the other hand, are engaging in an "I-it" relationship. They see their pet as a thing to be moulded exclusively in terms of their own needs. The dog has to be paraded, coiffured, cosseted, spoken to and ordered about like a servant. You might object that a dog, having evolved over many generations to be subservient to man, is essentially something that cannot survive outside its subservience. And you would have a point.

The counter-argument could go further: no relationship

can be wholly "I-it" or wholly "I-thou", particularly in the relationship between man and dog. A good owner would probably let the dog run free and allow it as much liberty as possible without exposing it to danger.

There are no references to dogs in Buber's book, but he does mention the other principal companion chosen by humanity from the fauna and adapted to household lives in a fairly typical passage:

> I sometimes look into the eyes of a house cat. The domesticated animal has not by any means received the gift of the truly "eloquent" glance from *us*, as a human conceit suggests sometimes; what it has from us is only the ability – purchased with the loss of its elementary naturalness – to turn this glance upon us brutes. In this process some mixture of surprise and question has come into it, into its dawn and even its rise – and this was surely wholly absent from the original glance, for all its anxiety. Undeniably, this cat began its glance by asking me with a glance that was ignited by the breath of my glance: "Can it be that you mean me? Do you actually want that I should not merely do tricks for you? Do I concern you? Am I there for you? Am I there? What is that coming from you? What is that around me? What is it about me? What is that?!" ("I" is here a paraphrase of a word of the I-less self-reference that we lack. "That" represents the flood of man's glance in the entire actuality of its power to relate).[1]

I can hear your sigh. Cameron's silliness is slightly more entertaining than Buber's intellectual somersaults. But let us

---

1 Martin Buber, *I and Thou* (New York: Touchstone, 1970), new translation and introduction by Walter Kaufmann, p. 145.

stick with Buber; he's worth it. I understand you, as we both belong to the same times, which are shallow, require no concentration and run on the modern fuel discovered shortly after petroleum and confusingly called "entertainment". I freely admit that Buber is not an easy read and sometimes his assertions are opaque and simply far too grand, such as, "Nothing can doom man but the belief in doom, for this prevents the movement of return." He is a mystic; I am a rationalist. He uses such terms as "soul" and "spirit", without giving adequate explanation, and in Walter Kaufmann's excellent translation (like his translation of Nietzsche's *Thus Spoke Zarathustra*) you feel that precision sometimes obscures meaning in order to avoid suggesting the wrong meaning. But like all good things, Buber's work requires a little effort, and then you start to hear some interesting intuitions.

An I-thou relationship requires the I to seek out the thou's nature and understand it, which is impossible. Hence the I-thou relationship is an ideal to which we should try to conform. We need to accept the nature of the thou and adapt to it. Attempting to change another nature is folly and rarely succeeds. If it does succeed, it is an act of tyranny. Many will object and ask, "What about teaching and parenthood?" Of course, there is a duty there, but it is not to change the thou; it is to help the thou to find its own way to change. When the thou is another I or an interlocutor, to use the normal terminology when speaking of human dialogue, the thou can be more or less disposed to seek out the I's true nature. This is a game of two players, and the ideal requires that both are ideal. The ideal I or saintly I will never give up, but always accept the thou for what the thou is. The ideal I will always turn the other cheek. Most of us will give up long before that. As I get older, I am less accepting of the ambitious and the manipulative (still less the violent, whom

I have always avoided). They cease to fascinate me, as experience has taught that they are wholly predictable. This is not commendable, but it is practical. Even if we have always fought against the commodification of time, we eventually have to accept that time holds sway, if we are to finish what we want to finish in life. We are never wholly free of ambition, however circumscribed.

The perfect I-thou relationship requires intelligence and understanding, for every dialogue produces degrees of misunderstanding and yet no one ought to say that I-thou relationships are the private domain of the intelligent, partly because the apparently intelligent are often only interested in displaying the virtuosity of their own thought processes. How many writers can deny this? Very few, if they're honest. In anyone who ever put pen to paper with the intent of communicating their words to persons unknown and unknowable, there is an imperious "I", who says, "I have something to say." Writers do not necessarily claim great importance for their words. Generally, they will not change the world or even a little part of it; they will only engage with a few minds, many of whom will silently receive them with disapproval or, slightly better, outrage. Nevertheless, writing is not the same as a chat in the pub or on the train – sublime things that can be as satisfying as they are ephemeral – nor are they the same as the dialogues we have in our own heads. The written word is outside time and evolves out of sequence and through a series of corrections and changes of opinion.

When we speak of human relationships, we inhabit the world of ideas, and Buber does not explain how we relate to the world. When writing *I and Thou* was Buber relating to the reader or the work? The writer has complete control over the work, and therefore it must necessarily be an I-it relationship. Maybe the work, like any other work of art, has its own demands. Would that make it an I-I relationship? Buber does not mention such things. The relationship with the reader is not really a relationship at all, as the reader is an essential but anonymous being, whose nature remains entirely unknown to the writer. Some writers imagine their reader, who is often very like themselves. One leading Italian writer claimed that he expected his reader to have read the same books as he had. It is questionable that the creative act – in the artistic sense – is ever an I-thou relationship. Something that should humble us.

I and Thou is a work that tries to change the world, not through economics or politics as is so often the case with such ambitious works, but through the individual moment of our existence, in our perception of the world and how we relate to all of it with sensitivity. Buber is not specific on this point, but I feel certain that he believed that everyone could access this sensitivity and the pleasure it can bring. This suggests the importance of passivity, a virtue I have argued for, often to be misunderstood, because the West is now so wedded to its go-getting philosophy. We live in an entrepreneurial society that is obsessed with seduction – that is persuading others to do things they do not actually want to do – and this is quintessential coercive thinking or, to put it in Buber's terminology, an I-it relationship with our human and material environment. We are expected to overheat the world and hammer it on the blacksmith's anvil. Very few get to do the hammering. Most of us are the anvil. The commonest type of passivity is the cowardly one, which submits to the powerful simply because they are powerful. That is not the passivity I speak of. I mean the passivity that says to the powerful, "I do not hate you, but I will not be moved by you. I cannot change you or stop you from doing what you're doing, but I will not assist you, even if there is a cost. I am sorry for you, because you have not understood what life is, and are alienated from your true nature. I hear your propaganda and I see your advertising and persuasive methods, but I will not be affected by them. I do not lift my hand against you, but I will do all I can to obstruct your plans. I know that my actions alone will have very little effect, but if enough of us sit down outside the palace of power, the assault on our planet and the poor will cease or slow down, at least for a while."

In *On Love*, Stendhal perceives love as something decidedly I-it: it is the conquest of another through a complex game that can include deception. It is seduction in the restricted sense of the word. "Love and war," we say, which is a grotesque association. A clearer encomium of the seductive arts is to be found in Machiavelli's *La mandragola*, in which the lover and the seducer are two distinct people, stressing the differences between the roles. The former is an inept young man rendered even more foolish by his uncontrollable passion, and the latter is a middle-aged man with experience of life who sets out to resolve the young man's problem for reasons that are not entirely clear, but most probably a desire to measure the efficacy of his own cunning. The seduction is planned like a political campaign, and the skills are those of the sophist and spin-doctor.[2]

The Arab Israeli who told his Israeli lover that he was a Jew did not deserve to go to prison for "rape", because the Israeli court would certainly not do the same to Jewish Israelis who lie about their jobs, their financial assets, their athleticism or any other factor they think might increase their chances of getting a woman into bed. These things happen all the time and are reprehensible. They reveal an awareness that the woman in question would not want sex with the seducer if they knew his true nature or status. That such women are probably shallow is of no importance. The Israeli woman was incapable of an I-thou relationship because she only sees race

2 Luigi Blasucci's introduction to Niccolò Machiavelli, *Opere letterarie*, ed. by L. Blasucci, (Milan: Adelphi, 1964).

and not the individual, even when she fails to detect it; this is a fine example of racism, but the rules of dialogic relations demand that the "I" acknowledge the "thou's" true nature for what it is and does not loathe it, at least within the act of dialogue. Deception in sexual relationships is common and certainly cannot be defined as criminal rape, but it is an act of disrespect – even when the motivation of the disrespected person is not worthy of respect outside the relationship, precisely because *all* human relationships should be characterised by that consideration we generally define as humanity and here we call the I-thou relationship.

This leads us to the strength and the weakness of Buber's argument, although it is perhaps unfair to subject his work to this kind of analysis. It is as much a poetic and moral work as it is a philosophical one. He purposefully rejected his first draft plan, because "its systematic character estranged me from it." In relations between human beings, the greatest damage is not done by violence and theft, but by mendacity and deception, simply because of the scale of the latter. Lives and families are devastated, but no law can do much to alter this fundamental law of the human condition. This is an area where philosophy, religion, morality, social pressure and various other forces can play a part, but their effectiveness will always be restricted. There is a cost associated with mendacity and deception, and for most of us this cost is sufficient to deter us. That we feel we have to be distrustful of others is a cost that remains. Given this centrality of honesty to genuine dialogue between human beings, is it sensible to confuse I-thou relationships between humans with those between human "I"s and inanimate or even abstract things, which can never be properly dialogic? The answer, I think, is yes: Buber's work is one of literary defamiliarisation, in which the author wishes us to rethink all our relationships. This book, published in 1922, was ahead of its time: in our current reality, we cannot restrict our considerations of reality to humanity while treating what is beyond it as a resource to be acted on as we wish without reference to its needs. Our own selfish needs demand that we treat this shrinking planet with care and respect, and I say this as someone perhaps too wedded to a humanistic mindset. Buber was perfectly aware that the human world is different and complex, requiring different rules and different moralities. He also believed that the I-it relationship was inevitable and could not be banned from our lives, even our interactions with other humans. He was also very insistent that any religious experience of any worth had to be within the physicality of human society and not isolated from it. Like many great works, you read the last page in a state of greater wisdom and greater confusion. Its inconsistencies are perhaps the cause of its charm and its efficacy.

We cannot mention Buber or *I and Thou*, without mentioning Walter Kaufmann who translated the book from German and wrote a "prologue" that is not only an introduction to a complex work, but also a gloss and a work of literature in its own right. When I was first acquainted with this work, over a quarter of a century ago, I was more impressed by Kaufmann's prologue than the main text. Kaufmann is more accessible than Buber, and he has many intelligent things to say. While praising and defending *I and Thou*, Kaufmann reveals what it hasn't done, and lists the other dialogic relationships: "In these five attitudes there is no You: I-I, I-It, It-It, We-We and Us-Them. There are many ways of living in a world without You."[3] It-It? Kaufmann explains,

> There are men who hardly have an I at all. Nor are all of them of one kind.

3 *I and Thou* ..., p. 14.

Some inhabit worlds in which objects loom large. They are not merely interested in some thing or subject, but the object of their interest dominates their lives. They are apt to be great scholars of extraordinary erudition, with no time for themselves, with no time to have a self.

They study without experiencing: they have no time for experience, which would smack of subjectivity if not frivolity. They are objective and immensely serious. They have no time for humour...

Here we have a community of solid scholars – so solid there is no room at the centre for any core. Theirs is the world of It-It.

Kaufmann takes Buber's ideas and develops them much further in a more rationalist key.

However, when I read *I and Thou* for this essay, I found that the book came out from Kaufmann's shadow. It says something that I had already come to believe: humanity is lost in an inexplicable world that becomes bearable and then even wonderful when we engage with its unknowability and avoid its "thinghood". I struggle at times with Buber's mysticism. But it seemed less of a struggle this time, and the subject matter could not be more essential. And it could not be more relevant now that consumer society has pursued much further our alienation from natural human relations. We need to think about them, and this is the good reason why Buber is the subject of my first essay. We face some difficult questions. Can we remember the dialogue when it was an end in itself? Can we communicate with our neighbour when we can communicate with the whole world? What does it mean to travel, when travel has been deprived of its power to surprise? Have we ceased to play with language since we became adding machines that assess everything in monetary terms? We thought we had entered an age of reason, but we have stumbled into the mysticism of the market, the greatest abstraction of them all. Compared with the mysticism of the market, Buber's eccentric religious mysticism feels like common sense.

It would be wrong to write this essay on Buber and human relationships without mentioning a magnificent novel which, I think, took or should have taken everyone by surprise. I had already read quite a bit by Stefan Zweig when I read it: a novel, his well-crafted novellas and a couple of non-fiction works, one on Erasmus and the other on Servetus, the former of which is still a serviceable biography. Yet *Beware of Pity* is, in my opinion, one of the great European novels. I argued over this book with an intellectual I greatly admire and whose opinions I reject only after careful consideration. He was a little dismissive of Zweig, which is not uncommon for reasons that to me are not clear. Zweig's novel is beautifully constructed, the characterisation is perfect, the dialogues are intriguing and the tragedy that unfolds with exquisite slowness is revealing of some important truths on human relationships.

Zweig undermines Buber, because he demonstrates very well that human relationships take place within society. Whether I-thou or I-it, relationships do not take place in isolation. Perhaps this is true of musings on the nature of a cat (which is not really a relationship anyway). Yet human relationships are acted upon by a thousand other forces: kinship interests, friendships, personal ambitions, rivals, language and social conventions (this last group covers endless subgroups). No human relationship is an island cut loose from society, even when those two persons are away in a remote part of a country whose language they cannot speak – because we always carry our relationships with us in our heads – and some people also carry their hatreds. In a way those we care about are more present when they are absent because they leave behind them an eloquent gap. That presence in absence may fade, if for some reason we never see them again, but others will take their place. There is no vacuum in human relationships.

This defect is not, however, fatal for Buber's book. His plea to assert the I not as source of manipulation and power but as a passive and independent interlocutor leads to an I that is strong enough to rebuff the pressures and conventions that caused the tragedy in the life of Zweig's protagonist. Beyond the possibilities of Buber's ideal and almost unachievable I, it is, as Walter Kaufmann points out in his prologue, sometimes necessary to simplify an argument in order to put it across more clearly and more forcefully. Buber's work should be read more widely, preferably with Kaufmann's comments, but these should be read after the main text. *I and Thou* should be approached without prejudice or preconception. The reader should not be put off by the occasional obscure passage. This is true of all good books, but it is particularly true of this one, which is so utterly itself.

And what does it say? Many things – too many to mention here – but essentially the author is urging you to treat every encounter – I think this is the right word – every encounter, however banal or fleeting, as a wonderful, God-given opportunity to do something new and discover something new. I use that adjective, God-given, in its literal sense, because Buber believes in God and that God is present in the human world in all its smallest mechanisms: it is there and only there that you can discover Him.

On Tolstoy's *Resurrection*

Tolstoy's *Resurrection* starts and ends with an explicitly Christian message, and to some small extent this mars the opening chapters with a narrative voice that is precisely that of one who shares Tolstoy's specific religious views – in other words the narrative voice appears to be indistinguishable from the author's voice (not simply exposing wrongs but also providing a moral gloss). This is not damaging at the end, partly because it is great writing but in any case because this is more appropriate for endings, which thus become undeclared epilogues – authors' glosses on their own works to assist anyone who hasn't, quite yet, got the point. And Tolstoy, like Upton Sinclair in *The Jungle*, was writing this novel for very particular non-literary reasons, which were both political and religious but more political than religious.

Tolstoy's *Resurrection* is a great novel. It may be that, today, it is not as great as, say, *Anna Karenina*, but at the time of writing it was the greater. Not only was it great literature, it was also something more important: a plea for clemency and a better world *addressed to his own times*. To some extent the important and original things in this novel had long been part of intelligent political discourse, although they are still largely to be implemented. Anyone interested in prison reform should read this book not in search of new ideas but to sober themselves with the depressing thought that over a hundred years later so little has been done to make his hopes a reality.

Tolstoy's *Resurrection* is also a great social document. In it we have privileged access to the "lower classes" of late nineteenth-century Russia. And Tolstoy manages to write without condescension, although sometimes he comes close, which is an achievement for someone living in a society dripping with class prejudice. Dickens does well, but Tolstoy does much better. He is scathing and even at times cruel in his depiction of his own class, but he never loses his humanity, his understanding for stunted lives trapped in their own affluence. The characterisation is occasionally judgemental but is always acute and profound. Some of the harshest judgements are reserved for the protagonist and autobiographical figure of Nekhlyudov, whose religious conversion is always in danger of tipping over into a new form of self-love.

I am not an expert on Tolstoy's life, and too much knowledge can hinder as much it can assist understanding of the texts. However, I know enough to be impressed to find that a man of such privileged background could in the nineteenth century identify not only with the virtuous and hardworking amongst the downtrodden poor, but also those who had drifted into crime and prostitution. More notably still, he understood that for the rural poor this distinction did not exist – nor did it in reality. One random, apparently minor misfortune could push them from one group to the other.

My relationship with this novel is not, however, that of an impartial critic; this is a book with which I have a close emotional relationship.

When I was thirteen or thereabouts, my mother would drive to some shops at the back of a wonderfully shabby hotel in Dhaka called the Shaghbagh (and renamed the "Shag-Bag" by my sister, as we had previously lived there for more than a year). On these trips, she would disappear for an hour or so, and my sanity was saved by something amongst the dusty greyness of the mini-arcade and the beggars that inhabited it. I knew the beggars well: a smiling little girl apparently healthy but for the pus that oozed from both ears – presumably only a short course of antibiotics away from a cure – a boy also smiling and the shadow of his elder companion, and a determined old lady who approached more slowly, bent by her years and a growth the size of a head dangling from her chin (I learnt much later that it could have been removed with a minor operation long before it took on those disconcerting proportions). She used her growth as a powerful weapon and if you did not close your window in time, she could hang it into the car interior, by which time you were utterly at her mercy. Smiling back at the children and fleeing the old woman, too terrified to consider her plight and the misery of her life, I could reach the sanctuary in which to lose an hour of my time more usefully. It was an English-language bookshop whose dimensions and aspect I have difficulty reconstructing in my mind. I'm sure that, like the other shops in the row, it had its name painted on a framed piece of plywood above the door and it was small. It was dusty and books were not organised in any kind of order; some were on shelves and others in teetering piles. If I remember correctly, the owner had little or no English and there were few customers – mostly Bengalis who could read English and couldn't afford new books.

It was here that I came across an American edition of *Resurrection*. It had a misleadingly romantic cover of a dashing nineteenth-century army officer whose extravagant military hat had an enormous plume. He was on horseback and a woman who looked as though she had dressed for a society ball was holding his hand and clinging to his leg in an act of utter subservience and devotion. Clearly the cover designer had not read the book and very probably nor had the editor who explained the storyline to him. I considered the book for a long time – almost certainly on more than one visit. Money was short and the cover put me off, but with time on my hands I read a chunk of it and was hooked. The book has stayed in my possession and my mind.

Not every book I read at that age I could understand, but this one I did. I have reread some books, such as Sartre's

Nausea, several times and each time they have felt like different books. Yet when I reread *Resurrection* for the first time as preparation for this essay, I felt that it is now for me exactly as it was, except for the strange, disappointing disappearance of an episode in which an odious aristocratic boy considers his superiority to the poor who surround his carriage in Moscow, affecting me profoundly. Whether it was deleted from the Penguin edition I have just read or I read the episode in another book by Tolstoy or even another Russian writer I do not know. Nearly fifty years have passed, and my memory was never good. That it feels unchanged is due to the nature of this book: it is simple and complex; it is focused on certain truths and is written with the intention of putting them across as clearly as possible; it goes straight to the most important things in human existence, about which it is often difficult to say anything very original. Surely this was one of Tolstoy's works that influenced Gandhi and through him the world.

Of course the impact is different now. When I first read at the beginning that one of the women in a remote Russian township would drown her unwanted babies, I was profoundly shocked in a way that perhaps I can no longer be, although there is much that shocks me today. Then I looked around at the poverty that devastated the country now called Bangladesh and Tolstoy's world did not seem so far away. There was much that could rekindle your faith in humanity; poor societies often display more human dignity than affluent ones, but at the same time I could observe the blindness of the middle classes, particularly the European expatriates. I remember hearing people discussing the strikes that regularly occurred in Dhaka's factories, which included some owned by Western corporations. They said that the owners were using the gundas, a local mafia that specialised in assassination, to kill the strike leaders. There was no outrage in their voices; these were necessary but inconvenient events. A Bengali friend of mine had seduced the family maid and made her pregnant: sent off with a couple of months' salary she could only turn to prostitution. Like Nekhlyudov, he felt guilty but could not do anything about it. Life, *Resurrection* explains, is a serious affair: our actions have consequences, often out of proportion with the pleasures that originally caused them. It's true that Tolstoy's attitude to sex is out of date, and rightly so. You feel that Nekhlyudov and perhaps Tolstoy himself never switched off for a moment, unlike Martin Buber who understood that we cannot maintain the same seriousness in all situations, nor should we. There is a scene in which Nekhlyudov has to plead the case of two of his protégés with an obnoxious and vicious prison officer. Nekhlyudov congratulates himself on his restraint following his conversion, but if you follow the dialogue you cannot help noticing that he treats the officer with contempt and obstinacy. He actually obtains what he wants, but you feel that Nekhlyudov and perhaps Tolstoy never really cease to be aristocrats, even though they have turned against them. But life *is* a serious affair, and a life spent in the pursuit of comfort and wealth is a life wasted. Tolstoy's principal arguments are as valid now as they were then, perhaps more so, given the shallowness of our times, although the credit crunch has gradually woken up many souls that slept through the previous two decades.

The surprising and for me slightly depressing thing that emerges from my rereading of this work is that so many of my ideas have grown towards Tolstoy's – most significantly his religious ideas, although I do not share his certainties. They are not identical: Tolstoy is still troubled by an afterlife, but the book, including its tone and documentary analysis, is about this world and how it functions, and that is where its strength lies. Did it take me nearly half a century to catch up with this book and my thirteen-year-old self?

Certainly, the only part of the book that stayed with me very clearly was Tolstoy's classism – but a classism that was not based on hate. That in itself was a very good lesson. You can only improve the lives of those who have too little by taking something from those who have too much and are afflicted too by their exuberant wealth. A political system requires its citizens to become complicit in its crimes, and by so doing it degrades them so much that the better ones have to seek solace in alcohol. This is a point that Tolstoy makes again and again, and it is an essential truth – not a bad point to start out on life. I am indebted to that little shop.

Another aspect I have always been aware of is that the motivation for being a socialist should be empathy and moral outrage at how other human beings are being treated, and not some analytical formula called "scientific socialism". For this reason I was always been much more at home with the label "communist" than "Marxist". Marx was right on so many important points, but I would not want to define myself by a single man's thoughts, as clearly I do not agree with him on everything and, more importantly, even if those analyses were wrong, I would still rebel against the way our economic system grinds people down and destroys the better part of their being.

By "communist" I do not mean any particular regime, but the holding of most assets in common, and in recent years I have become increasingly convinced that landownership has to be completely abolished as a prerequisite for any good society (some forms of private property may very well be acceptable; I do not claim to be a political scientist and I doubt anyone yet has the blueprint for a perfect society, but we can determine which things obstruct a good society: landownership and corporations). I was influenced in this opinion by Linbaugh's *The Magna Carta Manifesto: Liberties and Commons for All* which, along with a long period living in the country made me think that the land question is often neglected today. It might also be worth quoting the Gaelic proverb "Firewood from wood, a salmon from the river and a deer from the forest are never theft for a Gael" to demonstrate that such concepts have always had their roots in peasant society. I had forgotten how prominent the land issue is in this novel. Tolstoy deals with it almost exhaustively through a series of very effective dialogues expressing the different viewpoints of the different classes and within the different classes.

When I first read the book, I ignored the religious ideas because I was an atheist and could see no corner of this world where God could hide. The author's religious ideas did not spoil my first reading, but I sifted them out. I did remember them, but I did not remember exactly what they were. I don't believe that they sedimented in my brain and worked their way through very slowly, but who knows? We have little understanding of how the human brain works and retains or discards information, although I'm told that this new frontier is going to be opened up in the coming decades. The influences are more likely to be my reading much later about the "free spirits" of the sixteenth century who distinguished themselves from the equally unpalatable Reformation and Counter-Reformation. Nevertheless there is the hint of an interesting idea here: influences during our teens, particularly our early teens, are decisive in laying out the framework for our later intellectual development *almost unconsciously*. This would certainly help to explain why generations are such cohesive identities – more so perhaps than nations and political credos.

Marx and Tolstoy had one thing in common: they both were impractical when it came to the all-important question of how change could come about, although they pointed to entirely different routes. Marx put his faith in working-class organisation and Tolstoy in moral example. Working-class organisation did bring about changes, the most important of which were universal suffrage and greater freedom of debate, now claimed as an achievement of the middle class, which actually fought against them and has resumed its hostilities. Unfortunately for Marxists, the industrial working class proved to be a gradualist class on the whole, except in the period of early industrialisation. The truly revolutionary class capable of any sacrifice was the peasantry, and the peasantry is now a disappearing class.

Tolstoy believed society could be improved through example. Example is powerful (much more powerful than rational persuasion), and a more caring society can be built up slowly, but it can never go the whole way. Hobbes was right on this point: humanity is not as inherently depraved as he imagined, but neither is it wholly perfectible. A small part of humanity is always irredeemable: there will always be the psychopathic. It is also true that many, perhaps nearly all, people who engage in violent behaviour can be changed through careful rehabilitation. There is good in almost everyone, but not everyone and that is a fact that cannot be wished away. Let us shift for a moment to the more familiar paradigms of pacifism. There are three categories of pacifist: personal pacifist, moral pacifist and legal pacifist. The personal pacifist quite sensibly opts out and says, "The world can do what it wants; I will not personally or through others engage or assist in any act of violence." This is utterly commendable, but does not solve the problem. The moral pacifist sets out to persuade the whole of humanity of the benefits of pacifism, in the hope that eventually everyone will be persuaded and there will be no more war. The legal pacifist argues that such an event will never occur or come near to occurring, and that it is only by developing international law and *the means to impose that law through force* that war between nations can finally be overcome. Tolstoy wanted to achieve through the first two not only peace but the reorganisation of society. It cannot be said that he didn't have a powerful influence, but ultimately the state and the law, which he correctly identifies as the source of corruption, must be used to overcome the corruption they originally created.

This leads us to another thinker who did exactly the opposite: Machiavelli. He was obsessed with how the state could reform itself from inside, and he believed a little naively that good laws could be set up in perpetuity by a good lawmaker, and for that reason a good lawmaker – and only a good lawmaker – could be justified in using less than moral behaviour to achieve the situation whereby he could introduce good laws. Machiavelli was not the immoral man some people consider him to be, but he was mistaken. He and Tolstoy approach the problem from opposite ends: Tolstoy believed that change comes from the individual and Machiavelli thought that it comes from the state. Both are right and both are wrong. The two need to be merged, but they are almost irreconcilable opposites. For literature, this is a great gift, but for humanity it is an insuperable and tragic obstacle – a cruel sentence that reality has passed on humanity.

This does not mean that we should give up and it does not mean that we couldn't quite quickly achieve a much better society than the one we have today, but "heaven on earth" cannot transcend the Lord's Prayer, as Tolstoy contemplates in *Resurrection*. He sets a fine example, and analyses society quite brilliantly, and yet he cannot provide a credible way to achieve change – not because of any lack of intelligence, but because there isn't one or rather there isn't one that doesn't to some extent compromise Tolstoy's very high principles.

The question of how change should be brought about was

of great importance to the politicals, who appear at the end of the book. These were mainly the Narodniks, whose ideas are considered an early form of terrorism, although terror had always been used by power and goes back at the very least to the ancient and medieval siege, which used starvation and threatened annihilation of civilian populations to achieve desired results. The Narodniks could argue that they were merely using the same methods against the state as the state used against them. In purely rational terms, they were right, but the acts of terror had devastating effects on their own psyches. Tolstoy is particularly effective in his characterisation of the politicals and their inherent weaknesses, but at the same time he is respectful of their motivations. On the whole, they bear their sufferings lightly and show great courage, but theirs is a pointless exercise.

As an alternative, Tolstoy suggests in the final pages the implementation of a Christian ethic of non-violence, which has largely been ignored throughout the history of Christianity. At this stage he introduces the English proselytiser, who is a foil to the Nekhlyudov character. There is nothing preachy about Nekhlyudov, while the Englishman is irrepressible in his attempts to change people with simple arguments, even though he knows and understands little about the society he is visiting. He presumably did not take a pith helmet to Siberia, but he does wear a metaphorical one. There is an element of uncertainty about this Englishman: to us he is obnoxious, but Tolstoy may have looked on him more kindly. He provides Nekhluydov with the bible that completes the process of his conversion. In Tolstoy there is an appealing acceptance of the variety of human life, and he is not, one feels, like the English proselytiser who wished to homogenise humanity. In spite of himself, he remained a primarily literary figure, and not a political and religious one, although here he drifts in that direction. This was because he chose fiction as the most effective way of putting his ideas across, and this entails a degree of uncertainty and an acceptance of the irresolvable, which by definition cannot be resolved. *Resurrection* is further proof, if further proof be needed, of fiction's efficacy in analysing complex situations, even in a book like this that aims to put across important ideas the author is keen to propagate.

On Aphorisms

The aphorism is a very limited form. That is what gives it potential. It is a dishonest form, because it makes a bold statement without any attempt to justify it or consider possible consequences.

It may then appear to be a lazy way to pontificate, but it isn't or isn't when it has been done well. In some languages, another word for aphorism has the same root as "sententious", and the great danger to be avoided in writing aphorisms is sententiousness. No preacher or demagogue has ever taken to the aphorism in the West, but they've tried their hand at almost every other form.[1]

The aphorism is a scattergun and does not necessarily have a viewpoint. It can be, like satire, indiscriminate and vicious. It can be gentle, humorous and urbane. It can be philosophical, but in that case it is best supported by other prose works that don't have the limitations we've mentioned. It can be political, and I have published an excellent collection of aphorisms by the American Marxist Renzo Llorente.[2]

Oscar Wilde was not an aphorist, but his writings and conversations were extremely aphoristic and have been mined to create collections of aphorisms. When he said, "Youth is wasted on the young," he created the perfect aphorism (amongst many others). Why? First the brevity. Second the humour in the apparent contradiction, so the

---

1 I have to write, "in the West" because of Mao Zedong and his *Little Red Book*. Arguably Marcus Aurelius can be excluded because he wrote as a philosopher rather than a politician or theologian. No doubt someone could find some names to prove me wrong, but none spring to my mind.

2 R. Llorente, *Beyond the Pale. Exercises in Provocation* (Sulaisiadar: Vagabond Voices, 2010).

reader or listener is first struck by the impossibility of the statement and it takes a second or two to understand the actual meaning. Youth/young is being used in two different senses. The energy, health, strength, intelligence and ability to experience and feel of those who have not lived too many years are wasted on those who, because they have not lived long enough, are too innocent and lacking in experience to exploit those advantages. Thirdly there is the vagueness. The lists are mine, and other people might interpret "youth" and "young" in other ways. It could be to do with the beauty of youth, or its capacity for sex and partying. It might be that youth, being constrained by work and lack of wealth and other resources, is unable to enjoy its advantages, but I doubt that Wilde would have been motivated by such a mundane and practical consideration.

In my introduction to Llorente's book, I wrote, "Writers of aphorisms or fragments eschew the idea of systems, and prefer to snipe at those who do. Their power lies in their small ambitions, and the intention is to wage a kind of guerrilla war against the massed ranks of powerful but unmanageable ideological armies. They can only win by wearing the enemy down over a long period, but their actions are crucial." I was suggesting that the aphorism is well suited to our conformist times, when there is little hope of dramatic change. A lot has changed since 2010, particularly in Scotland, and when change starts to appear a genuine option, the essay comes into its own. How Scotland votes on 18 September will decide the relevance of either the essay or the aphorism. If the No wins, we will jot down aphorisms when we pause from the central task of weeping into our beer over a lost opportunity.

Did My Father Have Free Will?

I'm not an expert on my father, perhaps he wasn't either. Of one thing I am sure, he believed strongly in his own will – in his ability "to create his own luck" and mould his life as he intended. To put it in Sartre's words, he created his own essence.

He overstated his claim, of course: he was as much a product of his own time as the rest of us. And his time was one when the personal room for manoeuvre was restricted, although people pushed hard against those restrictions and sometimes broke through. I would not say that he did, but he came close.

My father was very much in the Western go-getting tradition and said that he wished he had been born at a time when there were still parts of the globe "to discover" and he could have been an explorer. On the other hand, he cultivated a more meditative side and dabbled in Eastern religions purely out of curiosity, practising meditative yoga long before it became a fashion. He had a penchant for random acts of kindness and, to his credit, he would never acknowledge them as such. They came from the heart without the heart noticing. He had utter contempt for many professions, starting with doctors who were always referred to as "perishing quacks", and then in descending order, accountants, civil servants, lawyers and teachers. He was middle-class but more hostile to other sections of the middle class than he was to other classes. This was a residue of two conflicting and mutually exclusive influences on his life. The first was his upbringing in what we now call a one-parent family: his mother was a war widow, and the Indian Army paid for his education. He mixed with the rich, but was from a family in which money was in short supply. The second was a brief shift to the left as a result of the war. In this he was following a widespread trend in post-war Britain, and he voted Labour in the first two post-war elections – for, as it happened, the winning side, only to follow the next trend – this time to the Conservatives and then like a weathervane back to Labour in the sixties (in 1970 he voted Liberal and continued to do so for the rest of his life, clearly having lost his instinctive olfactory skills for seeking out the prevailing political odour). Is the floating voter an example of a free spirit or a herd instinct? This was a question he posed himself later in life, without finding an answer or one he was willing to share with the rest of us.

He was, I think, both of those things. On many occasions, he clearly acted impulsively and recklessly *but not without an intellectual process*. He was definitely capable of making considered moral judgements that produced eccentric results, and then acting upon them with complete disregard to the risks he was conscious of. He was also capable of following the herd. He once signed a petition to prevent the opening of a home for children with psychological disorders. When my mother came home and he told her, she was furious. With a curl in her lip she asked, "So you did this to protect house prices?" This apparently had been the principal argument of the petition organisers, and my father, deeply ashamed, rang them to have his name removed from the petition (I'm glad to say the home was opened without any delays). In this episode, he was little more than a marionette – or was he? He was acted upon by various forces, but in the end had to decide whether he was going to stand his ground or humiliate himself, but by humiliating himself, correct a wrong. At its centre there's a tiny space in which a human mind has to make a decision, and that decision is, at least in part, the result of a rational assessment that takes into account moral and contingent factors that are quite complex. Even in his herd-like moment, he was still himself.

I listened on the radio to a neuroscientist called Dick Swaab, who claimed that "we are our brains", which seemed argu-able: at the very least we also our bodies, as our bodies clearly affect our brains and their performance. If we exercise, our brains seem more effective, and if we loll around and eat too much food, they feel about as active as a sloth's on a bad day. If brains are machines, then they're of the clapped-out kind that need a good kick or shove in a particular spot for reasons that are not at all clear. The secret method was only discov-ered because someone got so frustrated that they administered the kick or shove in a moment of hopelessness that turned out to be inspirational. Brains are erratic, and the product, no doubt, of evolution's clumsy and equally erratic process. Thank God they're erratic; that's their splendour. Brains are probably going out of fashion, now that computers can take over and be so consistent. We're told they are, at least, and surely they must be, because they really are machines.

The clever neuroscientist also defined himself as a neuro-Calvinist, because we are predestined by our DNA[1] and very early experience of life. He is right to some extent. No one can deny the influence of inherited traits and the early years of life, but that does not mean that we are without will. There is another factor, also extraneous to ourselves and our brains, which the good doctor failed to mention, and that factor is reason and rational ideas. If, for instance, Dick Swaab were able to convince me of the correctness of necessity or predestination, I might start to behave in a dif-ferent manner from what I do now. Necessity and predes-

---

1 By our parents, says Dr. Swaab, and most people would hope not, but they will find it increasingly difficult to avoid being like their parents as they get older, and to succeed in avoiding this, they will need an effort of will.

tination release us from moral responsibility, as we cannot fight against our natures and our environment. If we apply our belief, we have to let ourselves go, and float with the current.

Some people might argue that only a very moralistic person would believe in free will, and the determinist, whether scientific or driven by faith, is determined in turn by his or her self-assurance. The ideas reflect the traits of the people who hold them and are determined by external factors, thus assisting the arguments in favour of either necessity or predestination. The neuroscientist rightly pointed out that Calvin was the archetypal exponent of predestination, but he fails to see that this did not stop Calvin from hectoring people and trying to persuade them of their moral duties as he saw them. Again, some people might object that this proves nothing but the inconsistency of human nature and our inability to implement our rational analyses. This is also quite true, but … isn't it the case that we have to engage with those rational ideas to some extent – badly perhaps, stupidly perhaps, inconsistently no doubt – and that involves some considered decisions that are principally formulated in rational terms, and not because we're suffering from indigestion or our grandfather had an eccentric gene that we've inherited – particularly if we've been *trained* to think rationally and assess the always unreliable information put before us?

This is why education liberates. Most of us are like my father: we are often on automatic and simply following our instincts, almost unaware of our existence, and sometimes we're generous from the heart for no apparent reason and that behaviour can almost by-pass the brain, but we are also capable of making decisions after having carefully pondered a difficult problem and making those decisions by using the brain to get outside ourselves and into the abstract, where the abstractions are in control. The more educated we are, the better we are at doing this. In fact, isn't Professor Swaab living proof that his theory is wrong? He may be the product of the extremely high IQ he inherited from his mother and father, and all their forbears, he may be the product of influential teachers and lecturers, and he may be the product of an extremely well thought-out diet and strenuous runs at six o'clock every morning, but eventually when he sits down to think out how the brain works, he is free to move about amongst ideas and decide at will or at least on his own impartial assessment of the data. And this is crucial, he has to want to do it, rather than want to please his superiors, university funders and other external forces. He may also be affected by fashion, because there are fashions in ideas too. We have free will, but we don't have to use it. We can find our own way, but we need to get self-confidence or some self-confidence. We learn to use our will, because often during childhood, the will is not given a free run, and perhaps that's a good thing. It may be that too much freedom in the sense of lack of obstruction is, particularly in childhood, restricting on our natures and not liberating at all. Physical brutality and psychological bullying usually restrict a person's autonomy, but the impediments placed before us by living and sharing with others teach us to emerge from the claustrophobic company of our most obsessive and tiresome needs. In other words, society makes us what we are, and can enable us to interact with it as individuals with a margin of free will.

What is it that restricts us? Principally it is our own talents or lack of them. The tone-deaf cannot become opera singers and the badly coordinated cannot play for their national football team. We're restricted by the limitations of youth and old age, and deficiencies in our culture and education.

But these are not the restrictions that have caused so much ink to flow over the centuries; it is the moral implications that most concerned writers in the past, although I think we should widen the argument here. It is also about creativity – about not only the will to stand up to power on the basis of reasoned argument, which may of course be mistaken, but also about the will to create meaningful things for a society which may not be ready to understand them or may even be hostile. This can be as true of a mathematical theorem or scientific discovery as it is of a painting or a book. This is probably the case in almost any walk of life, as there are many ways in which we can be creative.

We should start with the moral arguments, which leads us to religion and much theological wrangling, some of it very foreign to our own times, but these arguments come from afar. Saint Augustine of Hippo in the fourth and fifth century AD is the important early proponent of predestination – the idea that God has predestined all our actions, and we cannot act in any manner other than the one we choose to, which effectively means we do not choose. This is not an easy argument to defeat empirically. The idea had been around for some time, and was a dogma of the cult of Isis, once an important rival to Christianity. Saint Thomas Aquinas came along much later, in the thirteenth century, to become the most famous proponent of the counterargument. The relatively liberal medieval mind had few difficulties with these competing arguments, which ran in tandem. With the Reformation, however, Protestants ran off with the idea of predestination (while paradoxically rejecting the Marian cult, which was the other legacy of the cult of Isis), and Catholics, perhaps as a reaction, embraced the idea of free will (there were Protestant heretics who believed in free will and Catholic heretics who believed in predestination, thus creating a perfect symmetry). One outcome of this wrangle, which we will mostly leap over, barely looking down, was a wonderful dispute between Erasmus and Luther, which is fascinating not just for the arguments they articulate but also and perhaps mostly for the tone and polemical, methods the antagonists deployed.

In reality, Erasmus was not just arguing for free will, but also for tolerance and scepticism, while Luther, more virile and aggressive, was not merely the proponent of predestination but also of unquestionable revelation and therefore the absolute truth, exactly as he understood it.[2]

Erasmus adopts the central argument for those who support free will: if human beings have no free will, they are in essence no different from an animal, a plant or even a piece of rock. This argument can also be used against the scientific theory of necessity, but Erasmus is arguing against the religious concept of predestination. He asks what the point is, "if man in his good as well as evil is just a tool of God's, like the hatchet for the carpenter."[3] This is not by itself a very convincing argument, as it is *a posteriori*: human beings are not like animals or stones, so their actions must be caused by something different, and the only other possibility is free will. This is effective against predestination, but not against scientific necessity, which is not concerned with the moral question. The Bible was the most important weapon in this battle, and on the whole Erasmus comes out of it slightly better.

Quoting Jesus in the New Testament, "Jerusalem, Jerusalem! Thou killest the prophets and stonest those who are sent to thee! How often have I gathered my children together, as a hen gathers her young under her wings, but

---

2 Continuum have published a splendid, well-translated and well-annotated edition, which has all the drama we associate with an Elizabethan play: Erasmus and Luther, *Discourse on Free Will* (London: Continuum, 2006).
3 *Discourse on Free Will*, ..., p. 39.

thou wouldst not!", Erasmus poses this question, "If all happened merely through necessity, could Jerusalem not have been justified in answering the weeping Lord, 'Why do you torment yourself with useless weeping? If it was your will that we should not listen to the prophets, why did you send them? Why do you blame us for what you willed, while we have merely acted out of necessity?"[4] The problem from a moral point of view is quite clear.

Erasmus also quotes the Apocrypha, "Let no man say when he is tempted, that he is tempted by God ... But everyone is tempted by his own passions."[5] Here we have an argument that resembles more secular ones. If we have free will which distinguishes us from the animals, we must be able to govern our desires, which clearly we do to varying degrees. However, if we are programmed by society – by our superegos – we still haven't gained free will. If society trains our minds to behave in a certain manner, then we are merely animals with an added mechanism which gives the species greater flexibility and adaptability. No one would deny that societies do these things, but the degree to which they can do these things can be argued over. The question is, "Do we refrain from murder because civilised society teaches us not to?" This could be followed by another question, which implies a different interpretation, "Do we refrain from murder because we fear the consequences in a civilised society?" But against both these arguments there is another one, which is quite popular amongst neuropsychologists at the moment, "Is there an innate morality that is hardwired into all human beings, unless they're suffering from some psychotic disorder?" All these arguments have some truth, but together they do not explain everything.

While Erasmus examines the counterarguments and seeks to find common ground, although firm in his underlying belief,

4 *Discourse on Free Will*, ..., p. 33.
5 *Discourse on Free Will*, ..., p. 37.

Luther sermonises ferociously and his occasional politeness is overlaid with sarcasm. This dramatic clash of different personalities strangely endears the reader to them both – not strangely in the case of Erasmus who still stands out as a great figure of tolerance and intellectual rigour, a forerunner perhaps of the better-known Voltaire. Strangely because the gentleness of Erasmus makes you feel slightly sorry for Luther, truly a product of necessity – his social background, the harshness of his life and the politico-religious reality of the early sixteenth century. Erasmus shows that you can rise above your upbringing and your time, because both men came from very lowly social rank. In the case of Luther, you can sense that behind the wretched dogmatist there is at least a man of principle, though you're forgetting perhaps that such individuals can be the most dangerous of all. He says, and you can envisage him on stage or in the pulpit declaiming madly these thunderous, menacing words,

> Therefore let me tell you, and I beg you to let it sink deep into your mind, I am concerned with a serious, vital and eternal verity, yes such a fundamental one that it ought to be maintained and defended at the cost of life itself, and even though the whole world should not only be thrown into turmoil and fighting, but shattered in chaos and reduced to nothing.[6]

Surely even the most magnificent and well-proven truth that humanity ever encountered could not possibly be worth such a price. Luther clearly thought that an argument won is won forever, whereas an argument won has actually initiated its decline, as the exceptions and provisos start to appear.

The terrifying illogicality of Luther's blind faith is starkly revealed in his response to Erasmus's mention of moral

---

6 *Discourse on Free Will*, …, p. 94.

responsibility: "You say, Who will endeavour to reform this life? I answer, Nobody! No man can! God has no time for your self-reformers, for they are hypocrites."

And yet there is more than a trace of elitism in Erasmus's position, which suggests that morality is not only a good in itself but also a means for maintaining order, an instrument of power, and this put him on this point alone in the company of Machiavelli, someone who would have disturbed him even more than Luther. He wrote that it is "better not to cavil and quibble about such matters, *especially not before the common people*."[7] Luther also believed in the importance of maintaining order but, as we have just seen, it came second to the absolute reign of religious truth as he perceived it. His response: "It matters little to you what anyone anywhere believes as long as the peace of the world is undisturbed." Luther is clearly wrong in claiming that Erasmus does not care what people think, but perhaps senses that Erasmus fears the people, not because they are poor and want his property as he has none, but because they lack his erudition and therefore cannot reason as reliably as he can. Many a liberal has been secretly happy that other, more illiberal clerics and state officials keep the people in their place and don't excite them with ideas they are incapable of understanding. The road to democracy had a long way to go – and still has – so we should not be scandalised by Erasmus's nervousness, because he had experienced the fierceness of hostile crowds – both Catholic and Protestant – and in old age had difficulty finding a place to live in peace.

Another famous dispute on this subject was between two Englishmen, but it originally took place in Paris. One of them, John Bramhall, is remembered now because he was the antagonist in a debate with Thomas Hobbes, which had

---

7 *Discourse on Free Will*, ..., p. 17 (my italics).

been organised by another exile from the uncertainties of the English Revolution, the Marquess of Newcastle. This was not a happy affair amongst exiles, as they were not comrades in a political struggle but intellectuals inconveniently displaced by events. Bramhall was an Anglican bishop and so there was again a certain amount of quoting from the scriptures, as well as the classics, but with the exception of God's omnipotence I will only mention the philosophical ideas, as this is the interesting part (and their religious ideas could not upstage Erasmus's and Luther's).

It will come as little surprise that Hobbes argues for necessity. As a protestant cleric, Bramhall was more unusual, because mainstream Protestantism is associated with predestination, but he was what is called an Arminian after a Dutch Calvinist who rejected the dogma. It is not such a good read, and it mainly demonstrates an interesting problem in this particular debate: differences are often not of substance but of definition.

Generally speaking the argument over free will is never about free will in all things. There are, as already suggested, enormous constraints on our lives and actions, which can then be divided into different categories. One fundamental distinction has always been between instinctive actions and reasoned actions ("spontaneous" and "voluntary" in seventeenth-century usage). Instinct belongs to the realm of necessity – even the bishop does not challenge that and writes, "the order, beauty and perfection of the world does require that in the universe should be agents of all sorts, some necessary, some free, some contingent [random]. He that shall make either all things necessary, guided by destiny, or all things free, governed by election, or all things contingent, happening by chance, does overthrow the beauty and the perfection of the world."[8] Some of our actions are

8 *Hobbes and Bramhall on Liberty and Necessity*, ed. by Vere Chappell (Cambridge: CUP, 1999), pp. 5-6.

governed by necessity, while it appears that only humans and the angels have election. Election is usually associated with will, but Hobbes uses the word "will" to denote the final stage of necessity where a degree of deliberation has taken place. Are you confused? Let me increase your pain with a quote from the famous political philosopher which combines awkward sophistry with now unfamiliar seventeenth-century syntax, when he examines a distinction used by his opponents:

> I am not ignorant of the usual reply to this answer, by distinguishing between will and permission, as that God Almighty does not indeed sometimes permit sin, and that he also foreknows that the sin he permits shall be committed, but does not will it nor necessitate it. I know also they distinguish the action from the sin of the action, saying that God Almighty does indeed cause the action, whatsoever action it be, but not the sinfulness or irregularity of it, that is, the discordance between the action and the law. Such distinctions as these dazzle my understanding. I find no difference between the will to have a thing done and the permission to do it, when he that permits can hinder it and knows it will be done unless he hinder it. Nor find I any difference between an action that is against the law and the sin of that action.[9]

Here we have so many threads to unravel that we have to go slowly. If your head is in a spin, don't worry; so is mine, and I am probably taking longer to write this than you are to read it. I will not go into all the inconsistencies on both sides

---

9 *Hobbes and Bramhall* on..., p. 23.

because they are now only of historical interest, but I think it fair to say that the argument Hobbes uses here is not against Bramhall, who does not distinguish between the action and the sin of action, and if he distinguishes between an immoral act (sin) and an illegal act, he is very sensible to do so. Both men have very similar positions, but are arguing to justify their own ideas rather than analysing in order to formulate their own ideas. This is *a posteriori* argumentation and there's a lot of that going on when it comes to this subject.

Bramhall accepts the existence of necessity in some of our actions and Hobbes quite perversely identifies "will" with necessity because, as I think it becomes clear, he has his reasons for organising the celestial realm in accordance with his own interpretation of the terrestrial one. He writes, "The last dictate of judgement concerning the good or bad that may follow from any action is not properly the whole cause, but the last part of it; and yet may be said to produce the effect necessarily, in such a manner as the last feather may be said to break a horse's back, when there were so many laid on before as there wanted but that to do it."[10] We can all agree that a great deal of external factors lead to our being in a situation where we have to make a decision, but this has no effect on whether that final decision is produced by free will or necessity. Bramhall writes, "An autonomous power of the sort the will is is a free power, because its operation is not necessitated by causes other than itself." This may be very restrictive, especially now we know more about how the mind works, but Hobbes does not appear to challenge this, and instead argues tautologically that in choosing between various possible actions which will be most agreeable to an individual, an individual will becomes necessity. The action becomes the only possible action because it is the only action taken.

---

10   *Hobbes and Bramhall on…*, pp. 20-21.

There are a couple of very interesting ideas here, which would become important in the development of English philosophy. The deliberation leading to the will in Hobbes's concept is, like Bramhall's "free power", sealed off in the self, although Hobbes admits that it aims at the individual's self-interest which could be in its relationship with the world around. Hobbes sees this as an amoral decision. "Power irresistible justifies all actions, really and properly, in whomsoever it be found." The individual must obey the laws of God and the state, but beyond that the individual can and should decide on the basis of self-interest. Luther disliked "self-reformers"; Hobbes doesn't even take their existence into consideration. Did the Anglo-Saxon idea of benign self-interest start with the man who is most famous for arguing the essentiality of the state and its dominion over the individual? There is a curious incongruence here, though this is not an inconsistency, such as the following one in his definition of the will:

> Now for his argument, that if the concourse of all the causes necessitate the effect, then it follows Adam had no true liberty. I deny the consequence; for I make not only the effect but also the election of that particular effect to be necessary, inasmuch as the will itself, and each propension of a man during his deliberation, is as much necessitated and depends on a sufficient cause as anything else whatsoever. As for example, it is no more necessary that fire should burn than that a man or other creature, whose limbs be moved by fancy, should have election, that is liberty, to do what he has a fancy to do, though it be not in his will or power to choose his fancy [instinctive action], or choose his election or will [reasoned action].[11]

---

11 *Hobbes and Bramhall* on…, p. 21.

This convolution on will almost destroys our will to live. Election is the power to choose a certain action, but Hobbes argues that we do not have the power to choose our election.

Bramhall argues that there is a difference between propensity and necessity, which is a useful distinction, although few of us would go quite so far in curbing our desires if they come too powerful for us:

> … concupiscence and custom and bad company and outward objects do indeed make a proclivity, but not a necessity. By prayers, tears, meditations, vows, watchings, fastings, humicubations [lying on the ground in an act of humiliation], a man may get a contrary habit and gain victory not only over outward objects but also over his own corruptions, and become king of the little world of himself.[12]

Like Erasmus and Bramhall, I think that human beings are essentially moral beings, and therefore I too am predisposed to the idea of free will. Hobbes and Luther are not interested in ethics, and therefore argue for necessity alone. One recategorises the will, and the other creates an equality of iniquity amongst all men, denigrating in particular those who attempt to behave more morally and possibly seeing this as a form of blasphemy. Free will has always been a battleground between a moral and amoral view of humanity, but should it be? Or should it only be?

Before answering that question, it should be clarified that believers in free will are not all moral people and believers in necessity are not all immoral people. People are not consistent with their beliefs, and this assertion can be used in favour of either free will or necessity.

---

12   *Hobbes and Bramhall* on…, p. 11.

As suggested, morality for Hobbes cannot be separated from the law. A person is moral if they obey the law and God; all the rest is necessitated "fancy". This is an important concept in the philosophy of law, as some believe, sometimes for good reasons and across a wide range of political credos, that the only rights are those enforceable in law. Again we have not so much a difference of opinion as a difference of definitions and distinctions. The very clear distinction is between those who believe that we have moral duties outside the law and those who don't. This is closely linked to the distinction between those who believe that human beings are naturally moral beings although, like every other facet of our natures, it can be nurtured or atrophied, and those who believe human beings are only capable of unselfish acts if obliged to carry them out by socialisation or the law, in which case they cease to unselfish acts. The question of free will is therefore a fundamental one that concerns our interpretation of human nature with considerable implications in both politics and religion. No wonder so many people argue this one backwards, and I wouldn't say that I am wholly free from this crime against logic.

The argument over free will has always been distorted by the problem of an omnipotent God, and the tetchy debate between Hobbes and Bramhall is no exception. Hobbes might be expected to secularise the debate, but this subject probably could not be secularised in his time, although the process was certainly there in other fields. What is interesting is how much the debate continues to be about morality.

The shift is from predestination to necessity, and necessity is much less damaging to deism than it is to theism. The God of the deist is the Big Bang (or whatever other first cause), and it is no surprise that Voltaire and Einstein were deists. The Big Bang, tantalisingly credible though it may be, remains a mystery. How could an event of this kind occur and is it in fact the first cause? Matter is energy, but where did all this energy come from? Where is the anti-matter? Of course, there may be further scientific discoveries that provide definitive answers, but they might just as easily produce many more questions. The God of the theist can no longer be omnipotent, as he turns his face to us and, as it is very difficult to believe in an interventionist God capable of overriding the laws of nature, He is becoming as dependent on humanity as humanity is on Him. We find however that the exclusion of God from the debate does eliminate some of the distortions, but it does not eliminate the moral question (which because of this does hint at the existence of some kind of God).

If everything could be perfectly calibrated and there is no free will, the process triggered by the Big Bang *must* lead to the inevitability not only of the history of the universe (relatively uncomplicated when physical forces were alone at play) but also the history of our planet and humanity. We are all a collection of chemicals interacting with each other and producing our decisions with only a semblance of autonomy. The immense instability of this model renders it impossible to understand: if Marx had died of pneumonia in his late teens, the working class movement would still have developed but possibly in different ways; if Archduke Ferdinand had died in a car crash on his way to Sarajevo, the First World War may not have started, Europe might not have lost so much power, many technological innovations might not have occurred, and I might be typing this book on a typewriter rather than a wordprocessor (but then I probably wouldn't exist, because my grandfather would not have died when my father was an infant, and my father's life would have been very different). The list could go on forever.

It would be easy for me to say that only the addition of the unpredictable free will of human beings could justify this chaos of our human world. It would make my job easier, but it would be wrong. Nature itself is the child of chaos.

Randomness drove the origins of evolution and has continued to this day. Moreover, humanity's desire to rationalise production and minimise costs may well destroy this planet or certainly many of its species, including ourselves. We should not be that too ambitious in our claims for free will.

We are subject to a thousand forces acting upon us externally and internally. We are most definitely not in control of our lives, although we are in the West seemingly more in control than ever before, because we have eliminated some of the risks of ill-health, we do not work so many hours and we have more reliable information on which to base our decisions. Illness can change our nature: we might become more accepting of the world in our illness or we might – in the case of strokes, for instance – become grumpier or even aggressive. Our selves are constantly changing realities governed by dominant forces. We cannot argue with this, but the human does occasionally demonstrate great independence, resilience and moral judgement, so the existence of these things cannot be denied either. The question is, what motivates them?

As mentioned, some argue that we are motivated by our socialisation, which includes our religion or ideology. It seems to me unlikely that punishment for our sins will be meted out in another existence or in another incarnation, but it does seem quite possible that moral behaviour does bring more pleasure in this life than does immoral behaviour. I don't mean a moralising life, which is just another form of immorality; I mean an ability to make decisions *not based on self-interest*. This may just be the product of our evolution as a social animal or it may be something of a more spiritual nature. Society needs people or some people to make decisions on a moral basis, so in genetic terms a population that produces a percentage of altruists will be more likely to survive. Worker bees work altruistically for the good of their small republics, as many Renaissance thinkers observed. I am unconvinced by this argument, because our altruism is much more complicated, and takes on different forms in different ages. It is surely in this area that human beings act with the maximum free will. And it is rightly called "free will", because we must will ourselves to it quite consciously, unlike most actions taken on the basis of self-interest, which may involve more instinctive or learnt reactions. Self-interest may well involve quite complex and even devious intellectual processes, but then we are, as Hobbes argued, totally trapped within the dictates of the external world (this was not a good or bad thing for Hobbes; it was the only way decisions are made). Most people eventually find self-interest to be a rather cramped dwelling, and perhaps after establishing themselves they look around for other motivations to fill their lives and make them meaningful. They want to do this, but they have to will themselves to it. It is a conscious decision. It may not in fact be that complex. Simplicity is often more generous.

I have answered my first question. Free will *is* about morality. And I have occasionally implied that it is not only about morality. It is quite often about creativity. Returning to Walter Kaufmann, we recall that he defined the relationship between academics and their subjects as an It-It one. Academics, it was implied, turn both themselves and their elected area of study into something a little dead. There's a touch of humour in this, and it should be added that Kaufmann was a talented academic and translator, who brought a great deal of life to his studies and translations. It could be said that the writer and painter have a thou-I relationship with their books and paintings. There is a dialogue between the artwork and the artist, but once the idea has suggested itself, the artwork becomes the primary interlocutor. The writer or painter has to accept the dominion of the artwork and work to meet its needs. The artwork appears to have autonomy but the artist dealing with the unexpected problems the artwork produces enters a world in which there is free will to respond and respond inventively. Artists have to purify themselves of all their resentments, rivalries and desires for self-justification (not unknown in the art world), because the work will consider these to be alien and inappropriate. This may look like arty-farty self-importance and perhaps it is, for no artist can approach their work without at least a touch of arrogance, but it also looks like arrogance because our societies communicate the idea that most of us have no access to the arts and we are obliged merely to consume them and consume them in the manner they dictate.

The example of *el sistema* demonstrates that any group of children chosen to learn an art can do so and do so extremely well. I'm sure that a *sistema literario* could produce just as good results; we are all born with talent, and while it is still possible to develop our talents in adulthood, it is much easier in childhood. An old Gaelic proverb says, "Learn young, learn well." This is why we should weep at the terrible waste of our children's talents in our current educational regimes: once, in the time of the "mass society", working-class children had to learn a degree of competence, because work required a minimum level of instruction and perhaps more importantly states became aware that an army with a higher rate of literacy could easily defeat the army with a lower one. These mass armies are no more, and most of the working-class and quite a few of the middle-class jobs are now unskilled. With all our smart technology, who needs a smart population? Thatcher's government first introduced the utilitarian approach to education: schools should only teach subjects that have a practical application in the jobs market. The barbarians had taken power.

Much more should be asked of our children, and if it were, they would overcome the challenge easily, because children are sponges – they are learning machines. Their abilities may vary in different activities but they all have the ability to excel. Not all of them can reach the greatest heights and if we were to improve the education system, the bar would of course be raised, but all of them will be able to appreciate some of the arts and produce good material. They will not be alienated from their culture either as producers or "consumers". Nobody ever became a poet without reading or listening to poetry, and nobody ever became a musician without listening to music.

Free will is thus a limited margin of freedom that is granted more to those who have had a chance to develop their abilities in childhood. This is not strictly a moral question, although some of the arts do also develop a sensitivity to others. On the other hand, there is little evidence that the educated are more moral than the uneducated. At the most, we could say that education frees children to be more themselves in adulthood, in both good and bad. In other words, it imparts free will.

The remaining margin of free will exists predominately in the mind. Individuals can succumb to outside pressures to the degree resulting from a balance between what they are comfortable with and what they feel obliged to do in order to survive. This is an important consideration in an authoritarian state or, I think, in a consumer society with its own methods of coercion, and could be influenced by free will, although also by mood and nature. But in the privacy of their own minds these individuals are able, if assisted by education, to develop ideas more freely. You may say that this is a very restricted form of freedom, and that it will have little influence on society or the future. You would be right about the first assertion, but wrong about the second. Where there are many people with a good education (and especially if they are disgruntled as well), then society is capable of changing in an intelligent and planned manner (which must be fairly gradual and conscious of the existence of unknown and unpredictable problems). For some time, we have been told that there is no other way of doing things. This fits with the mindset of necessity. If a people argue, debate and take decisions to change their society, they can do so. Things will never go exactly according to plan, but there is that possibility. There is a midway between arrogant, large-scale activism and subservient passivity. We can engage with the world, but we have to do so with an understanding of the limitations on our own role. To use Buber's terminology, with an I-thou approach. We have free will, if we will ourselves to be free.

And did my father have free will Well, if any of us have it, then he most certainly did. I possibly inherited a belief in my own free will from him, and this may be a delusion and a further constraint imposed upon me, but I used my putative free will in a manner he thoroughly disapproved of. We were hardly very original in that father-son relationship. All of us are a mixture of predictable instincts and erratic free will. Most of us – all of us except a few dogmatic philosophers and theologians – believe that we are if not masters, at least incompetent coachmen of our own destiny, and most of us exaggerate a little in thinking that.

My father was a mildly devout man who attended church fairly regularly, but wasn't concerned if he didn't. He did not go to socialise with clergy or congregation, returning promptly to his glass of gin and vermouth – or two. He was, in any case, a man of few words. He was not good at judging people, but was loyal in his attachments. Such people usually don't have much control over their lives, as these traits put them at a distinct disadvantage. Nevertheless he started life with the advantage of class at a time when the middle class was as assertive as it is once again today. It is difficult to know whether he overcame those disadvantages because of his class or because of his will. Without them he might have "done better", which meant he could have reached a higher rank and enjoyed more recognition, and almost certainly he thought that he should have and mistakenly thought he would have been happier for it. Part of him would have denigrated such things as rank and recognition, but such things have a terrible way of worming themselves into our brains and restricting our free will.

In Bangladesh there was a very young Englishman in the habit of meditating beside a tank, which was the local English word for small artificial lakes generally used for washing clothes. My father passed him every day on his way to work, and one day stopped and went over to invite the youth to lunch. It turned out that this hippy had walked and hitched from England, and lived some kind of ascetic life-style.[13] My father was not only being generous; he was also curious and, I believe, admired his guest because he admired all people who made their lives and did not simply accept the one that was given them by birth and society. It didn't really matter what they did. This is why I feel certain that he believed in free will even though we never discussed the subject (or much else other than an anecdotal presentation of his own life), and naturally he believed that he, in particular, had free will, but that does not prove that he did.

---

13 When lunch was placed before the free spirit, he declined pointing out that he had already mentioned his vegetarianism. As inevitably happens in this situation, an omelette was hurriedly made as a substitute. When he was about to leave, my father asked him if he wanted anything but the English ascetic said that he didn't – even money was refused. My father insisted, so possibly to placate his need, the young man said that he was short of underpants and wouldn't mind a few old ones. Underpants were provided. My mother told the story while my father interjected with these mirabilia which added to his fascination. I, on the other hand, could understand the journey overland with little or no money, but lonely meditation close to the murky waters of a tank I could not. I would have preferred the bazaar.

While he was exceptionally good at his own work, my father was not very good at knowing what was going on in the human world around him, but then few of us are. The unknowability of other human beings is the greatest barrier to meaningful relationships between us. We are capable of being tricked again and again by one kind of outgoing personality, and yet are diffident of someone pathologically incapable of deceit. The only way we can overcome these instinctive errors is by willing our reason to take charge of our behaviour. I'm not sure that my father was capable of this in his private life. But then a man who played his cards so close to his chest, as did so many men of that generation, was not an easy man to know. I don't think he knew other people, he may not have known himself – and this does restrict our free will. But I think – and I can say no more than that – that he did will himself in other ways to do things and create. Which is not of any importance to you, the reader, except in this: there are, very probably, different ways of exerting our free will, and I'm sure that we agree that it does exist when we're talking about our own lives. Perhaps even Hobbes made that exception; I'm sure that Luther did.

Nations and Nationalism

Ernest Gellner defined nationalism as "primarily a political principle, which holds that the political and the national unit should be congruent".[1] Gellner also believed that nations are something pretty new, although he is not very clear about when they appeared. At the end of his book, he says rather vaguely that he never claimed that men did not always live in groups (but, it is implied, those groups were not always nations). As most things in the modern industrialised world are not quite like anything that came before and are in some way a product of this modern world, and if the nation has to be the specific modern nation, then we have one of those circular arguments of which some academics are so fond. Gellner is proved right by his own definitions. If we are to go beyond such self-fulfilling arguments we need to ask what a nation is, irrespective of whether or not it is an entirely modern phenomenon. It appears to be an identifiable human grouping that is greater than mere kinship. It is large enough to mean that an individual could not possibly know every member (which does not mean that it is that large; tens of thousands could constitute a nation and this was roughly the size of the city-states, which in many ways were the closest thing to the modern nation in the ancient and late-medieval worlds). Moreover, there is unfortunately no specific criterion that defines this category, making" nation" an extremely elusive concept, and yet people always believe that they know what it is. Historical study appears to demonstrate that these features belong to both the modern and the ancient nation. Certainly the alacrity with which nationalism was adopted

---

1 Ernest Gellner, *Nations and Nationalism* (Oxford: Blackwell, 1983), p.1.

implies that the affected populations were not entirely foreign to the discourse of nationality.

On the modernity of nationalism, I believe Gellner is on much firmer ground, and besides the words themselves seem to tell us that: "nationalism" is a relatively new word, while "nation" is very ancient.[2] Nevertheless, because I am a little more circumspect and human history is full of surprises, I would prefer to say that nationalism on any significant scale is something that occurred in the late-eighteenth century and only firmly established itself as a powerful social and political force in the nineteenth.

Interestingly, it was culture and nation that were congruent in many parts of early medieval Europe, as well as nomadic, semi-nomadic and warrior nations in pretty much all eras. In Charlemagne's Europe, people were tried according to their own nation's laws and not the laws of any particular territory. To some extent this concept of nation appears to have been applied in the Ottoman Empire, where nations or *millets* were kept apart, not geographically but by carefully encoded cultural and social norms. The story of the Franks is an instructive one because it demonstrates the continuity and dramatic change in a nation over time. Nation is above all defined in historical terms, but it has little or no permanency (in that sense, it is similar to language).[3] The Franks arrived at the eastern borders of the Roman Empire as an independent nation speaking a group of similar dialects. At that moment, their political unit (albeit a fairly loose one), their culture and their nation were congruent, but they had no fixed territory. Some of them then became a mercenary people, engaged by the Romans to defend the eastern border they had come up

---

2 *The Shorter Oxford English Dictionary* vaguely defines "nation" as Middle English, while "nationalism" is very specifically dated from 1844.

3 Because humans hate impermanency, another kind of mortality, they long to believe that their nations and languages are permanent.

against (possibly against other Franks). Those Franks had therefore taken another political master, but still considered themselves to be Franks. The funeral inscription of a legionary who died in the third century in Pannonia (present-day Hungary and a few surrounding areas) bears this inscription: "Francus ego cives, miles romanus in armis", which we could translate as "I belong to the Frankish people, but under arms I am a Roman soldier". This typically layered identity shows however the predominance of national identity even though he was far from his Frankish homeland (and may not have been born there, given the difficulty of travel and brevity of lifespans).[4] With the fall of the Roman Empire, the Franks found themselves masters of several independent Frankish states (Neustria and Austrasia were the principal ones, but Frankish laws of succession meant that they tended continuously to split and reunite) and were also divided into subgroups (principally the Salian and Ripuarian Franks), each with their own laws. They now had a fixed territory, political units and nation that were congruent, but they no longer spoke the same language, as the western Franks had adopted Romance or Neo-Latin from the conquered peoples of what is now northern France.[5] This does not appear to have affected the unity of the Frankish nation. More interestingly still, when they conquered the territories of southern France, they did not assimilate them into the Frankish nation, but ruled them as a subject people. They were referred to as Romans, as was, not unsurprisingly, the population of Rome, but other Italians were referred to by the name of another German warrior nation, the Lombards. Indeed the Lombard identity

---

4 Alessandro Barbero, *Charlemagne* (Berkeley: University of California Press, 2002?), p. 14

5 See Alessandro Barbero, *Charlemagne*, p. 106: "the Franks of Neustria, who spoke the 'Roman language', were no less Franks than their compatriots in Austrasia".

survived long after Lombardy's defeat by Charlemagne, and I suspect it was Italian humanism's search for its glorious Latin roots that finally eradicated the name (nationalism may be new but national mythology is certainly not). In Boccaccio's *Decameron*, two Florentine merchants living in Gascony are referred to as "those Lombard dogs" ("quei lombardi cani"), which takes us to the fourteenth century. Lombard Street does not refer to the modern Italian region, but to Italy or at least northern and central Italy. The Romance-speaking Franks of Neustria seem to have been a little confused about the origins of their language. A ninth-century manuscript states: "It seems that at that time the Franks learnt the Roman language that we still use today from the Romans that were living there. Now no one knows what their mother tongue was".[6] The majority of a population can adopt the language of a small number of invaders (as occurred with English in Ireland or nearly occurred with Norman French in England), but it is unthinkable that a conquering majority could adopt the language of a conquered minority. Yet this is exactly what the Neustrian Franks believed. Chroniclers took it for granted that Clovis had either annihilated the Roman population of Neustria or driven them out. Any other version would have challenged their Frankish identity and reduced them to the same level as the "Romans" of Aquitaine and Septimania (now the Languedoc) to the south. The power of mythology in national identity is already clear and appears to be a constant. But mythology was based on the sound principles of power and subjugation, both of which are the key elements in the creation of strong identities.

The usefulness of Gellner's definition can perhaps best be demonstrated by quoting one of his ex-students writing much more recently. Professor Anthony Smith defines nationalism

---

6 Alessandro Barbero, *Charlemagne*, p. 106.

as "an ideological movement for the attainment and mainte-
nance of autonomy, unity, and identity on behalf of a population deemed by some of its members to constitute an actual
or potential 'nation'."[7] Smith, who is not dismissive of the
"perennialist" argument (i.e. the idea that nationalism has
always existed), is being cautious and circumspect, but to
such a degree that nationalism becomes too vague a concept
to be meaningful. Gellner identifies this crucial link between
nation and political unit, which in the modern world is
the state. What Gellner completely ignores throughout his
book, is the role of mass political involvement and the rise
of democracy in the creation of this new phenomenon. A
people's sense of nation, which had always existed, became
relevant because of their gradual transformation from subjects into citizens. By becoming one of the pieces on the political chessboard, that sense of nation became nationalism.[8]

Gellner claims to be a dispassionate observer of nationalism, while in reality he is something of an apologist for great-
nation nationalism, and for him small-nation nationalism is
ugly, counter-historical and rather kitsch. Social scientists
want nationalism to produce identifiable patterns of behaviour shared by all its forms. The fact that they have not yet
managed to identify them satisfactorily perhaps demonstrates that nationalism is too varied to be seen as a single
entity (Gellner does not seem to realise the beauty of his

---

7 Anthony D. Smith, *The Nation in History. Historiographical Debates about
Ethnicity and Nationalism* (Cambridge: Polity Press, 2001), p. 3.
8 Nationalism, in the specific sense of Gellner's useful definition, did not exist
before the rise of democratic pressures, but nationalism as intolerance of others
outside a large political unit has probably existed for as long as there have been
complex political structures uniting definable cultures. Let one example suffice
given that there are so many: Castilians objected to Charles V granting a monop-
oly over postal services in his empire, and demanded that "foreigners should not
be granted employment, posts, high office, governorships or naturalization papers".
See Henry Kamen, *Spain's Road to Empire* (London: Penguin, 2002), p. 55.

own definition, which ties nationalism down but allows for the variety of its forms). Unlike so many nineteenth-century "isms", nationalism is not even inherently left-wing or right-wing. Gellner starts a fashion for being dismissive of nationalism, which by his time was identified with secessionism and therefore concerned small-nation nationalism, while the important struggles of great-nation nationalism occurred in the nineteenth century: Germany, Italy, Poland and Hungary. Often it was assumed that small nations would be subsumed into these great nations, and therefore obliterated, which did not actually take place in Europe, but did in the post-colonial world on a grand scale, the Kurds being a notable example. Gellner writes sarcastically of "sweetly reasonable" nationalism, as though such a thing could only exist as an irrelevant intellectual construct. He seems to forget that both Gandhi and Hitler were nationalists and defined themselves as such, and yet what a difference between these two men and the effect they had on humanity: the difference between the prince of light and the prince of darkness.

Before expanding on these points, however, we must first consider the nation in agrarian societies, which Gellner disposes of in a typically schematic manner. He argues that there was an age of innocence when nation did not exist. I am unwilling to engage in discussions on the state of nature, which always say more about the arguments their proponents want to make about the present than any reality that may have existed in the past. What we do know is that modern historians of so-called "tribal societies" reject the word "tribe" and prefer the word "nation". Like western nations, these nations are not specifically ethnic or linguistic identities, and their boundaries are often extremely complex.[9] In fact, they can differ from "modern nations"

---

9 Gellner goes some way to admitting this, but comes up with the idea that tribes are unsuccessful nations and nations are successful tribes. Again, if Gellner

precisely because of this greater complexity. Amongst the Nzema of Ghana and the Ivory Coast, nation is both matrilinear and patrilinear, so the nation with which you engage in agricultural activities is not *necessarily* the nation with which you go to war.[10] This perhaps reveals one aspect of the modern nation: it ideally wants everyone to belong to one nation and one nation alone.[11] It rejects "layered identity". If we look at Scotland towards the end of the first millennium, we find that *Scotus* in the Latin sources could mean an Irishman (Gael in his original homeland), an ethnic Gael living in the territories either of Scotland or England as we now know them, an Ethnic Gael living in Scotland (which was then beginning to form), someone who came from the Gaelic heartland around the modern county of Argyll (historically Dal Riada), or someone living in Scotland of whatever ethnic background (Gael, Briton, "Pict" or Norseman, to name the principal categories). Of course the last definition was the one that eventually won out, but it did not firmly establish itself until after the Wars of Independence.[12]

---

wants to give these values to the words, who are we to argue with him. But if we start applying these definitions to Europe, it immediately becomes clear how absurd they are. The Cornish are presumably a tribe and the Welsh a nation. The Prussians (that is the original Baltic people and not the German settlers who took their name) must have been a tribe and the neighbouring Lithuanians a nation. Besides, many of today's successful nations could be tomorrow's dead nations. See *Nations and Nationalism*, p. 87: "Tribalism never prospers, for when it does, everyone will respect it as a true nationalism, and no-one will dare call it tribalism".

10   Pierluigi Valsecchi, *Power and State Formation in West Africa* (London: Palgrave Macmillan, 2011).

11   I find this aspect rather obnoxious, but Gellner would presumably admire it as it is all part of the rationalising and homogenising affect of modern nationalism. Gellner's somewhat Marxian analysis implies that nationalism is subjectively irrational but objectively rational in that it conforms to the requirement of the modern industrial economy.

12   Dauvit Broun, "Defining Scotland and the Scots Before the Wars of Independence", in *Image and Identity. The Making and Re-making of Scotland*

The second millennium can be seen as a process of identifying nation with territory (and ultimately the state), which considerably accelerated in the later centuries and spread out from Europe across the world.

Gellner provides a diagram that shows the upper layers of society as stratified horizontally and the lower layers of "insulated communities of agricultural producers" as divided vertically between each locality. This seems an incredible claim. The Ottoman Empire was made up of several nations and these nations lived alongside each other and had no clear geographical territory (as with our tenth-century Gaels). The empire encouraged these distinctions (as empires do) and demanded that everyone should wear their own national dress.[13] Sometimes nation was primarily defined by religion and sometimes by language (as in the case of the Albanians and Greeks). People were aware of their identities, which extended beyond their own valleys, and knew that some of their neighbours belonged to other nations.

Gellner appears to believe that the city-state was something was very different from the nation. In reality, the city-state was a nation that gave rise to a kind of proto-nationalism, particularly in its more republican and democratic forms. In late medieval and early modern Florence, citizens identified with their *patria* (Florence) and *nazione* (Italy – roughly modern Italy without the Kingdom of Naples). But the *patria* was perhaps the closest to the modern nation; it was the political unit, and Florentines or rather the higher ranks of Florentine society were mainly

---

Through the Ages (Edinburgh: John Donald, 1998), pp. 4-17.

13   Christians were banned from wearing brightly coloured clothing and from riding horses. Turkish functionaries wore embroidered green silk and turbans. Nations and religious communities were called millets. See Misha Glenny, *The Balkans 1804-1999. Nationalism, War and the Great Powers* (London: Granta Books, 1999), pp. 9, 18 and 72.

concerned with how it was run. The rest of Italy was the political forum in which their states jostled with the others, forming alliance and defending interests. It was a world more threatened from within, until foreign invasions started in the last decade of the fifteenth century.

The only society that fits at all well into Gellner's model of an agrarian society is the feudal one. But this is not proof that the peasantry lacked a national identity, but rather that the aristocracy did. Indeed, Russia had a popular national identity. Every year throughout the Middle Ages and the early Modern Era, Russia had mobilised massive armies to defend its endless border against summer incursions. Its whole structure reflected this isolated Christian state's need for survival. This moulded Russian culture and gave it a sense of its special role in history and its vocation for sacrifice, which to some extent was to be transferred in the twentieth century to what has been called a secular religion. It became a nation with an international mission.[14]

This brings us to challenge one of Gellner's great assumptions: the idea that rural society was entirely static in pre-industrial Europe. Apart from military duties, as occurred on a massive scale in Russia but also everywhere else to a greater or lesser extent, the roads of Europe were tramped by all manner of people: vagrants, merchants, tradesmen, Gypsies, and peasantry from the mountains in search of seasonal work.[15]

Even the peasant who never left his land had some idea of his national community, which was generally only one of many competing identities. His geography would also have been pretty vague. There is an interesting story of a man from St. Kilda who went travelling in the Hebrides in the nineteenth century. St. Kilda is a group of small islands

14   Tibor Szamuely, *The Russian Tradition* (London: Fontana, 1988).
15   Raffaella Sarti, *Europe at Home*, New Haven and London: Yale University Press, 2002), pp. 9-14, Chapter I, "Home and Family: Things Fall Apart".

far out into the Atlantic and the peasants lived an independent and egalitarian lifestyle that exercised a certain fascination on more "civilised" travellers from the beginning of the eighteenth century. Our St. Kildan reached the bottom of Skye where it nearly touches mainland Scotland, and looking across, said, "I suppose that must be England (*Sasainn*)". This story tells us that a nineteenth-century peasant could have a sense of belonging to a nation whose exact entity he did not know. He knew that it was bordered by another country called England, and the story implies that he also realized that the other country was much more powerful. Coming from tiny St. Kilda, he could not have dreamt the real dimensions of these nations.

Ideas, including ideas of national identity, had always circulated, but it was difficult to maintain momentum when communications were so difficult. The great change, which in the opinion of many ushered in the modern age, was the invention of the printing press. Without the printing press, the Reformation would probably have been no different to the many other popular Christian movements that challenged the Church hierarchy from time to time. The circulation of broadsheets, particularly in Germany, was fundamental, and the Reformation was the first step towards nationalism because it created national religions in many parts of Europe.

A sense of nation therefore existed before the advent of modern nationalism. It may or may not have existed in prehistory, but for our purposes it is a reality of human society. What was it then that turned a sense of nation into nationalism? What triggered this obsession that Gellner correctly identifies as a congruence between state and nation? Surely it has to be the greater desire of the population of a given territory to get involved in political affairs, itself a product of the greater permanency of ideas following the invention of the printing press. After Gutenberg's revolutionary invention, Europeans were initially more interested in the celestial republic and fought their wars of religion, but by the seventeenth century attention turned to the earthly one. It has to be admitted that much of the discourse was still couched in religious terminology, but the content had its feet firmly on the ground. In Winstanley's *The Law of Freedom in a Platform*, a work that was already calling for universal suffrage, we find clear indicators of a national consciousness that could be called nationalism. According to this radical thinker, England had once been free and had come under a pernicious foreign domination in the form of the Norman Conquest. Since then, the English had always suffered and the task, a quintessentially political task, was to set the English free and put them back in control of their own state and land. The English had been made servile by these centuries of subjugation. Historians rightly ridicule this interpretation. It was clearly a myth, and we know the importance of myths in nation-building. Like all good myths, it may have had a tiny element of truth in it. Anglo-Saxon society was no utopia; it was slave-owning like the Germanic warrior societies that founded it, and the Church had encouraged the various forms of subjugation to be abandoned in favour of the emerging and increasingly ubiquitous "serf". The Normans were to rationalise feudalism and strengthen the state. But a slave is always a slave, whatever name is used, and "serf" derives from *servus*, the classical Latin for slave. Norman society may have been marginally more repressive than the Anglo-Saxon one, but by the time Winstanley was writing, Norman French had long since disappeared from the country, following the premature demise of the feudal system which in turn was caused by the catastrophic effect of the Black Death in England. The historical veracity of Winstanley's ideas is irrelevant: what matters is that he perceived England as dominated by an alien group from which it had to be liberated, one of the typical phenomena of nationalism, as Gellner confirms. This is nationalism that is in no way concerned with military conquest (some of the army refused to go to Ireland on moral grounds; Fairfax refused to lead the army against its old ally, Scotland), and is one entirely interested in the political culture of the current state. The French Revolution was another great national event, and this time the nationalist nature is very clear. Europe looks to it as an example and a precursor to the new Europe that gradually evolves in the nineteenth century. The 1793 constitution may never have been enacted, but it makes clear that the Revolution was all about a democratic political settlement for the French nation. Again history was used to justify the nation and the revolution. Gaul/France was dominated by the Romans/Franks and Vercingetorix/ contemporary revolutionaries fought bravely against the oppressor. Like Winstanley, these revolutionaries used history to combine class and national identity. When Napoleon seized power, ancient Rome became the ideal model rather than the model oppressor. Modern historians can be a little precious about these obvious anachronisms, but they are simply arguments by analogy – the natural language of nationalism. According to Croce, "All history is contemporary history." An idealist position at the other extreme, but not without its element of truth.

Because history is a muddled and complex affair, the Revolution also led to Bonaparte and French expansionism, and as new tricolours were raised around Europe, a new political force had appeared and its name was nationalism. What may or may not have existed in the past as an isolated and partial reality, now became almost universal. It was a potent force, and one that was easily manipulated. It can undoubtedly produce intolerance and arrogance, as can all other ideologies. Johnson famously referred to patriotism as "the last refuge of a scoundrel".[16] Petty nationalism most certainly is. But nationalism is also the demand for a rightful political voice, a recognition of one's own culture and a place at the ruler's table. It should also be remembered that states were brutal and expansionist even before the advent of nationalism.

Nation is everywhere a reality and nowhere clearly defined. It is generated by various mixtures of language, geography, culture, religion and ethnicity or what I would call perceived ethnicity. Ethnicity is always pernicious myth. It may however be none of these. It may exist simply because a state has existed for so long that it has built up a culture of law and political activity that transcends any of the other identities that divide the nation. Switzerland is a good example of this. It has four languages (at least). It was the cradle of the Reformation and the ensuing fragmentation of western Christianity, but that fragmentation, which also occurred within its borders, did not break up the nation. Geography was undoubtedly essential in its formation, but only as far as the original mountain cantons were concerned. It developed a common culture, one that has become increasingly insular with the passing centuries, so that now it has something of a reputation for being a smug and slightly philistine nation, which belies its interesting history. On the other hand it is a well-functioning polity and its linguistic diversity means that it is inevitably tuned into the larger language communities beyond its borders. This diverse nation was perhaps the starting point for modern nationalism and democracy, although some might point to the Italian republics. The fact remains that Switzerland survived and the Italian republics did not,[17]

---

16   Quoted by Boswell in his *Life of Johnson* (1775).
17   The popular republics were the first to succumb, Florence in 1530 and Siena 1555. Two of the oligarchic republics, Venice and Lucca, survived much

an outcome that would have greatly comforted Machiavelli who always believed a virtuous republic had to be founded amongst a rustic people on a hostile and infertile terrain – and the Germans were his preferred choice, based bizarrely on his short sojourn in Bolzen, now Bolzano in northern Italy.

The only general definition for a nation is as unsatisfactory as it is tautological. A nation exists because it is a nation, and is widely accepted as such by a substantial number of people.[18] Others may deny its existence, but if it has meaning to some, it has a certain reality. It is after all a purely social reality, an entirely artificial construct. Most nations were formed through a degree of military conquest, but their ability to integrate new areas, gain legitimacy and effectively create a new and greater nation did depend on cultural factors. The conquest of minor Anglo-Saxon nations by Wessex to create England was not paralleled by similar success when it came to the annexation of Scotland, Ireland and Wales. The borders of France eventually settled along a linguistic divide. Not exactly, of course: Flemish is spoken in northeast France and a German dialect in Alsace, not to speak of the internal languages of Breton and Basque. Nations irreversibly assimilate small cultures. Cornish has disappeared in England, and Cumric has disappeared in Scotland (the classic Welsh epic *Gwŷr a Gogledd* or "Men of the North" is an account of the travails of their northern cousins). Gascony

---

longer until the Napoleonic invasion of 1799. There is some irony in the fact that a country that had recently been attempting to resurrect republican values was now annihilating the last vestiges of Renaissance republicanism, which was never to return. With the Restoration, Venice remained under the Hapsburgs and Lucca became a duchy.

18 Ernesto Sestan has claimed, "a nation is a human grouping that believes it is a nation". But it has to be stressed that it does so for good historical and cultural reasons. See Stefano Gasparri, *Prima delle nazioni. Popoli, etnie e regni fra Antichità e Medioevo* (Rome: Carocci, 1998), p. 14. Gasparri does not provide exact bibliographical information for the quotation.

was originally Wasconia (Basque-land), gaining the initial "g" from the dislike of neo-Latin and Celtic speakers for starting a word with the semi-consonant. It therefore follows that the Basque territories were once much larger. The process of cultural assimilation is as old as man himself.

Languages and cultures *influence* but do not determine borders and borders *influence* but do not determine languages. States *influence* the creation of national identities, and in recent history national identities have *influenced* the creation of states. Political structures enhance or suppress national identities. Necessarily then national identities, although historically determined, are constantly shifting. They shift territorially, they shift linguistically and most interestingly they shift culturally.

We have now come to the difficult part. So far I have reduced nationalism to a shapeless confusion, and I have heaped some, perhaps too many, unkind words on Gellner's fundamental work on the subject, *Nations and Nationalism*. It is time to put a little order back into nationalism by examining the possible kinds of nationalism. Gellner and many other social scientists and historians are most interested in the subjective and objective causes of nationalism, while the last two of my three distinctions concerns nationalisms themselves as they actually appear and influence events.

The first distinction is between the nationalism of great nations and the nationalism of small or subject nations. Gellner acknowledges this distinction and creates the categories of "Megalomanians" and "Ruritanians".[19] He then writes a witty but more than a little simplistic parody, which mainly concerns the reality of eastern European nationalism. His Ruritania is an absurd and ignorant little peasant

---

19 E. Gellner, *Nations and Nationalism* ..., pp. 58-62. The section under the title "The course of true nationalism never did run smooth".

country, which may or may not build the protective shell of a state. Either way, it remains absurd and ignorant. Like Marx, Gellner has a deep-rooted contempt for small-nation or Ruritanian nationalism. Like Marx, he believes that there are historic great nations that can instigate change, and in his opinion, nineteenth-century ethnographers have a lot to answer for. His peasant world (forever inhabited solely by peasants) appears to be one completely lacking any form of consciousness of itself or anyone else. It communicated in "context-bound grunts and nods".[20] This is my alternative ver-

---

20   E. Gellner, *Nations and Nationalism* ..., p. 50. This is the most outrageous of Gellner's remarks. The greater complexity of "peasant" languages implies that peasants had great linguistic control of their own particular "dialects". "Peasant" languages, often with ancient written vernaculars, tend to retain more complex grammar. Slovene is alone in retaining the "dual" (which goes alongside the singular and the plural). Gaelic retains the vocative. In conversation with a Welsh speaker, I was disappointed to hear that their complex but very elegant possessive pronouns are no longer used. This oldest written living language in Western Europe retained these possessives through well over a millennium of peasant culture. Modern culture, deskilled as it is, failed after little more than a century. Nor should we think that "peasant" languages are short on vocabulary. Gaelic distinguishes between the tiredness of hard work and the tiredness experienced in the early morning. They may not have known about low blood sugars, but they made a distinction that most "modern" languages do not. Gellner, who is absolutely certain that "modern" language is more complex than the "peasant" one, does feel a little perplexed about human development: "It is very puzzling that an institution, namely human language, should have this potential for being used as an 'elaborate code',..., as a formal and fairly context-free instrument, given that it had evolved in a milieu which in no way called for this development" (p. 33). Peasants probably appeared silent and diffident to city-dwellers, precisely because they were silent and diffident in the presence of city-dwellers. It should also be remembered that our image of peasant society is very much coloured by its lifestyle in the last two or three centuries of the second millennium, when it suffered from over-population, terrible diet (usually restricted to a single staple), endemic diseases (such as tuberculosis) and oppressive landowners (themselves coming to terms with a capitalist economy and often failing). Such conditions were clearly not conducive to artistic production, but in spite of the flippant superiority of such writers as Gellner, peasant society even then retained remarkable talents in song and poetry (the favourite art forms of pre-industrial society).

sion to Gellner's tale of passive Ruritanians: During the six-teenth century, most Ruritanians converted to Lutheranism. The Bible was translated into Ruritanian and broadsheets circulated amongst the peasantry with unheard-of radical ideas. The Ruritanians participated in the Thirty Years War, and were eventually re-Catholicised at the point of a sword. Although they never returned to Protestantism in significant numbers, the national poet and translator of the Bible, T., continued to be read and revered. In the nineteenth century, the Ruritanians rebelled against their Megalomanian rulers and were brutally suppressed. Following this traumatic event, there was a great flowering of Ruritanian literature and exiles in America sent money home to set up schools. At the same time unfortunately, Ruritanians were being cleared from the land to make way for Megalomanian farmers who introduced modern agrarian techniques (unfortunately it was discovered later that these techniques caused irreversible environmental damage and much of Ruritania became infertile, further reducing the population). Ruritanians were forcibly recruited for the wars against the other great power in the region, Domineeria, and for many Ruritanian men the stark choice was between emigration and the army. This meant that peasant families were robbed of young men at their most productive age and the rural economy was unable to sustain many landless peasant families, particularly after cheap agricultural imports came in from the New World. The two World Wars further decimated the Ruritanian population. After the War, the Socialist Republic of Megalomania questioned the loyalty of the backward Ruritanians and many were rounded up and put into labour camps. Now there are only 15,000 Ruritanian native speakers left (in the nineteenth century there were about one million), but we should not give up hope, because Megalomania, which has reinvented itself as a "free-market democracy", wants to become a member of the

European Union and has signed the European Charter on Lesser-Used Languages along with a wad of other charters. It will do all it can to keep this historic language alive, within the limitations imposed by prudent budgetary policy. There is the problem of the collapse of the Megalomanian economy and the scourge of organized crime, which means that all the young Ruritanians have emigrated to Germany. … You could do any number of these invented cases to back up your arguments, but I don't believe that mine is any less typical than Gellner's. The story of small nations in the nineteenth and twentieth centuries is a tragic one, and those cultures should not be despised simply because they lost out to more powerful forces. The Ruritanians suffered along with all Europeans, but they suffered more.[21]

Megalomanians say that in the interests of rationalisation you should conform to the national type. You may speak Catalan, but that is really just an affectation. Your real language is Spanish, which has international importance and a great literature. Or you peoples of highland India don't really have a proper religion; what you are actually practising is a kind of primitive Hinduism and you should start respecting the real thing by dressing properly and accepting the caste system. Or to use the arguments of Ernest Gellner, who is a Megalomanian of the first water, you really have to conform to the national culture because the modern industrialised nation with its division of labour, of which nationalism is simply an unconscious expression, requires a high degree of homogenisation in the interests of productivity and efficiency, otherwise we are all going to starve.[22] The

21 I seem to remember that Tom Nairn produced his own version too.
22 E. Gellner, *Nations and Nationalism* … particularly p. 39. He polishes up his Megalomanian credentials on page 45. Nationalism as a homogenising force is a natural consequence of industrialisation, while ugly nationalisms are the potential minorities. He overlooks that more atrocities have been committed by great

Ruritanian replies that he or she doesn't really care what the Megalomanians are doing, but would just like to carry on as before. Ruritanians are often considered reactionaries because they stand in the way of progress. In a way they are, but theirs is not the reaction of the powerful to a reduction in their power (the usual meaning of reaction), but the reaction of the powerless when faced with annihilation of their culture and identity.

All the colonial wars of independence were wars of Ruritanians against Megalomanians. All the battles and campaigns in aid of minority cultures, either aimed at independence or some form of autonomy, are between Ruritanians and Megalomanians. Gellner is his usual dismissive self: "To put it in the simplest possible terms: there is [sic] a very large number of potential nations on earth. Our planet also contains room for a certain number of independent or autonomous political units. On any reasonable calculation, the former number (of potential nations) is probably much, *much* larger than that of possible viable states."[23] States can come together or split apart, as their populations desire. Of course, we can all have views on individual cases. It could be argued, for instance, that the

---

nation nationalism than by small nations attempting independence. Even more seriously on page 45, the accusation is "that traditional, ideologically uninfected authorities, such as the Ottoman Turks, had kept the peace and extracted taxes, but otherwise tolerated, and been indeed profoundly indifferent to the diversity of faiths and cultures which they governed. By contrast their gunmen successors seem incapable of resting in peace till they have imposed the nationalist principle of cuius regio, eius lingua. They do not want merely a fiscal surplus and obedience. They thirst after the cultural and linguistic souls of their subjects. This accusation could be stood on its head. It is not the case that nationalism imposes homogeneity out of wilful cultural Macht-bedürfniss; it is the objective need for homogeneity which is reflected in nationalism." This wonderful bit of sophistry, which presumably justifies the Turkish genocidal campaign against the Armenians and the current near-genocidal one against the Kurds, could be used to justify just about anything, including the crimes of Nazi Germany.

23   E. Gellner, *Nations and Nationalism* ..., p. 2.

unification of Germany was unfair on other eastern countries like the Czech Republic and Hungary, which have had to wait for membership of the European Union. It could be argued that the break-up of Yugoslavia was absurd, because the republics already enjoyed considerable autonomy (their own police, their own army, their own parliament and laws, their own foreign debt, etc.). All they gained was the right to rid themselves of one of their flags and to take control of international borders – hardly worth the suffering of a brutal and senseless war. Nevertheless self-determination remains a valid principle as long as the rules of the democratic game are observed.[24]

But I cannot agree that the number of potential nations is in some way a problem. If the Karen of Burma gain autonomy or independence, is that to be regretted, while their annihilation to make way for a more viable national structure is to be seen as the onward march of progress? If democracy is our aim, then *all* national aspirations should be taken into account, which does not mean they can always be fully satisfied because, here I agree with Gellner, nationalisms are often competing and compromise is then the only way out.

One of Gellner's constant themes is that nations must be large enough to be economically viable in the industrial age. Nineteenth-century thinkers, such as Mazzini, John Stuart Mill and Friedrich List, dismissed small-nation nationalism as ridiculous just as vehemently as they supported great-nation nationalism, although they were not in complete agreement

---

24 Where, of course, the rules of the democratic games are grossly abused by an oppressor nation, then the oppressed nation has a right to respond. Current examples are the Palestinians, the minority nations of Burma, the Chechnyans and the Tibetans. Commendably, the latter have always rejected violent struggle in spite of terrible suffering and the systematic destruction of their culture. Tragically, the rest of the world has reacted to this impeccable behaviour by entirely ignoring the Tibetan cause – hardly an encouragement to non-violent action.

about borderline cases like Ireland.[25] There was some logic to this at a time when small nations would have had difficulty defending themselves militarily (ultimately that is why the Italian republics died in the sixteenth century and the Venetian Republic was annexed by Napoleon *en passant* in 1797), but there was and still is a considerable amount of rank prejudice. Unfortunately that prejudice is to be found amongst thinkers of the left as well as the usual band of racists, Great-nation nationalists and bigots.

It is often assumed that small nations with distinctive languages cannot produce great literature and art. Why then did such small nations as Athens and late-medieval Florence produce so much art and literature, while other similar contemporary and even larger states did not? How did the embattled Dutch Republic produce so much great art? Why did an almost completely illiterate country like Russia produce the greatest literature of the nineteenth century? The reason why the literatures of small nations are not well-known or appreciated is probably because not many people know them, and not because they are intrinsically inferior. Where the standard great-nation language is used, small countries and regions appear to kick well above their weight. The Irish and the Scots have contributed enormously to English literature, the Sicilians have spectacularly outwritten all other regions of Italy and many great Spanish writers of the twentieth century appear to come from small nations of Latin America. In art and literature, the metropolis is the most powerful place but not always the most productive. But it is the language of the metropolis that often has to be used in order to get a hearing.

But what was ignorance then, seems foolishness now. Two factors appear to determine economic success in early

25   Eric Hobsbawm, *Nations and Nationalism since 1780*, ..., p. 29-31.

twenty-first-century Europe: centrality and size. If you put a compass point into a central point in Europe and draw a circle of about five hundred miles, you will find the areas within the circle are generally richer than those outside. The circle includes south-east England, Benelux, most of France, Catalonia, northern Italy and western Germany. Europe's centre of gravity will shift eastwards in the enlarged Union, and this will benefit Germany greatly. If you then look at the small countries, you will find that they are performing considerably better than their larger counterparts. This is partly because Italy, Britain and Spain have large areas outside our golden circle that bring the national average down, but it does not explain why Norway, Sweden, distant Finland, Denmark, Holland, the Czech Republic, Austria and Slovenia are doing so well. Ireland, a republic of three million inhabitants and not even the whole Ireland that John Stuart Mill thought could just about make it, has gone from being one of the poorest regions of Europe to one of its wealthiest, in spite of dropping a few points after the financial crisis. It may not be up with Holland or Denmark yet, but its achievements are remarkable no less.[26] Small countries have many advantages as well as disadvantages. In the context of economic unions and possible super-states such as the European Union, small states may be able to have the best of both worlds. Even if neither independence nor autonomy are granted to minority cultures, they should still receive proper protection and rights within the existing national structures, rather than being treated as if they didn't exist.

---

26 The commonly-held belief that Ireland's economic growth in the nineties and early zeroes was due to EU subsidies is a rather ungenerous distortion. Its growth rose to an incredible 8%, but only 1% could be put down to EU subsidies, which were in any case considerably smaller than the subsidies being injected into the Northern Irish economy by London to little effect.

The second distinction is between ethnic and cultural nationalisms. It is agreed that nationalism is built on myth. Myths are often quite innocuous, as with Winstanley's myth of good liberty-seeking Anglo-Saxons and greedy and oppressive Normans, because the Normans were no longer about and the word came to mean the landowning class. Some myths are dangerous however. Ethnicity is always about dangerous myths, if by ethnicity we mean some kind of genetic affiliation. All nations have undergone various degrees of migration. At the height of the Roman Empire one third of the population was made up of slaves mostly imported from abroad. As those slaves were manumitted, more were brought in. Italy must be the oldest melting pot in the world. I consider that to be a plus. Germans very probably are a purer race than the Italians, but not as pure as they would like to think. Nietzsche said in his provocative manner that "Germans had entered the line of gifted nations only through a strong mixture with Slavic blood".[27] A language is a reality, a religion is a reality, and set a of legal traditions is a reality. Ethnicity is not.

There has recently been some debate about the Celts and whether they ever existed. Both sides appear to take up extreme positions because they confuse culture with ethnicity. The Celts were reported by Greeks and Romans to be tall and blond, and they belonged to an Indo-European warrior race similar to the Germans. As they gradually moved across

---

27   Quoted by W. Kaufmann, *Nietzsche* (Princeton: PUP, 1968, 1950[1]), p. 284. Nietzsche's anti-nationalism has none of Goethe's humanity (or perhaps it would be more correct to say that Nietzsche liked to keep his humanity hidden). It is based on his contempt for the "human herd animal". He also wrote, "No, we do not love mankind! On the other hand we are not German enough ... to advocate nationalism and race-hatred. ... We are too unprejudiced for that, too perverse, too fastidious; also too well-informed and too well-travelled" (*The Joyful Wisdom*, London: Penguin Books, p. 377). Precisely because it is of the right, Nietzsche's anti-nationalism is intellectually extremely interesting.

Europe, assimilating peoples as they went, they became the darker people we generally associate them with today. We know almost nothing about this history, but DNA evidence now shows that both the English and the Scots predominately belong to some pre-Celtic people (apparently the English are 80% and the Scots 90%, although these statistics are always being refined. There is no great ethnic difference between us, but there is a cultural difference and a linguistic difference, although the latter is diminishing. It was not a Celtic race that came to Britain and Ireland, but a Celtic culture or, if you like, a Celticised people. In other words, the Celts were already a mixed people when they got to Western Europe and started to mix with whoever was there. It has some sense then to say that Ireland, Scotland and Wales are Celtic countries, because at least part of their peoples still speak a language from the Celtic group (although only in Wales does a substantial part of the population speak such a language). The Celtic languages are a reality and the affinities are there for all to see. On the other hand, Bossi, a dangerous proponent of xenophobic nationalism of the worst kind, claims that northern Italians are Celts. It is true that northern dialects with the exception of Venetian have a typically Celtic phonetic substratum, but clearly that does not make them Celts. They are neo-Latins, whose history has been influenced by the Celts, the Lombards (a Germanic race), the French, the Spanish and the Austrians (in chronological order). If Bossi could convince enough people that they are a Celtic race, then in a sense they become one, or rather the behaviour that flows from this belief becomes a reality and a dangerous one at that. Why is it dangerous? Primarily because when your Celtic-ness is only your race or your supposed race, because the Celtic culture has long disappeared, then the only thing to do is to maintain your imagined purity by keeping the foreigner out.

Abram Leon, the left-wing Zionist and later Trotskyist,

wrote that "the Palestinian Jews were not dispersed to the four corners of the earth by the Romans".[28] Their descendants were mainly converted to Islam during the Muslim invasions, and therefore became the Palestinian Arabs. The Diaspora already existed in the large Jewish communities that had built up around the Mediterranean over many centuries before the destruction of the temple. History was written by the literate, the intellectual class of scribes, Pharisees, lawyers and merchants, and therefore with a view to their vicissitudes. The great ignored mass of Jewish peasants and shepherds stayed where they were, but now lacked a political leadership. However, Leon claims that Jewish battalions of Tiberiad, Nazareth and Galilee assisted the Persian king in taking Jerusalem as late as 614 AD, demonstrating some kind of cohesive presence. Whatever the case, the myth of a Jewish race can be easily disproved by looking at a Kurdish Jew, an Ethiopian Jew and a European Jew. They all look like the peoples they live amongst or used to live amongst until recently. Both anti-Semites and extreme Zionists conspired to keep alive this absurd myth, but the reality of the Jewish religion and culture cannot be denied. The Jewish poet writing

---

28   Abram Leon, *The Jewish Question. A Marxist Interpretation* (New York: Pathfinder Press, 1970), p. 121. Leon's extensive reading of classical texts and histories means that this is still an extremely useful book, in spite of it being written under the oppressive conditions of Nazi occupation. He can be forgiven then for the occasionally over-simplistic analysis typical of the times: "Whereas Catholicism expresses the interests of the landed nobility and of the feudal order, while Calvinism … represents those of the bourgeoisie or capitalism, Judaism mirrors the interests of a precapitalist mercantile class" (p. 76). Nor can we accept E. Germain's assertion that he had liquidated "the Jewish question as a problem from the historical materialist point of view" (p. 21), as no historical question can ever be definitively resolved. But Leon's book retains its brilliance, precisely because he never lost all his passions as a left-Zionist and does not surrender entirely to Marxist-Leninist orthodoxy. Wanted both for his political views and his "race", he amazingly avoided capture until 1944 and death followed shortly afterwards in Auschwitz at the age of 26, thus ending his short life so full of intellectual and physical courage.

in Hebrew in eighth-century Muslim Spain, the Yiddish playwright in Soviet Russia and the Israeli journalist who tries to wake up his or her countrymen to the situation in the West Bank are all part of a cultural continuum, albeit a rather fragile one and one that crosses many other cultural and linguistic identities. Judaism is one of the great transcultural cultures, like the Rom, the Bedu, the Arab traders and the Chinese in south-east Asia. Judaism started the early Middle Ages as the most privileged of these cultures. The fact that they could practise their religion at Charlemagne's palace in Aachen demonstrates the esteem in which they were once held in both Christian and Arab society. Unfortunately the history of Europe in the second millennium has been the history of increasing intolerance until the eighteenth century, when the continent seems to have moved in two directions at the same time: towards greater tolerance and greater intolerance. The twentieth century has seen terrible events (the most terrible events) and also many forms of liberation.[29] Racial myth has destroyed cultures and endangered peoples. Ethnicity can therefore be associated with the dangerous aspects of nationalism and cultural identity with its more positive values. Both are a direct result of democratic involvement, but racial myth is a form of false consciousness.

It must be made clear that by making this distinction and showing a marked preference for cultural identity, I am not equating potential cultural nationalism solely with linguistic difference as Gellner does. He makes such a surprising claim about Scotland that you have to question whether our leading expert on nationalism really understood what a nation is: "The linguistic distinctiveness of the Scottish Highlands within Scotland is, of course, incomparably greater than

---

29 It has been called the "short century" by Hobsbawm and the "people's century" by the BBC, both entirely appropriate names, but I would call it the "century of destruction", in human, cultural and ecological terms.

the cultural distinctiveness of Scotland within the UK; but there is no Highland nationalism."[30] Marx himself made exactly the same point about the Gaels (Highlanders) and the Welsh, and despondently remarked on the irrationality of it all: "no state boundary coincides with the *natural boundary of nationality*, that of language."[31] He also observed that perfidiously "the Germans in Switzerland and Alsace do not desire to be reunited with Germany, any more than the French in Belgium and Switzerland wish to become politically attached to France."[32] If Marx could partially understand this reality in the nineteenth century, in spite of his considerable perplexity, surely Gellner must be able to understand that language is only one factor and not the decisive one in the Scottish situation. Both Highlander and Lowlander, often hostile to each other in the past, have always considered themselves Scottish, and that Scottishness is expressed through a religion, an education system and a legal system, which are all part of the state without a government left behind by the Union of the Parliaments (and partly rectified by the reintroduction of the parliament in 1999). The diversity within Scotland's borders in no way detracts from its status as a nation, any more than the diversity within England's borders detracts from its, or indeed the extreme linguistic diversity in Switzerland which has already been mentioned. The totally homogeneous nation exists almost nowhere, which is disappointing for Gellner, but for me very heartening. The problem is not that nations have complex layered identities; the problem is that some modern nations do not want to accept that this complexity exists.

---

30   E. Gellner, *Nations and Nationalism* ..., p. 47.

31   Karl Marx, *The First International and After* (London: Penguin Books, 1974), p. 383; the italics are mine.

32   *The First International* ..., p. 383. Note the term "reunited", as though Germany had once existed as a united whole in the past.

The third distinction is between inclusive and exclusive nationalisms. Ethnically based nationalism has to be exclusive, but a cultural one may or may not be so. For instance an exclusive nationalism may claim that only speakers of a certain language or followers of a certain religion can aspire to belong to its ranks. Inclusive nationalism ultimately makes no requirements of its citizens at all (it goes without saying that there are many grey areas between these two types; indeed nearly all actual nationalisms take up a position somewhere along a spectrum between them).

It may be felt that I am hardly entitled to attack Gellner so fiercely, as he was a university professor and an expert in his field. So let me quote another university professor, one who is of moderate or centrist views but who lives in a country where a sense of great-nation superiority does not come so easily. Indeed, as an Italian his main concern seems to be with the completion of the national and democratic revolution to create a modern state: "… the civic virtues of loyalty and solidarity, which have the role of legitimising democratic state power, are not in some way inborn, they have to be generated. This educative process is based on the recognition of *both* one's *common historical roots* of a shared ethno-cultural nature, *and* the current *good reasons* for keeping our democracy alive. The fusion between the acknowledgement of historical roots and the reasons for democratic coexistence give substance to the 'nation of citizens' in the fullest sense of the term."[33] Here we have someone who understands much more fully the complex equation that makes nationalism a modern phenomenon.

Let me first clarify a few points that are fundamental to understanding this difference between Gellner and Gian Enrico Rusconi. Gellner quite correctly identifies state

---

33   Gian Enrico Rusconi, *Se cessiamo di essere una nazione* (Bologna: Il Mulino, 1993), p. 30.

education as one of the prime causes of national homogenisation, although he incorrectly believes this to be connected primarily to industrialisation. In fact, universal education was not introduced in England and Wales until 1871, long after the commencement of industrialisation and later than other European nations where Calvinist and Lutheran emphasis on personal knowledge of the scriptures had led to higher literacy rates. The reason why the British establishment hurried through the Education Act was that they had just witnessed the crushing defeat of the old European power, France, which had a remarkably low literacy rate,[34] by Prussia which had a remarkably high literacy rate and was in the process of unifying Germany. It was the flexibility required of the soldier and not the worker (whose duties were becoming increasingly repetitive) that awoke the European states to the need for education. In other words, the destructive force of war brought the change and not the wonderful bounties of economic progress whose praises Gellner sings. Lord Shaftesbury, the paternalistic conservative politician, opposed the bill because he understood, quite rightly, that universal education even of a fairly restricted kind would accelerate the process of political involvement by the "masses", which had been building up pressure for nearly a century (Chartism, after all, had been and gone).

Nationalism is therefore part of the demand for active citizenship, as can be most clearly demonstrated in the anti-colonial wars and movements. Nationalism is not just about territorial division; it is also about a shift in power within society.

Just as cultural nationalism is preferable to ethnic nationalism, inclusive nationalism is preferable to cultural nationalism of an exclusive nature. Inclusive nationalism, by definition, is a rejection of ethnic nationalism, but it goes

---

34 Hobsbawm, *Age of Capital*, when Algeria was invaded, its literacy, of a medieval, scriptural kind, was higher than France's.

much further. At the risk of slightly misleading metaphors, I would say there is something maternal about inclusive nationalism, in that the state values all her citizens equally and is concerned for their health and education. She is the maligned "nanny state", rather than that wonderful creation, the paternal state that is concerned with control, surveillance, discipline and displaying virility through endless warfare. She is less concerned with how they grow up than that they should grow up. She accepts their failures as her own and commiserates with them. The paternal state is moralistic. He demands that his children act exactly as he does and share his values, which are eternal. He punishes failure severely and will not look his failed children in the face.[35] Suggesting a parental relationship between the state and citizen is perhaps unwise, but what we mean is all of us taking responsibility for all of us.

Inclusive nationalism is not, however, an entirely new invention. Like so many other aspects of our modern world, it goes back to the prophetic qualities of the English Revolution. In his argument with Cromwell at the Putney Debates, Rainsborough announced that he wanted to live in a nation that affords full rights and dignities to all those who live within its boundaries, *irrespective of their origins*. In over three centuries, we have not been able to turn that generous imagination into reality.

---

35 I am indebted to Antonio Gambino for his concept of maternal and paternal societies as expounded in his clever and amusing book *L'inventario italiano* (Turin: Einaudi, 1998). Like many Italians (and displaying one of their endearing traits), he is very self-critical of Italian society, which he considers to be particularly maternal. The book would be worthy of translation not only for what it has to say about Italy, but as an example of national self-awareness that could be usefully applied elsewhere.

On Friendship

Friendship, which many have written about, covers a wide variety of relationships, most of which provide us with a helping hand through life, as long as we understand in each case which kind of friendship we're dealing with.

Loyalty to our friends, including those who are disloyal, is important, but there must clearly be a limit to that loyalty. Surely we should remember who they are and try to reconcile differences where possible, and though even here there must be a limit, it should stretch tolerance as far as is possible for our own natures.

Friendships can be associative, and therefore based on joint interests or similar backgrounds. You enjoy each other's company because you can take so much for granted, having shared experiences and come to similar opinions on the fundamentals of life. You argue pleasantly over minutiae that have little importance beyond analytical precision. Such relationships are relaxed and fall into two categories. The first is of those who look outwards to a world that is to some degree hostile – varying from very mildly to oppressively. This is the collaborative world of those who join in a cause, which may vary from some minor community project to high politics. These are friendships that do not require a great deal of dialogue; these are collaborative friendships that deal with problems and ideally solve them with the minimum fuss. The second is of those who look inwards to those minutiae and discuss them endlessly. These are relationships that can produce an enormous intellectual stimulus, and may become essential to our creative activities (as, in a different, more practical way, can the relationships in the first category). These relationships are extremely garrulous, and some might consider them unproductive, particularly in these utilitarian times, but they are some of the most important relationships in our lives.

Friendships can be complementary, and therefore bring together people of different backgrounds, skills and knowledge. Some of these relationships are very important, because they're instructive, and they bring us out of our comfortable shell. They introduce us to other people's obsessions, and require an ability to listen and to try to understand. That "try to" is important, because we can never quite understand as they do, because we haven't put in the hours that they have. They talk of things that are familiar to them. They may be good at coming down to our level, or they may not, in which case we have to listen harder and ask questions. They enjoy proselytising their own heartfelt beliefs and profound experiences, and we enjoy peering into this other world and sensing its wonder, even though we have no intention of immersing ourselves in it completely. Some of these relationships are simply very enjoyable, because our friend is wittier than we are or more skilled in his or her ability to tell a fine story or even conjure up an anecdote of doubtful veracity.

This all suggests friends must not be judged. We should not attempt to change them, although in not attempting we may end up doing this, perhaps in ways we would not want. All relationships, including non-judgemental ones, change people, but friendship is essentially acceptance of the other person as they are. In the age of networking, coercive relationships are often passed off as friendships, but they are not. These are properly called hierarchies, which have always existed, but people did not always pretend that they don't exist.

Proverbs and writers on friendship often stress the importance of frank advice between friends. This is an idealised friendship, and refers to a particular kind of friendship. We all have friends who would take our advice as an insult, and that advice should be withheld as it would be either wasted or, much worse, counterproductive. Besides, we should question whether we, with all the mistakes we've made in our lives, are qualified to provide unwanted advice. The Gaelic proverb claiming that friendship is the mirror of the soul should be covered with a small mound of salt.

This leads to another important differential in friendship: its longevity. Friendships made in our early twenties tend to be lasting. By that age, we have become more or less what we still are. The ageing process and experience change the tone and vehemence of our thoughts, but we retain the essence of our invented selves. In our teens, as Kundera once suggested, we are trying on various personas like masks in an attempt to find which one fits. Friends from this period can become very different as you grow older, but still a residual affection can remain. But friendships from our twenties can be broken off by circumstance and taken up again with little interference from the missing years. These are often relationships in which advice can be dispensed in both directions without offence on either side. It can be sought out. Are these then the most important friendships? Only in a way. When we revisit these ancient friendships, we find our friends in the midst of other short-term friendships that are often more intense. Some of the most important and instructive friendships in our lives are short ones. They come out of a contingency, and have no purpose beyond it.

I am not talking here of what I call professional friendships, which are based on mutual respect and perhaps admiration for the other's work, but are also characterised by a degree of distance and formality. In a culture that denigrates formality or at least language that reflects a more formal relationship, this is often hidden, but hiding it is not a good idea. That formality is admirable where it is appropriate, and we should not pretend we're all close friends when we're not. In any case, a professional friendship is only on the very boundary of friendship. What I am talking of here is a contingent friend-ship based on an original encounter between dissimilarities, which is intensely revelatory in the initial period.

This in turn leads to another important differential in friendship: its capacity. It is often said that friendship is the most important ingredient for marriage, but this is a cliché that holds only a small part of the truth – to the extent that it is highly misleading. The validity of this assertion mainly rests on its implication that it takes more than sexual attraction and compatibility to make a marriage (or long-term sexual relationship, whether heterosexual or homosexual). No one would argue with that, but marriage (or sexual partnership) in the West requires a great deal – some might say too much. How many of our friendships would last, if we spent the same amount of time with our friends that we do with our spouses. Good marriages overcome the problem of overfamiliarity. I was talking to the wife of a friend whose conversation and wit I admire. She told me that her marriage lasted because she found him so amusing. I immediately leapt to confirm this truth. She looked at me as if I were a fool and said, "But I don't find him funny when he's trying to be – only when he's taking himself seriously." This revealed many things: that she might have been wittier than he was, but also that she knew all his jokes and the mechanisms he used to create new ones. Perhaps he too had to invent her persona in order to love her, and I remember that he was an extremely uxorious man.

Montaigne excluded women from friendship, and never bothered to consider the nature of friendship amongst women, and he excluded closeness from marriage because "women are in truth not normally capable of responding to such familiarity and mutual confidence as sustain that holy bond of friendship, nor do their souls seem firm enough to withstand the clasp of a knot so lasting and so tightly drawn." Fortunately we have progressed, but not that much, at least amongst heterosexuals, for whom friendship still remains predominantly homosexual (i.e. between people of the same sex). You would expect then that for homosexuals friendship would be heterosexual, which to some extent it is, but homosexuals also have many friendships with people of either sex. In this sense, homosexuals are showing us the way friendship should develop in the supposedly open society of the twenty-first century.

The great burden we now put on sexual partnership in the West and increasingly beyond it may not stand up well, if we apply the utilitarian dictum, "the greatest happiness of the greatest number". The problems these relationships encounter today are exacerbated by the modern consumerist culture, which turns everything into a product or commodity – even a human relationship – which must be judged for its usefulness to the individual rather than the couple or family, and also bombards the consumer with an endless series of adverts that, amongst other things, conjure up the unobtainable image of the perfect family of consumers busy at their consumerist duties. In spite of this, there are many successful marriages and sexual partnerships, and today many, perhaps most of us, would expect great loyalty to be reserved for this more meaningful relationship and not friendship in general, as Montaigne argued. For the French essayist, friendship should seek perfection and for him one particular friendship was all-consuming; the death of that friend was a blow from which he could never recover. It was, as he describes it, homosexual love but not sexual. What we call Platonic love: "There is no deed nor thought in which I do not miss him – as he would have missed me; for just as he infinitely surpassed me in ability and virtue so did he do so in the offices of friendship." On the other hand, he says, "in my bed, beauty comes before virtue". If, as he claims, he did in fact separate sex and passionate love, which is not really friendship as we understand it, then perhaps this separation has the advantage of compartmentalising relationships and demanding less of each one. But his description of friendship is not consistent: the friendship as a monogamous Platonic love surviving even death coexists alongside "common friendships" – a more recognisable kind of friendship which includes a clique of close friends vying for priority. He agonises over the resulting conflicts without resolving the problem: "If two friends asked you to help them at the same time, which of them would you dash to? If they asked for conflicting favours, who would have the priority? If one entrusted to your silence something which it was useful for the other to know, how would you get out of that?". Here we have the clubbishness and hierarchy of traditional male friendships. Today, each friendship should be its own thing, and not in competition with other friendships, which may have very different functions. Nor should friendship override an individual's personal morality, although personal morality also needs a degree of flexibility – but not to the point of corruption. Montaigue's three unanswered questions lie at the heart of the kind of freemasonry that degrades society.

Sexual love in a partnership or marriage is to some extent an exercise in self-deception, while friendship is an exercise in knowing another as deeply as is possible and, of course, never succeeding. Friendship should be as promiscuous as possible, as it is better to learn from a great variety of people and viewpoints. That is why friendship does not have great capacity. Many a long friendship has come to grief due to a prolonged holiday in each other's company. That every human relationship is unique is a truism, but a friendship has no ideal form, nor does it require a purpose. It is enough for two people to wish to be regularly in each other's company, either by themselves or with others, for no other reason than that companionship and not for some other purpose, such as financial self-interest or ambition.

On Writing about Ourselves

In her collection of blogs, *On Writing*, A.L. Kennedy refers to the practice of basing fictional characters on real people as "body-snatching". The *roman-à-clef* gets a hammering. Some of the great *romans-à-clef* come to mind, including Tolstoy's *Resurrection* which I examine in an earlier essay. Kennedy is right to point out that there are terrible dangers in this kind of writing, and to write about someone with the intention of harming their reputation would be reprehensible (unless they're a politician and the satire is political rather than personal). Sometimes you read a flawed novel or short story in which you get the impression that the writing is an elaborate private message delivered publicly to a particular individual, and the writer cannot wait to post off a copy to the victim.

But "body-snatching" has produced many good novels, and to some extent all characters must arise from the author's experience of life and other people, even when a character is invented. Moreover, the distinction between an invented character and a real one is not clear. Many a character might start life in the author's brain as someone drawn from life or even a mixture of two real people, and then take off in a slightly different direction once the novel evolves. A character may be invented and then come under the influence of a real person, because the author perceives the appropriateness of this to their changing ideas of how the book should be written. Never say never in literature, and in many other things. Much of the current advice on writing is to avoid risk, but art is primarily about risk.

My own experience of writing is that real people tend to

make caricatures, and are only useful for very minor parts. This is counterintuitive, but given our inability to really understand other people's motives, it should not surprise us too much. I have also noticed that readers want to attribute autobiographical influences where none existed. I wrote a dialogue at the end of my first novel, *The Golden Menagerie*, in which the three main participants were originally called "c.v.", "l.v." and "s.v.", which stood for cynical voice, liberal voice and socialist voice. Only after the dialogue was complete did I attribute names and describe them in a manner that appeared to suit the different viewpoints they embodied. This did not stop people from identifying these characters with real people. I had originally written this book in the south of England and the story ended up in the west of Ireland. As it happened, my life copied my book and I ended up living on the periphery, in a village near Stornoway on the Isle of Lewis, and so I decided to relocate the final dialogue to a place that I knew rather than one imagined and never visited. From the moment I used Stornoway, readers who knew I lived there felt that the story must have been at least in part based on actual events, which in the case of some more minor characters was partially true.

Another book that comes to mind is Evelyn Waugh's *The Ordeal of Gilbert Pinfold*, which is a wonderfully extreme example and therefore instructive not only about "body-snatching" but also the whole business of writers writing about themselves both in fiction and non-fiction, because the book became famous principally because of its closeness to real events in the author's life and also worked well as a novel in itself. The body Waugh snatched and abused most readily was his own, and the book is an act of courage and almost self-harm. He subjects himself to unremitting ridicule. The saving grace of Gilbert Pinfold, Waugh's alter ego, is that he deals with the prolonged bout of temporary madness on his own and comes through, something of which Waugh was justifiably proud.

In brief, Pinfold/Waugh is suffering from insomnia and rheumatic pain for which he is taking a cocktail of different drugs and alcohol, in particular bromide and chloral. In hope of respite from the two oppressive symptoms of aching joints and sleeplessness, he departs on a sea journey for Ceylon during which he starts to hear voices. The drugs may have been the cause of a derangement that resembled in many ways paranoid schizophrenia. The current Penguin edition contains a useful introduction and some fascinating appendices.[1] When asked "how far *Pinfold* is an account of your own brief illness?", Waugh replied, "Almost exact. In fact, it had to be cut down a lot. It would be infinitely tedious to have recorded everything. It's the account of three weeks hallucinations going on absolutely continuously." Later in the same interview, he makes an intriguing observation, "… it was not in the least like losing one's reason, it was simply one's reason working hard on the wrong premises." You don't have to be mad to fall into that deluded state. Life is a deluded state in the midst of lies, misunderstandings, wrong interpretations, betrayals and an unrelenting flood of propaganda. Delusions that originate in ourselves and delusions imposed from outside, but poor Mr. Pinfold had something more – a serious clinical condition.

Waugh goes into great detail on Pinfold's cocktails of drugs and alcohol. Too much so, as though to justify Waugh's own experience of madness, which would be understandable. Here he is most certainly copying from life. But self-justification, generally the greatest pitfall of autobiographical elements, is not the pervading tone of this book, quite the

---

1 Evelyn Waugh, *The Ordeal of Gilbert Pinfold* (London: Penguin, 1998), reprinted by Penguin in 2006 and originally published by Chapman & Hall in 1957.

opposite. It is the author's unrelenting and cruel examination of his own character and temporary madness.

When Pinfold, before his departure, says, "Why does everyone except me find it so easy to be nice?" the reader feels, but cannot know, that this was an expression Waugh often used in his own house – something familiar to his children that they would greet with exasperation, smiles and filial indulgence. I imagine a cantankerous man driven by a powerful sense of duty "to do the right thing", and nearly always failing. Is this desire to think about the author, rather than the protagonist, the other characters or even the narrator, a distraction that impedes the flow of the novel? It feels at times as though Pinfold and Waugh are jostling for centre stage, and the reason is that Waugh made little attempt to cover up the link between his own experience and Pinfold's fictional one, although he may equally have exaggerated it. Our imaginings of the real Waugh are not reliable.

When I read of the drunken and drugged-up Pinfold, who "prayerless … got himself to bed", I immediately infer that Waugh would consider his nightly prayer a significant duty. In spite of his very public conversion to Catholicism, this may not have been the case. Even if the inference is correct, it doesn't tell us what kind of prayer: is it that idiotic prayer to a patriarchal god for happiness, help in an examination or some other bounty missing from the pious person's life, or is it a meditation away from all selfish considerations – an attempt in frivolous times to regain a sense of the seriousness of life? I would think that on political and religious issues Waugh was very distant from me, but this book suggests that I share one important thing with him: contempt for the pettiness of life – the guarded ego, self-importance, the hollow courtesies, servility, deceit. We all disdain these things, and indulge in them too, more often in some periods of our lives than others. In fact Pinfold,

disastrous and inept as he is – a malign Charlie Chaplin –
is ultimately as likeable as he is disagreeable, because he
is most contemptuous of pettiness when he discovers it in
himself, and throughout the high point of his derangement
a nebulous self-awareness endures, although it also succumbs to his persecution mania or his "pm" as Waugh and
his wife referred to it in their correspondence, suggesting
that the condition was not entirely new.

Thus Waugh provides us with an intriguing novel which
we would read differently if he hadn't publicised the source
of its content. But this too may not be wholly reliable. While
in his conversations with his wife he put the whole blame
for his condition on drugs and alcohol, outside the family he
was less protective of his reputation. On meeting a friend in
London who commiserated on his illness, Waugh reportedly
"burst into laughter" and replied, "I know that Laura [his
wife] has been putting it about that I've been ill. But it's not
true. I've been off my head." We possibly have here someone
who is so determined to be ruthless in his self-assessment in
public that he may be distorting the truth.

The Pinfold story is not just about the book and its account
of his illness, there is also the possibility that the illness itself
arose from his relationship with the media, and concerns the
way authors relate to their public, a subject which is more
relevant today than it was then. Waugh appears to have been
upset by a couple of interviews by a BBC journalist who then
became the object of his paranoid delusions. The family and
in particular Auberon Waugh supported the argument that
Stephen Black's interview drove Evelyn Waugh mad, but
when I read the relevant excerpts in the Penguin edition I
can find nothing in the first interview, which was at his home
and supposedly the offending one, that could justify Waugh's
ire or even his offence, although the second one does throw
more light on the disagreement. In the first interview there

are those techniques, probably part of BBC training, whose purpose is to inform the audience of things the interviewer already knew:

> Black: You are a Roman Catholic, Mr Waugh?
> Waugh: I am, yes.
> Black: Have you always been a Roman Catholic?
> Waugh: No, for the last 25 or 30 years.
> Black: You became converted to the Roman Catholic faith?
> Waugh: Yes.
> Black: Would you like to tell me something about the reasons for your conversion?
> Waugh: Well you know, I don't think I would. Because they aren't interesting. There's no human story in it. It was simply a fact of recognising a plausible rational system, of following the arguments with proof of the historic truth of Christianity.[2]

The first three questions are unnecessarily long-winded. Black could have simply reduced all four questions to: "Mr Waugh, could you tell me something about the reasons for your conversion to Catholicism?" The third question was idiotic, given that Waugh was in his fifties at the time of the interview. It is unsurprising that someone like Waugh was irritated by this line of questioning, which in its pointlessly slow developments of the basic facts, resembles a cross-examination in court. That it did more than simply irritate him demonstrates that Waugh's relationship with the media was already damaging his psyche. The modern media world was knocking at the door, and Waugh was too old to adapt. He would not be alone in that. However, he seems to have

---

2 *The Ordeal of Gilbert Pinfold*, pp. 135-36

coped well with the much more hostile interview by John Freeman, although the excerpt on *Pinfold* does suggest that it was not a happy experience.[3]

Waugh's staccato answers give the impression of someone who has decided not to engage. His fourth one reveals a religiosity I find difficult to understand as the claim to "a plausible rational system" seems overstated and I, for one, would like to hear his reasoning, whether or not there's "a human story in it". But he is on firmer ground when it comes to his clear understanding of how the relationship between author and reader should work. "There's no human story in it," if applied to fiction alone, has some weight in it. Everything should have some relevance to the reader, whether or not the reader is aware of this before reading the book. All the rest is mere gossip and self-indulgence. He knows that his religious ideas are important to him, but not to anyone else, unless he can put them in a form that does become relevant, as he did in some of his books. His reticence is very sensible, however alien it might seem in the age of Facebook.

But how this reticence contrasts with Waugh's willingness to expose the darkness and unpleasantness of his madness! His friends must have been horrified, although his wife may well have expected it and possibly even valued it for some therapeutic benefit. According to the introduction, his friend Christopher Hollis refused to categorise *Pinfold* as a novel in the bibliography he wrote for the British Council, commenting, "some have professed to find the chapters of near-madness amusing, ... but a reader has to be hard-boiled indeed who finds madness funny... What remains odd is that one who has been through such experiences should be willing to tell the world of them in such a comparatively casual fashion, and, as it were, to lunch out on them." There are

3 *The Ordeal of Gilbert Pinfold* ..., pp. 163-166; Waugh was clearly in more robust psychological health during this 1960 interview.

some serious misunderstandings here: there is nothing casual about *Pinfold*, which was not easy to write, and has clearly been as worked on in a literary sense as any other novel by this author, which means a great deal. Consider the grandeur conflicting with self-irony in the sentence, "Mr Pinfold stood confounded, the only troubled thing in a world at peace" or simple irony in "A good officer knows the enormous ills that can arise from men brooding on imaginary grudges" with reference to events imagined through voices in Pinfold's head – the imaginary grudges were his not the imaginary seamen's. At one point, Pinfold imagines a mutinous situation met with threatening retorts which is resolved with an Indian seaman being entangled in machinery, and followed by the captain's speech justifying the incident to the rest of the crew: "… a great quantity of valuable metal was sacrificed last night for the welfare of a single seaman. That metal was pure *copper*. One of the most valuable metals in the world. Mind you I don't regret the sacrifice and I am sure that the Company will approve my action. But I want you all to appreciate that only in a British ship would such a thing be done. In the ship of any other nationality it would have been the seaman not the metal that was cut up. You know that as well as I do. Don't forget it. And another thing …" Does this sound like madness or nightmare? It sounds to me like pure satire. This is a literary work, but it is also a hybrid, and it may be that in his drive to be honest to events, he slightly damages the literary value of the work. That is a fine point I leave to the critics; what is clear, and we can take his word on this, is that this book is not a verbatim of his troubled journey to the east. It is written for public consumption as a novel, and it must not be boring – his word not mine.

What is fact, what is fiction, what is for public consumption, and what is for self-justification, because no author is entirely unconcerned about what his public think of him, even when, as in Waugh's case, he constantly denies this? In this labyrinth of unknowability we come to an element for which I have no reasonable explanation. The hostile voices that Pinfold/Waugh hears during his trip often express their prejudices against leftists, homosexuals and Jews. Like all such prejudices, they are not accompanied by any explanation, assuming as they do that such prejudices are almost universally agreed upon. Pinfold is accused of being a communist, a pansy and changing his name from Peinfeld to Pinfold. If I hadn't read the appendices, I would have simply considered such prejudice to be typical of the time and the society Waugh moved in. I remember such common-places very well from the fifties and sixties. But it appears that these were the kind of quips that Waugh himself was in the habit of making against other people, particularly the anti-Semitic one about changing names. Two possible explanations occur to me. The first is that he was continuing in the satirical vein we have noted above. Waugh is a confusing and thus fascinating writer in part because he is quite capable of running with the hare and hunting with the hounds. But the persistence of the remarks on name-changing suggests otherwise. The second possibility is that this really is what he heard in his madness, revealing perhaps a guilty conscience in his undoubtedly anguished soul about such base prejudices. The accusations are directed at him, and they cause some hurt. When asked by Freeman, "Were those the kind of hallucinations that you yourself felt?", Waugh replied, "Oh yes, those were the voices exactly." This is slightly more convincing, but not entirely. The episode, along with the information in some of the appendices, demonstrates that the text is somehow sealed off from us and will never be fully understood. This may have been intended or it may just be the inevitable product of mixing fact and fiction on such an Olympian scale.

Would I be testing your patience too far if I were also to

suggest that it is not impossible that Waugh played up the exactness of his account in order to help sales? I think he was shrewder at projecting his literary personality than some might think. If he did, he did well because part of the book's attraction is its backstory.

It would be an interesting experiment to have *Pinfold* read by two groups of readers of similar profile or sociological mix, one that knew nothing of the author's background story and one that did. In this case, it would be like reading two very different books. But *Pinfold* is an exception, even amongst Waugh's works, and we must be careful about the conclusions we draw.

A great *roman-à-clef* is usually a vehicle for the author's ideas. The experience drawn on may or may not have been sought out: the naturalist authors of the nineteenth century made a point of carrying out research. When reading Tolstoy's *Resurrection*, you *feel* that he has visited several prisons and you *feel* that the accounts of how the peasants reacted to his offer of giving them the land were drawn exactly from his own experience. No doubt these things are known, and can be found in any good biography of the author, but knowing these things would not change the book at all. It stands exactly as it is. That is its greatness.

A failed *roman-à-clef* is one that constantly feels like unprocessed experience of people and events from life – and in the worst cases motivated by a desire to offend. Some such works offend incidentally, as authors might know that the material will be recognised and will offend, but cannot resist the material because it is funny or instructive or in some other way apparently essential to their purpose.

In between these two extremes, there are infinite varieties of mixing invented material with material based on real or perceived events.

The admission of characters and events being drawn from

life can change the way a book is interpreted. Surely in many cases it could ruin a book – even a good book. But not in this case – or not entirely

An author's life, as described by Waugh, is a pretty miserable affair, and if we follow A.L. Kennedy's life in her collection of blogs, it seems no better now. She is a talented writer – and a successful one. Hence there are two good reasons for expecting her to produce great wisdom on the subject of writing – although it would always only be an expectation, because not all good writers can. She is contributing womanfully to keeping what we now call the literary novel alive. Even her detractors will have to admit that. She strikes me (more so after reading this book) as an energetic woman and one of small needs – two factors very useful to a writer's productivity and independence. The principal problem with this book is that three-quarters of it is a blog, and a blog composed over several months is not designed to be read in a couple of sittings. Blogging creates a relationship that has nothing to do with literature – it is a correspondence society with a lead correspondent, a group of internet friends, a forerunner of the social networks, with which it shares several features. So when, in Blog XXI, readers of the book encounter Kennedy's intimate words, "We are, I think, all in this together," they know that this is not directed at them, but at the original followers of the blog: a fan base interested in the immediacy of Kennedy's movements, health and current activities. For the reader of the book, it is like chancing upon a round-robin sent to someone else three Christmases ago. And I was never an admirer of round-robins. It's true that these blogs are by an accomplished writer and there are moments of brilliance, but far too few. Whose idea was this? You sense that a publisher was looking to exploit what is probably a very popular blog for a quick profit. The editor could at least have put the essays at the beginning, and deleted the many repetitions, including the endless apologies for not having posted a blog for some days (oddly the editor does not provide any dates, so you have to gauge the timing of the blogs by Kennedy's shifting opinions on Nick Clegg).

Among the author's endless, punishing itineraries, her ulcer, her fear of flying and latterly her labyrinthitis (an inflammation of the inner ear that can cause distressing dizziness), Kennedy finally comes out with a coherent if arguable statement on writing: "Aiming yourself at a clique of pals, or a market, or up your own private right of way doesn't make for particularly appetising prose. Viciously selfish, compulsive, obsessive and odd though many writers may be, we do everything we do for other people." The first of these pronouncements is undoubtedly correct; here are the principal dangers for a writer: elitist hermeticism, subjugation of one's own voice to fashionable concepts of "good writing", and self-obsession, which is exacerbated by this kind of blogging. The second of them attempts with little or no explanation to present writers as Mother Teresas with bad manners. In my opinion, writers, more than any other artists, are a disparate lot, although, strangely for people who work with words, they are generally less sociable than the others, particularly the ever affable musicians and actors. They do what they do because they want to. Art is not an act of selflessness – more likely an act of useful arrogance. I have called the literary novel "an exercise in empathy", and that is beneficial for the reader and, if enough copies are read, for society beyond. Outside the act of writing, the writer may display any of the human qualities or vices, and there may be entirely unrelated to their works. Ultimately fiction is a work of imagination, and even the most dedicated authors have to take a holiday from imagining.

Waugh seems to have always understood that he had

to distance himself from his readers, although sometimes he was plain rude in how he described them. *Pinfold* was a departure, and he probably achieved what he set out to do, even though I'm not quite sure what that was. Here he is with Freeman again,

> Waugh: …, I'm afraid that if someone praises me, I think what an ass, and if they abuse me, I think what an ass.
> Freeman: And if they say nothing about you at all and take no notice of you?
> Waugh: That's the best I can hope for.
> Freeman: You like that when it happens, do you?
> Waugh: Yes.
> Freeman: Why are you appearing in this programme?
> Waugh: Poverty. We've both been hired to talk in this deliriously happy way.[4]

Waugh here is thoroughly unreliable. A writer who doesn't want public interest in his private life is not unlikely and would also be a quite sensible person. There might be a financial loss in terms of sales, but there would also be a psychological gain. But a writer who doesn't care at all about what critics and the public say about his books is not credible. Writing requires obsession, one that is often beyond the writer's control. Writing is for a readership, without which there seems little purpose. Some of us, myself in lead position, are dangerously close to little purpose. Waugh was not, and an unsuccessful book would have hurt him profoundly, I'm sure.

There is a reason why Kennedy's novels work and her blog doesn't. In her novels as with all others, the author

---

4 *The Ordeal of Gilbert Pinfold* …, p. 165

and reader enter into a contract involving, I suppose, that famous suspension of disbelief but also a willingness to accept the characters as the author has constructed them. The reader expects to gain as much information about the characters as the author is willing to provide. I feel that I now know more about Kennedy's life than I do of many of my friends' lives. She points out at one stage that her much interviewed friends reveal little of themselves in interviews, which suggests that newspaper and magazine interviews are a form that encourages interviewees to be defensive of their personal lives, whereas blogs and social media encourage not only Kennedy but many people to reveal sparse and sequential data similar to that of a personal diary.

"Since I last wrote I have, Dear Reader, been in Glasgow, Ullapool, Aberdeen, Oxford, London, Bakewell, Tissington and various bits of leafy Warwickshire." Kennedy confesses to not always knowing which city she's in, and if you read this book, you will not blame her. Her hyperactive lifestyle seems more suited to the pop star than the writer, and is founded in part on the mistaken Romantic belief that writing has to involve experience of life. And she herself has decried direct observation from life. On the other hand, Waugh was chided by his interviewer for living in reclusion in Gloucestershire. Waugh sensibly replied that some writers like Austen can write excellent works "out of just what they see within five miles of their own rectory. Others, like Conrad, have to go to the seven seas to find stories."

Unless Kennedy is making a fictional narrator of her blog persona, just as Waugh would appear to have been doing on occasions (often to put himself intentionally in a bad light), it's clear that she is not enjoying her writing career except in those few moments in which she sits down at her computer to write – usually at some time after midnight or on a train (she writes, "You want my life? You have it, matey"). Performance is the drug that keeps her away from her true calling and the calm she appears to need – with good reason, if half her stories are true. That is the lesson about writing that I take from her book, but it was not one that she intended.

In *Ars Poetica*, Horace advises the author to listen to established authors and then put the parchment away in a closet for nine years. "What you have not published you can destroy; the word once sent forth can never come back." In those days, publishing meant commissioning scribes to make several copies – a tiny risk against that of the blog, which within seconds of it being posted could potentially be read by millions (I should clarify that some writers' blogs are not at all personal, but simply articles published on the web, just like those in newspapers, and some of them are excellent). Although we can all agree that nine years is now too long (a historical era in our times), we can also agree that the essential element of literature is there – in the waiting. We are all a little impatient about publication dates, but those months in which the text rests and is rewritten count for a lot, as Kennedy also believes. Her other books are carefully reworked, and yet she openly admits that before publication in book form the blogs were not. Their immediacy is sacred, but in being published they cease to be immediate and therefore demand a higher level of coherence and a different relationship with the reader.

There are aspects of Kennedy's *On Writing* that are attractive: her modesty, her humour, her political views, her fierce self-deprecation (a trait she shares with Waugh). You feel, however, that she is also weighed down by a duty to self-promote, another feature of modern society, not only present in publishing. Self-promotion leads to the blog, and the blog leads to a dictatorship of the self. Even the self-deprecation, which leaps from every page – the only forceful element – ends up, by dint of repetition, resembling self-obsession.

My contrast between Waugh and Kennedy is not so much between two writers as it is between two generations. Social media are particularly unkind to writers, because they are a written conversation and follow the rules of the spoken word. The question of how much writers should open up to the world around them remains unchanged and Waugh's fear of the interview was based on similar reservations, but the pressures for us to get publicity are now extremely powerful. We are all affected, and writers are expected to be their own self-publicists. My advice – and on writing I have even more reservations about formulating an exact opinion than in most other spheres – is that writers should avoid Twitter, Facebook, personal blogs, and all outlets that entice immediate opinion or revelation, or at least use them very sparingly. The author is best served by a degree of mystery, and should remember that what appears to be only a minor lapse could turn into a flood. So I will end perversely with a self-revelation of my own.

I wrote a long and rambling introduction for my book on language, *In Praise of the Garrulous*, which for some reason I was very pleased with. It was seventeen thousand words – about a third of the book again – and I wrote it in three or four days. Both my sister[5] and Eric Hobsbawm politely advised me to drop it and replace it with something more succinct. I resisted only briefly, although it took a little longer to understand the enormity of the error I was about to make, not to speak of all that wasted paper. Hobsbawm added further advice: to write about why I wrote the book and to speak a little about myself. I took his advice in the right measure, I think, but if he were alive to read this book, he might think that I have now taken his advice further

---

5 Bertha Husband, radical artist and co-founder of the Axe Street Arena, which was active on the Chicago arts scene in the eighties and nineties. She has often been obliged to read my manuscripts and provide advice.

than he would have wanted. The essay too can encourage a writer to say too much that is personal, because personal experience provides part of our understanding of the world. It is, as nearly always, a matter of balance, but the best defences against getting that balance wrong are time and the advice of others.

On the Soul

The soul is out of fashion, except amongst fanatical believers who have, no doubt, a different idea of what it is. For them it is a rigid, unchanging thing, and for some of them a thing ordained and controlled by a God who marks our behaviour in schoolmasterly fashion and has his favourites – his elect. But "soul" is an essential word and like many of the really important words, it defies definition. Significant words say significant things or, to put it more clearly, they assume premises on which most people have already made a judgement. If you reject the word, you reject the premise. The premise that the word "soul" shouts out so loudly that it offends materialists and utilitarians is "Man does not live by bread alone." It is a word hated by both worshippers of the market and humanists. The latter, for whom I have a certain sympathy, are worshippers of humanity alone, and I wonder if it's good for anything to worship itself.

"Ah but," I hear some people say or sneer, "if the soul exists, where is it to be found? In your head, your heart or your big toe?" Consciousness must exist for everyone, and yet it has no place. We sense that it's behind the eyes which are the windows through which we view the world.

The soul also has no place. It is where we transcend the self, and by doing so become more alive. It is a rash person who opines too much on the nature of the soul, but I suffer from rashness, which hopefully is moderated by doubts. Or shall we say, everything in the following paragraphs is a metaphor for an imprudent hypothesis. We all have a soul, but if we don't nurture it, it shrinks to the size of a pea. If it is nurtured, however, it grows and grows and grows. I don't know exactly what that feels like, because mine is only the size of two and a half peas, and wanders mournfully around the area of my belly. It is not easy to nurture the soul in this society, and few of us are going to follow the path of Saint Francis and start talking to the animals.

What evidence do I have for these ramblings? The evidence of more than sixty years on this planet and in that time I have frequented many more milieus than most people have. I have met sadists and friendly drunks, intellectuals and saints, the perennially enraged and the unshakably calm, the sad and the content, the selfish and the generous. Certainly, but aren't all these behaviours the product of DNA, diet, education, culture, society and the list goes on? Of course, but wouldn't all these people behave slightly differently – better perhaps – if they admitted another dimension to their being, if they engaged in some kind of moral exercise beyond all that jogging on the way to eternal youth, and sudoku, crossword puzzles and all that cerebral jogging on the way to clarity of mind?

A large soul could be identified with spirituality, another term which is, I admit, a little unsatisfactory. It is a presence that can be felt, and I have noted it in some religious people and a surprising number of atheists who would deny its existence. Surprising? Perhaps not, given that nothing deflates the soul like smugness, and beyond a certain degree, religious faith (particularly in one religion) does lead to smugness.

A soul does not have to be immortal, as a soul without a body seems more improbable than a body without a soul. An immortal soul would lead us back to the self.

A mortal soul leads us to God. It is the way to shake off that bearded, patriarchal God who dictates certainties to his children. God, after all, has always been a reflection of human reality. Warriors had warrior gods. The fragmented classical world before Christianity had a god for every profession. Ancient Israel took a leap forward and produced a god for a whole people. From there came the God of all humanity in which Christians and Muslims believe. Some early twentieth-century Jews believed that Judaism had developed an even more universalist approach, because suffering had produced an enviable cosmopolitanism (term of denigration for the supposed Marxist Joseph Stalin and of admiration for the civilisation of the left). Religions last much longer than political movements, but they do so by changing incessantly. God in our own age will have to adapt again, relinquishing a little power and taking on more responsibility. Why should we care? Every concept has to evolve.

Perhaps the soul is a fragment of God, and God is the totality of all human souls. When the last human being dies, God would then die with her: a blasphemous thought, but isn't the moral world He represents a human one? It is also a Manichaean thought, and I like the idea that we all have to work to make the world a better place, starting modestly and generally remaining with our own most immediate human relationships.

Liking an idea is not evidence of anything. God is, I suppose, the indefinable and unknowable absolute. We have to live with that, but the soul as something we are responsible for, and leading to a form of spirituality beyond the banal and self-indulgent, approximates to what many of us perceive to be a truth. It is a starting point, not a very stable one, I admit, but in this subject nothing is.

On Publishing

The book was the first object to be mass-produced. It had always been there, but in the mid-fifteenth century the printing press made it more accessible and literacy gradually increased. Only at the start of the sixteenth century did the magnitude of change it was bringing become clear. All the new kinds of writing that are familiar to us still were then invented. The book challenged the sacred or, to use the clumsy academic word, it desacralised the written word by spreading it like confetti, and it created the need for religious and political censorship. The book started as a liberating force and aroused the demons of repression, who would come and go over the following centuries, and still do.

It is said that modern technology is changing the publishing world. In the sense that other technologies are squeezing the printed word out, that is true, but the publishing world has always been unstable, and has always gone through fallow periods. Many writers have made a good living from writing, but they are not usually the ones we remember. Some of those who had both talent and success, like Dickens, had difficult lives because the printing press also created the first celebrity culture – not on the modern scale, but dramatic nonetheless. Celebrity can so often destroy the celebrated person. It was a new form of fame, alienating the person from their own personality, which becomes a form of public property. If this is the case, the demotion of the written word might be a good thing for writers and publishers, as they will find a little peace in neglect, and will be able to get on with their job without all the clamour. On the other hand, the written word remains more dangerous and potentially subversive than many of the other arts that have a wider public.

The technology that has been inimical to writing has been around for a long time, and started with television. Modern printing technology, however, has been good for publishing, and has made it possible for quite a few hand-to-mouth publishing enterprises to be set up and survive in the shadow of the big corporations. E-books have been damaging for independent booksellers, whom small publishers rely on greatly, but on the other hand they have brought in extra income. On the whole, printing technology has offset some of the disastrous consequences of getting rid of the Net Book Agreement.

We are quite possibly on the brink of a period of increased literary and artistic activity, because economic crises often produce such outcomes. When crisis makes people more curious, publishing can survive in the harshest environment. Insane commercialisation of the arts is more damaging than any authoritarian rule. The splendid and varied Soviet writing even during the darkest years of Stalinist repression demonstrates this truth. Different societies react in different ways, and literature varies much more from one country to another than painting, music and architecture. This is partly because countries usually have different languages, but also because literary culture and reading habits can differ dramatically even between nations with the same language. If we look at twentieth-century architecture, the most striking thing is not the variety but how each decade produced clearly defined global styles. People talk about Stalinist brutalism, but actually this architecture was produced more or less everywhere. Some great architecture was produced in the Stalinist era, and also in Fascist Italy, along with some appalling architecture often reflecting more closely the governing ideologies and the harshness of those times everywhere. If you look at literature, you encounter huge differences across the globe, and the quality and influence vary too.

When I come to examine publishing, even in the light of my own experience of it over the last two decades, I am struck by the continuity. Naturally there are ups and downs, and the disappearance of the Net Book Agreement gradually destroyed most of the innovation in the British publishing industry and created lifeless corporations run by accountants and managers. But in the last five to ten years, a new generation of publishers has been created. It exists because there are people who are not motivated solely by economic self-interest, as the spirit of our times dictates, but by a passion for books. Of course many people make a great display of their "passion for books", and we have all heard rhetoric devalue those words. We hear them from bureaucrats, broadcasters and academics who would not cross the road to look at a new idea; they would rather recycle old ones. Some of the best people in the book trade have no pretensions; they just get on with it because they quite simply love the humdrum mechanics of it.

Publishing is a business, and people who run businesses can get bogged down in margins and income streams and bad debt and all the jargon of modern business culture. I will try to avoid such things which are dull for anyone who isn't in the business, but ultimately independent publishers have to sell enough books to cover the costs of producing them and this is where they come up against the corporate world. Business being business, not everything in publishing is as it appears. An apparently thriving publishing business may rely on authors paying the costs of publication – a form of hidden vanity publishing with no risk to the businessman. It is a good business, but makes a bad publisher.

Publishing is a craft, and people who engage in a craft can get bogged down in its minutiae – flaps, formats, covers, paper, fonts and all the wonderful things that make a book apart from the most important thing – the text. When I started publishing, I happily pumped out a series of books with ugly, indistinguishable covers, white paper that could blind you on a sunny day, and fonts that hadn't kept up with the aesthetics of fonts – something I still don't really understand. I was ignorant of these things and arrogant enough to leap into the business without any knowledge of them. I thought that people shouldn't judge a book by its cover and it would be enough to get the editorial part right. But I was mistaken: publishing is a craft and every element is important, and no one person can have all the skills. This is the collaborative nature of publishing, and that's why it becomes so compelling – that's why you have to continue, even when you're lurching from one crisis to another.

The author is the central figure in publishing, certainly literary publishing. The publisher has an essential, auxiliary role, and should keep out of the limelight. Some authors produce work that needs a lot of editing; others only require a few typos to be corrected. But the author always remains at the centre, or should do. As in all walks of life, self-knowledge avoids crass errors, and authors who need editorial assistance are wise to stay with a publisher who knows how to work on their kind of book. The publisher takes the artwork, frames it and arranges for it to be hung on the wall. The artwork is the author's, and the modern author has to seek the limelight to survive – something that does not come easily to all of them, including some of the best.

I heard a publisher quoting another publisher, and clearly the truth contained in the quote was immediately understandable to all the publishers present: "A publisher should not expect an author to be grateful, but should be grateful when the author is." Gratitude for the risks a publisher must run is an unnecessary plus, but I would add that the real but unspoken gratitude comes from the work itself. The published work thanks you every time you pick up a copy.

Occasionally there will be a defect (hopefully a very small one) and then the book will reproach you. It is difficult to explain the pleasure that derives from publishing another person's work.

My first two books, both novels, were published by Luath Press in 2004 and 2005. When it came to my book on language, *In Praise of the Garrulous*, Luath was less convinced and this led to the establishment of Vagabond Voices.[1] I had no idea about what I was getting into. Shortly afterwards I met Allan Massie at an event in Glasgow. I knew him and knew from others of the existence of an unpublished manuscript of his – a book called *Surviving*. He agreed to let me publish it. I remember very distinctly that during the editorial process, someone rang and, as I was talking on the phone, my eye rested on a particularly well-formed sentence. I felt pleasure passing through my brain as I realised that this sentence was being published because I was making it happen. Of course, I made all those mistakes with the look of the edition, and the book did reproach me many times, until I made up for it and brought it out in a new and much better edition. Now the book thanks me, and it's once again a pleasure to pick up a copy and read a couple of pages. All books I publish are important to me, but there is another I have to mention for no particular reason other than its brilliance. It is Chris Dolan's *Redlegs*, another great work of art and this time a great Scottish novel in terms of its vocabulary and content, but also entirely accessible to any reader of standard English.

Anyone thinking of going into publishing should remember

---

1 The publisher of this book. I never noticed who the publisher of a book was until I got into publishing. Why should you? A reader's disinclination to care about such things is helpful in my opinion, although I now want to know the minute I pick a book up, just as I examine its physicality in a way I never did before. Occupational hazards.

this. Don't go in for the money, there's little to be made and you will probably have to work at least part-time on something else. Don't go in for the kudos, as you'll be at the back of the queue behind wealthier and better networked people. Go in for the pleasure of making these very special objects that can engage a reader's mind for several hours and give them, hopefully, a new experience. The more people come into the business to revitalise it, the better. Every book is an entirely different thing, so publishers are not in competition in the same way that toothpaste manufacturers are.[2] If we could create more publishers here in Glasgow, we would all benefit. There would be a greater pool of skills, and the reading public would grow as well. I would like to see a *sistema literario*, *el sistema* for writing. Most human beings have enormous untapped creativity, which atrophies in this society governed by monetary profit. I proselytise and hand out information on publishing, particularly the importance of digital printers who have taken some of the huge risks out of small publishing. I'm not talking about print-on-demand, because you need to believe that a book is going to sell a reasonable number, as each well-edited book does require some considerable costs that are not going to be covered by tiny numbers of books printed on demand. This brings us to the publisher's most important task: choosing the right books and, having chosen, putting as much care and energy into the process as possible. Very good books don't always sell, but across the range enough sales can be generated to survive. Generally speaking, survival is the target.

Can a writer be a publisher? It's true that writers are generally absent-minded, disorganised and occasionally grumpy loners. None of these attributes are appropriate for businessmen, but

2 You will understand this immediately, but the corporations never will. They have one template for all businesses.

as I have suggested, publishing is not only a business, it is also a craft. Moreover there is a long history of self-publishing – going all the way back to Gutenberg no doubt. But we don't have to go back that far. Let's look at some of the more illustrious examples: Virginia Woolf and Marcel Proust. They are simply the pinnacle of self-publishers on top of many thousands of less successful attempts, but they represent very clearly the two principal models for self-publishing.

Proust went down the more obvious route: he went along to a printer and paid him to print a number of books. This method has cluttered bedrooms and garages for as long as anyone can remember. In the sixteenth century they presumably had broken carts that were used as receptacles for unsold books. Its main problem is that no thought is given to how those books are going to be sold. Potential Proust-readers have been thin on the ground everywhere, I suspect, especially before his fame, so there would be little hope of selling them from a stall improvised in a market square. Nevertheless Proust proves that it can work. Italo Svevo tried this system twice, and tragically became so disillusioned that for at least two decades he abandoned writing, before starting on his masterpiece, *La coscienza di Zeno*, which only got published because his English teacher happened to be James Joyce and Joyce perceived its brilliance. It and those failed early books are never out of print. The lesson here is that luck is also very important, and you have to give luck a chance. You'll never be published if you write and show your work to no one. Luck does not knock at your door. Luck comes mainly in the form of good and preferably wealthy parents. That is why so many authors, good and bad, come from middle-class backgrounds. Even working-class writers who win critical acclaim, like Gwyn Thomas and James Kelman, to some extent struggle financially all their professional lives. Both of these are great stylists and depict working-class life through highly innovative syntax and diction. They sell, but they should be selling more.

Virginia Woolf, to my mind the greatest English-language novelist of the twentieth century, set up Hogarth Press with her husband Leonard in 1917, while humanity was killing itself on an unprecedented scale. I expect that he did most of the work, although that assertion is based on nothing more than ill-informed opinion – my feeling is that her fragile brilliance was unsuited to the rigours of the publishing world. I may well be wrong. This publishing company published all her great works, and their joint management survived until 1938 and her husband's until 1946 when it became an imprint of Chatto & Windus. It survives to this day as one of Penguin Random House's many imprints. It had all the hallmarks of a great literary concern: a combination of dilettantism and extraordinary literary talent. Many such ventures fail quickly: perhaps because they ought to or perhaps because they were too good, too innovative or too short of funds. The problem facing arts councils is which ones are which. This model involves engaging with other authors and creating a resource – perhaps a local resource – for literary innovation. In my opinion, they all provide something, even if it's training for more publishers and writers. Naturally this form of self-publishing has more staying power than the purer Proustian model, which however also makes a valid contribution. Self-publishing should not be hidden; it should not dress itself up as something else. It has nothing to be ashamed of.

The question is, however, whether self-publishing in either model is second best. I would say that in part it is. But it is often necessary, as can be seen from the names we would be deprived of without them. We would presumably also be deprived of many minor talents as well. On the other hand, we had better get used to it: just as poorly produced samizdat was the inevitable release of literary talents in the Soviet Bloc, there appears in the shadow of the corporations to be a return to the unity of production in the first century of printing, during which writer, printer and publisher could be different men working together under the same roof – in the same crowded workshop. Publisher and printer are unlikely to come back together in the case of what we now call "physical books" (although the wealthy but impractical Woolfs bought themselves a printing press). These roles are divided by technology, at least for the foreseeable future, but the distinction between writer and publisher may become less distinct. Some time ago, Timothy Mo, finding courage not to be redundant at least in literature, struck out for independence and produced his own books in spite of being well-established as an author. He was the first to see that modern technology had made publishing much more accessible, and that was before the e-book, which makes it so much easier for writers to become their own publishers and in a sense their own "printers". But let me stop you short just when I'm starting to convince you of a literary dawn about to break across our harsh and arid cultural desert: we can produce the books and e-books, but selling them remains stubbornly difficult. Particularly in the Anglo-Saxon economic model, small businesses are extremely difficult to sustain, and most of them are probably agencies that have taken over tasks originally provided directly by the state, and are therefore dependent on a culture of nomenklatura. Small publishers have few channels for selling their wares to the public.

So writers can be publishers, but are they likely to be good publishers? Clearly the skills would appear to overlap, but writing requires reflection and detachment, while publishing requires involvement, collaboration, understanding and organisation. For someone who has scarce organisational skills, publishing is so all-consuming that it leaves little room for writing anything except fragmented works: short stories, essays, aphorisms and poetry. But the novel's the thing, and that is still the preferred form for most writers today.

My detractors, many of whom have not met me or even read me, will be pleased to know that I am going to go silent and start work on a historical novel that takes Machiavelli as an opportunity to examine intellectuals and their various foibles. It should take two or three years, but may never be finished. Publishing has its demands and it has its pleasures, as does writing. Where there are shifts between the two, writers gradually become publishers or the publishers writers. It is unlikely that the two can coexist in perfect balance for a long period of time.

A writer is an intellectual in the restricted sense of a hare-brained person who in their muddled existence sometimes comes up with original ideas, as a child can see the idiocy of adult certainties. Intellectuals worthy of the name should be able to stand their ground and are always in a minority, because they disagree promiscuously and therefore can never develop a network that can protect them. They would be fools to try. Machiavelli and Winstanley, the first constantly revisited and the second almost universally ignored, were both courageous enough to stand their ground and not complain about their sufferings, but both foolishly deluded themselves that they could make a difference in their own times. That these two excellent political thinkers dedicated their most famous works to powerful men (the former to Lorenzo de' Medici whose uncle had had him tortured and the latter to Cromwell, no less) demonstrates the stupidity of intellectuals – their foolish trust in power and in the power of reason and reasoned argument.

Intellectuals are fools, but their great merit is that they're also dangerous to the powerful (an intellectual in power is dangerous, but this time to the powerless – an intellectual in power is an aberration). Intellectuals should acknowledge their foolishness and use it sensibly. And sensible intellectuals do not even seek power, conscious that it would corrupt their single virtue – their ability to stand outside certainty and undermine accepted truths.

I admire polemicists and publish them gleefully, but when I write, I argue constantly against myself, and often don't know which side I'm on. I'm not an advocate in court; I'm the member of the jury who abstains. This is why I like writing fiction. If x is the commonly held opinion and I appear to suggest y, I would like the reader to say, "Yes, x cannot be right or wholly right, but y, which this confused author appears to believe in, is also wrong. Surely it must be z," where z equals as many opinions as there have been readers.

And these last few paragraphs are a case in point. I was uncertain whether to put them under publishing or produce yet another essay on writing. On balance, the essay on publishing seemed more appropriate because, although publishing inhibits my writing, it may well do what I want my writing to do, only better. Through publishing different things, I can generate a mass of conflicting ideas more effectively than through anything I could write. I find it easier to believe in other people's writing than in my own. I feel that if I'm ever going to be a footnote in the history of Scottish literature, then it will be for my publishing and not my writing. There you have it: an intellectual's vanity.

On Nation, Polity and Cosmopolity

When a small country comes up against a large country, the small country pays a high price, whatever happens. If it rebels, it pays disproportionately in defeat and is crippled in victory. If it succumbs to pressure to avoid the pain of a one-sided military encounter, it is treated with greater contempt, because it is not feared. Vietnam defeated the United States, but continues to pay the price for its audacity and courage. Afghanistan continues forever to fight off invaders, but is reduced to a pulp of misery and hardship. In the fifties Egypt and Hungary sought autonomy without firing a shot, and were invaded, did shoot and were humiliated. The legacy of those days remains today, particularly in the case of Egypt. In 1968 Czechoslavakia gave in, as Dubček wisely avoided a battle that was lost before it was fought; ancient Czech independence of spirit was lost, possibly for many generations.

Two films – Neil Jordan's *Michael Collins* and Ken Loach's *The Wind that Shakes the Barley* – were good in their own way but too partisan. Each film blamed the other side in the Irish Civil War for Ireland's continued misery in that war. They missed the more interesting story: both sides were right, or at least at the moment war broke out the arguments were finely balanced. Always supposing that you believe in the use of violence to obtain justice from a more powerful force, there was no simple solution to the fact that Ireland in that moment could not defeat Britain, while Britain, if it had wanted to pay a high price, could have defeated Ireland. Collins correctly argued that, in such a situation, a partial victory was better than no victory at all, a pragmatic acceptance of the balance of forces. De Valera correctly argued that, having fought, Ireland had to fight on for complete independence of all its territory, otherwise it might remain divided, as it has.

Given that De Valera himself would very soon become the long-standing Taoiseach or prime minister, and *gradually* dismantle the imperial link by 1937 (though cautiously leaving the final declaration of the republic to the opposition in 1949), it may be said that he proved Collins right – that what could not be achieved by force could be achieved by stealth. But it could equally be argued that if there hadn't been part of the IRA willing to continue the struggle, the British would not have conceded enough levers of power to Collins to create a situation in which either Collins or De Valera could gradually achieve more powers by stealth. Politicians act within the real world and are obliged by the balance of power to choose between unpalatable options. Some intellectuals and politicians who have never tasted power delight in their moral purity and fail to distinguish between those who have choices and those who don't. Only the great powers have real choices, and generally they get them wrong and must take full moral responsibility for them, as in the case of Britain's brutal suppression of the Kenyan rebellion, America's war in Vietnam, the Soviet Union's treachery and repression in Poland, China's unremitting strangulation of Tibet and Russia's obliteration of Chechnya. You could add to these Burma's annihilation of its minorities, once almost half the nation, and Israel's war in the nineteenth-century style against its indigenous population guilty of having being born in their own land. Even small nations can be brutal to smaller and weaker nations. Good and evil are universally human.

Ireland, or rather Ulster, suffered a terrible event that heralded centuries of future suffering that would spread out from Ulster. It was inflicted by an English court under the first king of the united crowns who used his English power to implement a Scottish policy aimed not so much at the suppression of Catholicism as the protection of Scotland's western seaboard from the Gaelic or "Erse" world that straddled Ireland and Scotland, and which James VI now considered foreign to Scotland. His grandson, James VII, would one day seek and obtain the support of those Catholic Irish who were dispossessed by the ethnic cleansing of the Fife Adventurers, but long before that another grandson, not yet crowned Charles II, sought and obtained the support of Gaels on Scotland's western seaboard. Such are the paradoxes of history. Needless to say, Charles did nothing to assist his loyal subjects when he did become king, a lesson entirely lost on generations of that bloody and absurdly romanticised political movement, Jacobitism.

From the very beginning of that union, then, Scotland has been more privileged and less oppressed by the English than other dominions. It retained its institutions, and its own elites, subordinate now but surviving in some form, which was not true of Ireland and Wales. Scotland became a headless state.

Scotland is by European standards quite an old nation, but one constructed out of five different "ethnicities" (or perhaps language communities might be a better term). Those ethnicities were the Gaels, the Britons, the Norse, the Angles and the Picts. The first four language communities were definitely not part of the original peoples, who presumably were subsumed into them. In this it was like almost every other European country. The dominance of Gaelic came on the back of the spread of Christianity, also a common feature of early nation-building. Gael, or *Scotus* to use the Latin term in surviving records, originally applied to someone or a community living in any part of Britain or Ireland, which sometimes meant what would become northern England, just as other ethnicities had large or fragmented communities north of the current border. Gradually, through the usual misery of military conflict, a nation was randomly formed and *Scotus* no longer meant those belonging to the culture that came over from Northern Ireland and instead meant those living within a certain unified territory under the rule of a king. In other words, Scotland is a historical construct, which like every nation, is an abstraction that exists precisely because people believe that it exists. *This does not mean that it is not real*; ideas are as hard as steel, even if they're intangible and have no spatial reality.

Ideas have to be maintained from one generation to another, and can be greatly assisted by power, although they may also be revived by the abuse of power, as in the case of Scotland. It is common in our homogenised media today to claim that Thatcher's introduction of the poll tax one year earlier in Scotland had no influence on the rise of what is a little misleadingly referred to as Scottish nationalism. Everybody knows the story, but I think it is worth restating, because it is so stark and so obvious. Thatcher had promised to introduce this tax, and had been elected overwhelmingly in England at least in terms of seats. Instead of introducing it there, she decided to do so in Scotland where the electorate had rejected her politics even more overwhelmingly (the Tory vote dropped by 4% and 11 seats to 25% of the vote and 10 seats in 1987). The tax was introduced by her Secretary of State for Scotland, acting like a governor in a subject province. Scots campaigned by non-violent means for a year and were not listened to, but when the poll tax charges fell through letter boxes in England, riots in London and Birmingham lost Thatcher her premiership and the poll tax was withdrawn. Should anyone be surprised that this had a lasting effect on the Scottish electorate? There are those who point to the fact that the Conservative vote in Scotland held up in 1992, but the important change in that election was the SNP increasing its vote by around 50% thus affecting Labour. It is true that the poll tax affair only accelerated the increasing divide between the political cultures of Scotland and England, which started perhaps with the disappointment of the devolution vote in 1979 (due to the 40% rule), and without doubt as a result of the brutal deindustrialisation under Thatcher's first government. However, there is an argument for saying that the poll tax pushed the discontent more firmly in the direction of nationalism, because it divided the experience in Scotland from that of other deindustrialised areas in the UK, namely Northern England and South Wales. Nationalism was rekindled after an extended period in which Scotland's cultural and linguistic identity had been losing ground quite dramatically. In other circumstances, there might have been convergence, and the current situation, which offers Scots great opportunities if they have the courage to grasp them, is a creation of British politics over the last thirty years and the blindness of the British establishment (including New Labour) to the crisis it inflicted on Scotland over the same period.

Peoples come together and quite often they divide again. It is pointed out that Britain was united during the Second World War. This was undoubtedly true, as it was of many other states that no longer exist, including the Soviet Union, which had extended Russian as its lingua franca over its entire territory except, perhaps, in the Soviet Socialist Republic of Armenia. When it all fell apart, the British establishment was perhaps the loudest in its applause, but few of the states created by this tectonic shift had anything like the durability of Scotland, including the Baltic states, whose previous existence was limited to the interwar years. Two years after the Union of Parliaments, Peter the Great defeated the Swedes and wrested from them the Baltic nations along with many other territories. Before the Swedes there were the Danes and before them the Teutonic Knights, although the story is complicated by the Grand Duchy of Lithuania, a vast state facing southwards and nearly reaching the Black Sea, which lasted for three centuries. Scotland may have suffered, but in the slaughterhouse of history, it comes out as lucky on the global scale as it was on the local one.

However the longevity of a nation is not necessarily an argument for its revival. A dangerous word in debates on nationalism is the word "forever". Forever is the enemy of doubt and implies an unchanging nation in the past as well as the future. The eternal nation can be suppressed like the Jews in Babylon, but eventually it will return, as though it were a single entity that can quickly be revived. Nations are inconsistent on just what eternal means. Germany claimed French territory such as Lorraine because in the Middle Ages it had been German-speaking (indeed the cradle of German literature), but in the east it claimed Polish and Czech territory because they had become partly German-speaking in relatively recent times. Nations are constantly in flux. The argument that the state created by the Treaty of Union should be kept solely because it has been around for a long time is irrelevant. Three centuries is more than the average lifespan of a state, and if a state ceases to have legitimacy amongst its citizens or citizens of one of its constituent parts, it will not last. Equally there is no reason to believe that Scotland will exist forever. Apart from the likelihood sooner or later of a federal solution for the European Union, this coming century could be as brutal as the last, if the slow build-up of xenophobic forces in the continent continues because the economic system is incapable of maintaining the social rights people have become accustomed to. Europe is at a fork in the road: it could become more liberal and social-ist or more authoritarian and racist. But then these have perhaps always been the two conflicting spirits of Europe.

Nation is not about ethnicity and never has been. There are so many ways you can approach this argument, but let us just take one curious example. The untypical sometimes instructs us on the typical by virtue of its extremes. In her fascinating book, *Captives*, Linda Colley provides an interesting account of how Irish troops dealt with the problem of English desertions from the garrison in Tangier, then an English possession: "During the siege of 1860, Irish Catholic soldiers and officers defending one of Tangier's forts on behalf of the Kind of England were obliged to call out instructions to each other in the Gaelic language, so as to avoid being understood by some English Protestant renegades who were serving with the Moroccan forces outside the gates."[1] This historical gem conjures up the idea of English deserters continuing their service to the Sultan long after the inevitable defeat of the army they had abandoned, and their descendants walking the streets of North African towns and cities. At the same time the descendants of the Gaelic speakers now are, in all likelihood, speakers of English in Ireland, England, America or Scotland (where they might speak Scots). History is chequered with these complex exchanges that make nonsense of ethnic myths. Given this precedent, it is difficult not to be disappointed with Linda Colley's brief work for the referendum year, *Acts of Union and Disunion. What had held the UK together – and what is dividing it.* The historian has not proved to be as adept when dealing with the present day. She has no understanding of the political debate in Scotland, which is driving the independence question and, perhaps worse, she appears to have made little attempt to understand it.

Colley does reveal one important aspect of the British state and touches on another concerning the circularity of the "British" nations. The British state has failed spectacularly

---

1 L. Colley, *Captives* (London: Jonathan Cape, 2002), p. 39.

to retain its huge empire, because it never got to grips with institutionalising it. Born as a mercantile empire, Greater Britain could never transform its institutions into something more inclusive. It wanted to do business, but it didn't want to be changed in the process. Even the Roman Empire, not remembered for its charity, extended citizenship to all its provinces in 212 AD through the Edict of Caracalla, who may have done this to increase taxation. Roman historians do not paint a pretty picture of Caracalla, and as far as I know, no one has attempted to revise it. However, Caracalla, who was of East Mediterranean (Syrian and Punic) origins and brought up in Gaul, appears to have never returned to Rome or Italy after killing his brother and securing the imperial throne for himself, and ruled the empire from the provinces. He may have seen the move as shifting the political axis away from its traditional centre.

Britain failed to understand the logic of empire, but should have learned because it had paid a high price for ignoring the American demand for "No taxation without represent-ation". Even the islanders on Montserrat were prevented from visiting the "Mother Country" in a moment of crisis, while islanders nearby under French or Dutch rule are part of the metropolitan state with representatives in Paris and Amsterdam, and the rights of members of the European Union – including the right to live in Britain denied to sub-jects of the British crown on islands like Montserrat. The British like to think of themselves as the good imperial-ists. This claim is highly debatable, but they were certainly the most ungracious and have remained so, even now the empire has been reduced to a few rocks sticking out of the water. Colley tells us of "a succession of schemes, devised and discussed from the later nineteenth century to at least the 1950s, 'to federate the Empire by a great act of political reconstruction'." Needless to say, nothing was done, as with the reform of the second chamber (still not complete) and home rule for Ireland, Scotland and Wales (still not complete in the case of the last two). Like the American empire today and the Soviet Union up until its demise, it was undermined by a monumental inability to act and to adapt, motivated by the certainty that what had worked in the past would always work in the future. The security of power is not a good counsellor. It is stunning that people believe in the absolute stability of such states right up to the moment in which they collapse. Afterwards they shrug and say they saw it coming. As I say, ideas and their lesser companions, perceptions, are as hard as steel but more brittle.

The other point that Colley touches on and which is quite significant in this independence debate is the triangular relationship between the nations of Britain and Ireland. Once the triangle was made up of England, Scotland and Ireland, and now that Ireland – or at least the part of it called the Republic of Ireland – has achieved not only complete independence but also a strong identity within the European Union, it has been replaced by another triangle – that of England, Scotland and Wales. What happens on 18 September will not affect Ireland, but will affect England and Wales, and affect them in different ways. If the British establishment learned from history, it would respond to a Yes vote in Scotland by granting a devolved parliament with real powers in Wales. But it won't. A "yes" vote may help the English to rediscover their radical past and reject the narrative of the British establishment. This outcome is worthy of further examination.

In the mid seventeenth century, an English republican army invaded Scotland and Ireland, and different Scottish armies invaded England (one to help parliament overthrow Charles I and later one to restore his son to the English throne) and Ireland to support the covenanting cause of fellow Calvinists. A small Irish Catholic army invaded Scotland to support an army of Highland irregulars mainly made up of moderate episcopalian protestants of the kind that would later be called non-jurists, in a brutal clan war with vague religious overtones. This highly successful ragtag army eventually came under the leadership of Montrose, but then as such armies do, it demobilised to take booty home and left him to his fate. Ireland and Scotland fought the last of Europe's bloody religious wars, but England fought the first European revolution and within its ranks all the ideas of modernity were at least imagined and argued for, even if they never got too close to the centre of power – the closest being the Putney debates.

Whatever the brutality of Cromwellian armies in Ireland and Scotland, the English changed politics forever, not only in Britain and Ireland but also across Europe. If Winstanley or Lilburne had been French, there would be central squares named after them. As it is, hardly any of their fellow countrymen have heard their names. Hobbes, Locke and Milton were giants of that century, but most English only remember that an apple was supposed to have fallen on Newton's head. England, which was perhaps the most egalitarian of nations, became as a result of the failure of its Revolution the least egalitarian. Like all revolutions, England's was a traumatic affair, leading to widespread economic disruption and poverty that exhausted the nation. When the Restoration occurred, the identity of the nation turned against its egalitarian past that went back at least as far as Wycliffe. In the late eighteenth century and the nineteenth century English radicalism would return again. Nations change from century to century and from generation to generation. Every political argument has to be fought and won or lost again and again.

As in Scandinavia and the Iberian Peninsula, this island of Britain is made up of closely linked nations, whose joint histories include rivalries and antagonisms as well as shared experiences and enterprises, although those two peninsulas were never as divided in their political cultures as Scotland and England are today. Perhaps in the new triangle, Scotland could become the radical force, but not in the bellicose way of the mid seventeenth century – quite the opposite, the new radicalism will have to be built on non-violence, starting by dismantling that huge arsenal of nuclear weapons the British state felt appropriate to locate twenty-five miles from Glasgow and the largest conurbation in Scotland. The English left understands Scotland's difficulties but argues that they need Scottish support. This argument is alluring, but false. No post-war election result would have been changed by the Scottish vote, and that is why the Scottish voice is never heard. Scotland would be much more useful to the English left if it set the example of how social rights can be defended in the modern world. Scottish independence would hopefully also release the English establishment from its terrible yearning to maintain the role of a great power, even if it breaks the bank. Scotland will not get involved in future illegal wars, and England might well become more reluctant to do so. The only way that the English-Scottish border would cease to be an open one, as is the case in most of Europe and indeed in Ireland, and become subject to passport controls as the media constantly speculate, would be if England decided to leave the European Union. This is another disturbing possibility, but Scottish independence might discourage English withdrawal. Scottish independence would force England to perceive itself in a different way. This may lead to increased xenophobia, but it is just as likely or more likely that it would lead to a revival of post-war values. If England or a federated state of England and Wales would at last engage with Europe, it could still be a major player, and not the haughty, reticent and ineffectual member the British state is today. Ultimately, Scotland, England and Wales could become equal states within another union, a properly federated Europe-wide one with a more democratic structure than the current EU. Scotland, England and Wales would often have shared interests within the EU and could speak with one voice – a voice in which the interests of Scotland and Wales would finally be properly represented.

As has already been hinted and only noticed by a few commentators down in England, the independence referendum is more about social rights than it is about nation. It is not about the Scots being better than the English. I have given an example of greatness in English history, and in the immediate post-war period England was if anything to the left of Scotland, excepting some of Scotland's most radical industrial centres. In the fifties Scotland had a Tory majority and the Labour Party was strong in large parts of southern England. If we go further back to 1922, we find that two Communist candidates were elected to Westminster, one in Motherwell and one in Battersea. The one in Battersea was an Indian, Shapurji Dorabji Saklatvala, and in both cases the Communist had been endorsed by the Labour Party. They both lost their seats in 1923, but in 1924 Saklatvala tried again without a Labour endorsement and in the wake of the fraudulent Zinoviev letter which lost Labour forty-two seats, and he won by a small majority, the only Communist candidate to do so. During the 1926 General Strike, he was arrested on the charge of sedition and jailed for two months. He kept his seat until 1929. We could go further back to the nineteenth century and the Welshman Robert Owen's social experiments at New Lanark or back to the late eighteenth century and find considerable parallels between the two countries: both deep into the imperialist reality of slavery and plunder, both at the centre of radical ideas swirling around the Atlantic, both curious and driven sometimes by humanity, sometimes by greed, but more or less on the same political and cultural cycle.[2] This brings us to perhaps the most important point in this essay: Scottish independence could be extremely important if it is success- ful now. If independence loses on 18 September, the quest- ion may very well return in another referendum in twenty years or so, but the moment will be lost. The left should be supporting Scottish independence not only in England, but across Europe, because Scotland now has the will and the vision to create not revolutionary but radical change. There is always a turning point, and Scotland could be it. In spite of the political tribalism, there is a consensus across all the Scottish parties, or at least their memberships, that hard-won social rights need to be defended or restored. It is unlikely that this determination will survive for twenty years within the British state. The SNP decided on a lengthy run-up to this referendum and they did this, I think, so that the flood of scare stories released by the British state and its obedient media would gradually become less effective and finally appear a little ridiculous. Scotland, alone amongst the nations, is incapable of survival, according to our weekly dose of negativity from a propaganda campaign that named itself "Project Fear", and a more appropriate label could not have been invented by supporters of independence. Scotland now has a real chance of inventing something new, which for want of a better name we could call a polity rather than a nation, at least in the traditional nineteenth-century meaning of the term.

Traditional nationalism required all its citizens to believe that they are the same, even in the face of clear evidence

2 Peter Linebaugh and Marcus Rediker, *The Many-Headed Hydra. Sailors, Slaves and Commoners and the Hidden History of the Revolutionary Atlantic* (London: Verso, 2002).

to the contrary. When I worked in Florence, I had for a time a colleague who came from the town of Ururi in the south where they speak Albanian. Occasionally her husband would ring her and they would converse in their own language. "Che roba!" another colleague would say and raise his eyes to the ceiling to express the outrageousness of this situation. Albanian in Italy! Before modern nationalism, this would not have been important: who cared what the peasants or a few townspeople spoke? With the spread of elements of democracy, it started to matter what people thought, and if they were exchanging ideas in Albanian or Welsh, how would the rulers know what was going on? Many of these linguistic islands are disappearing, but border areas are still interesting places for sociolinguists to visit. Slavia, a Slovenian-speaking area that has been part of Western Europe since the time of Charlemagne, is, unlike other ones in Italy, a place where language and national identity are not connected. A language campaigner in that area told me that in the mountains when he was talking in Slovenian to the peasants, they would tell him without a trace of irony that they were Italians and not Slovenians. Of course they were Italians in the sense that they carried Italian passports and could presumably also speak Italian, but they also *felt* Italian. Not so when I visited a town in Slovenia close to the border with Austria. Here the local population spoke German or whatever Austrian dialect they speak in that area. It was one of the strangest places I have ever visited. The entire population appeared to get up in the morning with the express purpose of being as Austrian as it is possible to be Austrian, which means they weren't very Austrian at all. They all wore those Austrian hats with a feather to the very last man. They were all engaged in the serious business of downing huge quantities of beer, as though this was their occupation along with being very Austrian. I have never seen so much bottom-pinching, which the waitresses suffered with contempt but also resignation. I have been to Austria proper and it is very different. A little austere perhaps, but the people dress differently from each other, as they are not employed in the business of being as Austrian as possible. There I felt as though I was in the real world, while in the Slovenian Austrian town I felt that I was at some tedious theatrical event, which gave the impression of going on forever.

Across the border there are areas that until very recent times were Slovenian-speaking. Unfortunately the modern national state has done there what such states often do: it has eliminated the "alien" language, linguistically dividing parents from their children. It is a dismal story that has been repeated all around Europe and no doubt the world, and it is less amusing than the excessive, self-conscious Austrianism in Slovenia. The likeable thing about liberal regimes is that they allow people to be daft. Better that than everyone the same. Better to allow a little tattiness. Bad taste should have its place.

If there's a country that wishes to shed its stereotype, it is Scotland. There is the invention of tradition and there is the invention of invented traditions. It's true that tartan was standardised and identified with clans on the basis of no historical evidence at all. That was an invention. But it wasn't invented out of nothing. Behind the tat, there is something well worth saving, principally Scotland's languages and its musical tradition. But the revival of Scottish culture does not have to be inward-looking. In fact it cannot be revived without opening itself to immigration and new ideas. Like all cultures, Scottish culture has developed through foreign influences, and to develop further – because revival is not repetition but renewal through change – Scotland should be open to a process that will take it in a direction about which none of us can be certain. But change will come, so better that it is controlled by the whole of its community, including those who have just joined it. If you breathe the air, you belong. And if you don't breathe that air any more, then you don't belong at least until you return. That is the essence of a polity: it is community not based on ethnicity or even language and culture; it is a community based on residency.

I lived in Italy for several years in the seventies and eighties. I was well-acquainted with its politics at the time, while my knowledge of British politics became a little vague. Why should I have had a vote in general elections in a country I was no longer fully acquainted with, and yet not be able to vote in the election of the government that regulated my life and to which I paid my taxes? Surely in this world of increasing geographical mobility we need to move past the idea that nationality is based on who our parents were or where we were born and not who we are now. This concept of civic nationalism, as it is sometimes called, is not mine and has been around in Scotland for some time. It is its most important contribution to the debate on nationalism.

Scotland, however, is not a monolith. It has its shares of xenophobia and intolerance, no doubt. It may be that at the moment it is on the wane, and that is why this moment is crucial. Nations change dramatically from one generation to another. The forces arrayed in England are similar, including the south of England, but the percentages are different. If Scotland is successful with its new economic plan based on openness and immigration, the pride it takes in that may protect the ethos on which success was built. Equally and perhaps particularly if success is spectacular, Scotland may change so dramatically that it becomes smug and sealed off from the world. Switzerland, the first country to implement democracy rather than just speculate on its possibility (Britain arriving late with universal manhood suffrage – 1918 – and even later with universal suffrage – 1928), was once a country of poverty and emigration, but is now considered the antonomasia for accumulated wealth – aloof, trapped in its self-perception and distrustful of the foreigner. Success brings its own problems.

The Better Together campaign hit on the idea of Project Fear because they think they can win without conceding anything and feel that only those who propose change have to predict the future, but the future cannot be predicted accurately by anyone. In any event there are a wide range of scenarios, not just yes and no. If either "yes" or "no" wins by a few thousand or even ten of thousands of votes, there will be a need for compromise. If the "no" wins by a large margin, Scotland will suffer terribly. Devolved government may be in danger, and what little industry is left in Scotland may go. Britain is in a greater economic crisis than it knows, and the current government is exacerbating it by using the crisis to push through a full-scale dismemberment of all the social gains of the post-war era. There are many uncertainties if the country votes "yes", but there are at least as many if the country votes "no".

The vote on the 18th of September is not on where our country will go; it is on whether we will have the right to decide on where it will go. It is not sensible to divide the two things entirely. If, for instance, Scotland was going through a period of sectarian violence, which has been a danger in the past, independence might be risky. We have seen the woeful effects of such sectarianism in the tragic break-up of Yugoslavia. No one in their right mind would want to follow that path. But Scotland is very united in its condemnation of sectarianism, which still exists, but is marginal. History shows that such evils can return from the margins, but this would be more likely in the unionist scenario than the independence one, because the Union has always fostered sectarianism for its own political purposes.

Independence appears to point in the direction of a polity – a new kind of state based on citizenship (*politeia* meant "citizenship" or "government").

The nation in the nineteenth-century perception never existed and was always an "ideal", although not one that many of us would consider ideal today. The ideal nation was one homogeneous people united by language, culture and often religion. They were considered to be an ethnic identity and, ignoring all historical evidence, an unchanging entity which occasionally finds itself under foreign domination, but always returns to its pristine state – as though the nation were not only a discrete entity but also a natural one, rather than a political community shored up by a legal and cultural tradition. This perception continued into the twentieth century, and started to become more of a reality. Dialects died out, "inaccuracies" in national borders were at least partially removed, often forcibly through education or internal migration,[3] obligatory national education systems standardised language, mass warfare mobilised and mixed populations, and television came in like a cultural tsunami. As often happens, defeat was engendered by victory or near victory. The delayed backlash of minority cultures against dominant national ones came in the sixties, when television brought the prospect of annihilation. The deindustrialisation and fragmentation of the workplace, a human tragedy in many ways, did bring another myth to an end – that of the mass society, the cousin of nationalism. I would always claim that "mass society" was actually more variegated than our consumer society, and people had more autonomy within the undoubted regimentation of industrial society. And most importantly, the global free market eventually set off a chain of mass migration on a

3 The Fascist regime in Italy relocated Slovene railway workers to southern Italy, and southern Italians to Slovene areas in the north.

global scale, similar in magnitude to the migration coming out of Europe in the nineteenth century. This created the potential for a much more variegated and exciting society, in which cultures mix and create new cultures. This is the kind of society that could be created by the Scottish Polity based on civic nationalism.

However, we could go yet one step further. The idea of the polity is looking outdated even before it has been established: the creation of a truly open society with a strong commitment to social rights and the use of the state to guarantee education and health could become one of those insular utopias that end up a generation or two later as sealed into their pasts and unable to keep up with the pace of change they helped to start. The ideas and values that created success are undermined by that success. Perhaps what we need is a cosmopolity. Immanuel Kant wrote of a cosmopolitan right, which is the right of every human being to travel everywhere on the surface of this planet, the only imposition on travellers being that they have to respect the laws and customs of the societies they visit. In Kant's time they almost had that right; it was not a revolutionary demand. It will now take a long time to get back to Kant's time, let alone to the full implementation of the cosmopolitan right everywhere. But we could make a start. This is not just about a more liberal approach to immigration, which most nationalist forces in Scotland are committed to; it is also about getting out into the world – about Scotland exercising its cosmopolitan rights and responsibilities. Jim Sillars in his book, *In Place of Fear II*, argues that Scotland should build and operate hospital ships to deal with the healthcare crisis in the Third World. It appears that the Westminster government has ordered two aircraft carriers without having any aircraft to put on them and only enough seamen to man one of them, so it could at least sail out of port.

Sillars believes that the time has come for Scotland to rid itself of its military tradition, of which it has been so proud in the past, and replace it with another one:

> Juxtaposed to that military tendency, there is a broad streak of idealism in the Scottish people, which makes them ready to respond to those in need or danger across the world. This policy gives expression to that tradition; it tells the world that we are committed to helping and healing, and that we can take a weapon originally intended for war, and turn it into an instrument that is wholly peaceful. The policy is idealism in practice. If not swords into ploughshares, then a war ship into a peace ship.[4]

This is an example of how the cosmopoly works: it acts towards other states in an I-thou fashion, to use Buber's terminology (or should it be an I-I relationship?). It does not think that its duty is to stymie contrary developments in another state, because those trends come out of another reality and another tradition, which may make sense to its citizens. It does not see itself as a separate and sovereign unit entirely in control of its own destiny and in competition with all other states, but as a part of a whole. It is built on citizenship which in turn is based on residency, so it does not believe in citizens and aliens, as it does not perceive a great distinction between the citizen and the non-citizen, who can become a citizen by becoming resident, just as a citizen can become a non-citizen by becoming a non-resident. A cosmopoly does not believe in the homogenisation of culture or political systems. Because certain policies and structures work better in different countries and different periods, variety is the better

---

4 J. Sillars, *In Place of Fear II* (Glasgow: Vagabond Voices, 2014), p. 53.

way of developing a global economy. Each country should be able to follow its own economic strategies without the IMF and the World Bank interfering, as long as certain basic liberties exist. Only these should be protected by the UN. For instance, the right to property should not be considered a fundamental liberty, like freedom of speech or the ban on torture, even in the selective way it is protected now (currently only the property of the rich is protected). Each state should develop its own system for dealing with property, as long as it is equitable. If property exists, then it can only be confiscated, taxed or requisitioned in accordance with laws that apply to all citizens. The outward-looking cosmopolity should coexist with other traditional nations, and if it prospers, more countries may follow. The struggle to the death between economic systems that started after 1917 distorted the development of both and must be brought to an end; economies should pick and choose, and learn from each other. This may seem utopian and unlikely, but the nineteenth-century nation-state would have appeared equally so to a merchant of Cologne or Milan in the previous century. In urban areas of such fragmented nations, there was already feeble pressure for change, which would grow. Today there is already an increasingly global consciousness, which may be the one positive thing brought to us by extreme free-market capitalism in the late twentieth century, and it is this shift in ideas that will eventually bring change about. Independent Scotland is hopefully going to be born into this new cosmopolitan mix and it seems to be in the mood for radical experimentation. States could develop in a new direction if they respond to the current mood amongst most populations of the world to a greater or lesser degree. That is a big if, and it too concerns only a moment in time. If states do not start to relate to each other in a new fashion, then in times of financial crisis and an increasing global population we will inevitably slip towards xenophobia and war. The small nation is some way more manageable, and with a population of over five million, Scotland is around the average size for nations on this planet: unheard of by many, it could find its place in the world by becoming the first cosmopolitan state. It cannot change our globe, but it could set a precedent and become part of a movement of small and smallish countries.

Some people – often those who support our insane wars, despise the European Union and talk of British tolerance and honesty – say that it is not good to increase the number of borders. Their internationalism goes no further than their own country's right to decide the fate of other countries. It is not about borders; it is about the types of border, the worst of which are often within a sovereign state. Can you think of a more absurd border than the one that divides communities in Northern Ireland and calls itself the Peace Line, adopting the Orwellian tone of bureaucratic euphemism? Of course you can; there is the border between the two halves of Cyprus. Surely you can't think of an even more absurd border than that stretch of wired-in no-man's-land. But you can; there are the multiple borders within the land now under Israel's sovereign control between Israel and the open-air prison called Gaza, Israel and the West Bank, and around all the little bantustans set up by that apartheid regime. Now think of the border between France and Germany or the endless one between the USA and Canada: there's nothing there. To achieve this you need balanced economies and a perception that hostilities between the two countries could never happen again. That is what we need for the whole world, although it is sadly a long way off and may never be achieved. The balanced economies have to come first and at the moment they're becoming increasingly imbalanced. In fact the redistribution of wealth between rich and poor countries is the most pressing political issue, because from it flow all the other ecological problems and conflicts over resources. Redistribution of this kind can only be achieved by creating a genuinely cosmopolitan culture on a global scale. This could be more likely in small nations. For a long time, intellectuals have argued that only large countries are viable, but the self-sufficiency of these nations is what can make them so insular. Small nations have to go beyond themselves and their citizens are much more likely to travel abroad. In Schengen, people are constantly crossing borders; they can do this for a meal or a trip to the theatre.

Independent Scotland should be open to the rest of the world and it should not laugh at foreign cultures but learn from them. It should be different and inventive in seeking solutions for its considerable problems created by decades of neglect, but it should be aware that invention requires the stimulus of other peoples' successes and failures as well as its own. It should defend its culture by absorbing a little of other ones. It should be relaxed about having to change in order to continue to exist, but govern change in the interests of people not profit. It should contribute to the day when borders are no more than an open field, a dilapidated customs house and a rotting kiosk for passport control.

On Class, Work and Politics

I left school at sixteen and throughout the seventies and early eighties I did all manner of working-class jobs, mostly unskilled but skilled when working at sea. I did these jobs in two countries, Britain and Italy, producing what is now a very unfashionable CV. Nevertheless they provided me with experience and information I would not have been able to assimilate in any other way. I was able to see that beneath the different prejudices and cultures, working-class life and middle-class life were equally varied and complex. Many things that divide people are transversal to class.

At that time, the working class was feeling stronger and more self-confident with every passing year in both Britain and Italy, but more so in Italy. It was enjoying greater afflu-ence, although this was, as always, greatly exaggerated. The middle class was feeling that its primacy had been eroded, although this was fantastically exaggerated.

Both countries had good state education – Italian educat-ion was even better at school level and British education was better at university level – and this was leading to greater social mobility, which has now all but disappeared in both countries. Unemployment was low and large sections of the middle class sympathised with working-class aims. It was just a particular moment in history, but at the time it felt like an unstoppable trend. Some of the left had unrealistic hopes, but what we now call centre-left parties were gain-ing a firmer grip on power. After a surprise Tory victory in 1970, the Labour Party returned to power in 1974. Until the Falklands War in 1982, Thatcher's 1979 government appeared to be on course for electoral annihilation. In Italy, the Communist Party was kept out of power by a fragile coalition of five parties with just over 50% of the seats, while it continued to extend its grip over local government, particularly in Central Italy and Emilia-Romagna. By the early eighties, even leading industrialists were arguing that the Communist Party would eventually have to share power in government. The left faltered every now and then, but the direction of travel seemed clear.

It was a long time ago.

Since then, it has been fashionable in Britain to assert that class is a thing of the past, but quite the opposite, the victorious middle class in both countrieshas become increasingly assertive and the working class is increasingly humiliated. Being humiliated makes people very aware of their status, even if they don't have a voice.

Class is perceived differently in different countries, and also in different classes. In most European countries – and Scotland is one of them – there are two classes: the working class and the middle class, and this has been the prevailing view since the Second World War at least. In England, the country that was the first to shake off serfdom in the fourteenth century and had the first modern revolution in the seventeenth, attitudes were much more complex and old-fashioned until more recent times: the middle class was flanked by the upper middle class and the lower middle class, and there were and still are references to an ill-defined upper class. Marx spoke of the aristocracy of the working class in relation to the English situation, but his other term, the petit bourgeoisie, still has currency in France and Italy where until recently there was a large number of small businesses, shops and artisanal concerns, and there still is to some extent. Like lower middle class, this is principally a term of abuse.

The petit bourgeoisie or lower middle class, which are more or less the same thing, is an intermediate class which has been unfairly treated since Marx, although it can be radical. It is a fragmented class that looks in two directions, so it can also be reactionary. I like the varied, and in Italy I worked for many small businesses and found them to be extremely varied, covering almost every political colour. It is a class in which all sorts of oddballs and pleasant eccentrics mix with folk who would claim to be bourgeois, although the bourgeoisie would not accept them as one of their own. Thatcher was one of these, but she was by no means typical of the whole class. I was told of a shopkeeper on the Isle of Lewis in the post-war period who was a great reader. If a prospective customer came into his shop while he was in his sitting room at the back engrossed in a good book, he would deny the apparently innate human desire to turn a coin and ignore the customer no matter how many times that customer opened and shut the door to set the bell ringing. Capitalism has now squeezed out this class, and I think that on the whole we are the poorer for it. The typical petit bourgeois had more money than the average worker, but his expenses were not that much higher. That small amount of money created more freedom perhaps than that enjoyed by wealthier people with standards to keep up. They could spend it on aping the more affluent and identifying with the next class up or they could enjoy the margin of freedom offered. The Lewis shopkeeper had a horse and every Friday rode into town to get drunk. At the end of the evening, the publican would balance him on top of the beast, which knew its own way home. He could afford not only to turn customers away, but also supply himself with books and booze in sufficient quantities.

The dismissive term "underclass" was invented in America for low-paid workers, casual workers, part-time workers and the unemployed. This term was quickly embraced by New Labour. The name says everything about how the working class is treated, following the assault on their organisations.

Changing a name is a means of spiriting away an inconvenient reality. Organised labour had become an embarrassment to an organisation called Labour. Since then other strange terms have been coined – the precariat, emergent service workers, traditional working class and new affluent workers – and these further fragment the working class. But the working class remains, because those who have only their labour to sell are constantly moving between employment, semi-employment and unemployment. They don't feel that they belong to different classes, and they have good reason.

Lumpen proletariat, another Marxist term, is also derogatory. It equates roughly speaking to the unemployed in the underclass, but where there is no welfare state, as in Victorian Britain or seventies Italy, the unemployed had to fend for themselves and this often meant criminal or unlawful activities. I lived on Via Ghibellina in the Santa Croce district of Florence in the seventies. It had been abandoned by the working class following the 1966 floods and replaced by the lumpen proletariat or *sottoproletariato*, if for a moment we accept this distinction. What did they mean by this expression? Mainly Southerners who came north to work on building sites and in other unskilled labouring jobs, Southerners who ran businesses on the back of the low rents in the area, such as dealers in old furniture, which then was just called old furniture and not flattered by the word "antiques". There were plenty of students, a number of petty thieves and a scattering of prostitutes, transvestites and others who found a trade in the city centre. Finally a few drifters like myself. Conveniently for the authorities, the prison was in the same street. One night the guards shot a prisoner, and the next morning there was a crowd below my window. I remember a portly, middle-aged man who was reputed on I know not what authority to be a lawbreaker: he may have known the inside of the institution which was for short-term prisoners only. He was the self-appointed rabble-rouser and he had every right, because he was agitated and clearly cared. He said that they were still shooting people in the prison, although this turned out to be incorrect. It was the only riot I have been part of, although it would difficult to say whether it was the citizens who were rioting or the police. They certainly made the first move with a barrage of teargas canisters. The crowd responded as though they knew the moves. I remember an athletic young man with a goatee beard picking up a canister and hurling it back – an image we have all seen in a hundred newspapers. Old ladies passed oranges down to us, as these gave some relief from the teargas. A friend said that we needed barricades and smashed a car window with a brick so that it could be manoeuvred into the road. The owner left a nearby bar and remonstrated with us. He called us *ragazzi* in a friendly way: "Come on lads, can't you see that the door's open." He opened and shut the doors to demonstrate that he hadn't locked the car. There had been no need to smash the window and lean in through it to release the brake and turn the steering wheel, while others pushed. The owner got into his car with a bemused smile and drove off. It was no longer requisitioned. If this was the lumpen proletariat, it was very polite and quite organised. The next day, the Communist Party newspaper, *L'Unità*, which was always nervous about any disorder and being accused of fomenting it, declared that the clashes with police had been caused by outside elements that were quickly distinguished from the democratic population of the district. There was little truth in this, and for days afterwards locals complained about the beatings the police had administered in an entirely random manner.[1]

---

1 Today the Santa Croce district is very different and has been partly gentrified. The prison has been removed, and the building turned into an arts centre. The Italian Communist Party is no more, and its paper, which was not at all bad in

Class is elusive, because it purports to make clear distinctions between individuals when those distinctions are never clear. There are really only two important sociological distinctions, the one between the middle class and the working class, which includes the lumpen proletariat, and the one between the middle class and the owners of large concentrations of capital which includes what we might call a new managerial aristocracy – the boards of large corporations and large investment funds. And there are only two important political distinctions, the one between those who want to redistribute wealth and those who want the distance between wealth and poverty to continue to grow, and the one between those who believe in freedoms, social rights and transparency, and those who believe in authority, property rights and secrecy.

Norman Tebbit is upset that the values of the working-class world of the fifties have disappeared. These values should surely include community and solidarity, but they get no mention from him. He is concerned about values based on shame, and for a Tory he has an unusual explanation for their disappearance: the working class has adopted the nastier values of the middle and upper classes. It is certainly true that the "Anglo-Saxon" version of middle-class values, based almost exclusively on economic self-interest, is more dominant now than at any time in the past – even the mid-Victorian period when it started to dominate the middle class. Tebbit is unaware that the government he was a member of introduced the policies that led to this ethos, although I don't agree that the working class has entirely given itself over to middle-class values of any kind. This is

spite of my comments, is now in private ownership. I wrote about this incident in a short story "In That Moment", part of the collection, *On the Heroism of Mortals* (Glasgow: Vagabond Voices, 2012), pp. 113-16.

sad for Tebbit, and it is probably better that he doesn't realise the part he played in bringing about this change, because it's equally true that Tebbit was not primarily motivated by his own economic self-interest, and this demonstrates once more that ideologues do not live in a manner consistent with their ideologies. He wanted to improve mankind, and he thought that this could be achieved by making each individual economically independent and working the market. This was freedom as the right perceived it, and he was willing to work hard to bring in these policies that people like me consider to have been disastrous and which will take decades to put right, even if we were to start reversing them tomorrow.

Thatcher was horrified when her national airline, British Airways, went international and exchanged its British livery for a global one. This was the airline she had privatised, and its decision was the inevitable consequence of her policy, and yet it appears that this obvious truth never passed through her brain as she scrambled impatiently to find a handkerchief to cover the offending tail fins of a model aeroplane British Airways had displayed at a trade fair. We could add in passing that Thatcher was as bad as her ideology – in fact, even worse.

Both of these politicians had mediocre intellects, and self-awareness was not their strength, but the real reason for their inability to understand what was happening around them was an obsolete nationalism of the worst kind. They identified very strongly with a nation – England – but not the real England of all its citizens. Theirs was based on an ideal nation that never existed. Its ideal people was the middle class, to which everyone could and should aspire. Neither of them were middle class in origin, and both had successfully joined its ranks. Although their backgrounds were not without relative privilege, they could not see that for many it would be much more difficult than it was for them, even in the times of much higher social mobility that followed the

Second World War and lasted until the election of their government. Their nation did not include "the enemy within" who were potentially the entire organised working class and their fellow travellers of whatever class.

It has to be admitted that the left, at the time, focused on a similarly abstract nation, consisting of an abstract or imagined working class. Nation is a powerful tag, and it is constantly used within class conflict, purposefully stirring the mud to obfuscate political questions of equity and social justice. Nationalist issues are divided by the fundamental difference between great nations and minority nations, but leaving that important point aside, you will often find that just beneath nationalist discourse in political debate lies a fundamental difference of class interests. It may conceal either left-wing or right-wing arguments. The current independence referendum in Scotland is no exception: it is about the defence of hard-won social rights which are under attack throughout the UK and have been most clearly eroded in England, which continues to vote Tory. Those social rights were introduced by the post-war Labour governments and generally speaking left in place by Tory governments before Thatcher's. After Thatcher both Conservative and Labour governments have set about dismantling those social rights, which now are most effectively defended by the Scottish National Party. Some might say that the SNP is too cautious; I might agree with them, but their programme of gradual reversal may prove to have been well thought out and pragmatic in the "current political climate".

Class interests always have a sounder basis than national interests, but national interests have more demagogic force, because class interests are wrapped up in a web of lies, class propaganda and sectorial interests. A national identity is, for some reason, easier to imagine than a class one, even though there are in fact always two imagined nations – one imagined by the working class, the other by the middle class. Left and right are not about class membership, but about whether or not to distribute wealth and social rights more equitably. Nothing else. Members of the working class can identify with a middle-class ethos, as Tebbit argues and strangely finds regrettable. Members of the middle class can identify with the working class, either because they or their parents started out from that class or, more simply, out of a shared sense of social justice, which has always made the left such a potent force and is why so many obfuscations have to be introduced to keep it from successfully achieving aims that are very widely supported.

Classes are represented by political movements, and political movements develop interests that can diverge from the class they are supposed to represent. They act within a national and international context in which all manner of cultural forces are in play. The significance of those cultural forces has been underestimated.

We have to consider the time and place of each class. The values of the European nineteenth-century middle classes were best preserved by the Soviet bureaucracy and Soviet society at large. Similarly the English revolution preserved the values of the rural middle class or gentry long after these had disappeared elsewhere, except in America where they have, if anything, been better preserved than in England. Was the Cold War a conflict between two entirely different views of what the middle class should be? No, but there was a little bit of that – most noticeable in the different attitudes to education: a social approach with a profound reverence for classical European culture in the Soviet Union and a pragmatic and vocational approach with subtle methods for stymieing social mobility in America. The Russian Revolution was also a revolution in social behaviour, but this was partly reversed under Stalin, more or less at the time when social change began to gather pace in America. Modernity travelled by different paths towards a single end. The superpowers were mirror images in many ways, but the differences were also very clear and above all they concerned class – each peddling absurdly distorted self-images.

I have been emphatic about class, but my classism is not based on hatred of anyone. When I read Marx's and Engel's *Communist Manifesto* in my teens I was impressed by the ideas, but uncertain about the tone, although it did have undoubted literary value. When I understood better that there was in fact no communist party, only two energetic young men stirring up a lot of trouble, my uncertainties increased. The line, "A spectre is haunting Europe – the spectre of communism",[2] appears to have been designed to terrify the middle classes. But why wave a red rag at a bull? The middle class by its very nature is a paranoid and somewhat jittery class. There are good reasons for this: they enjoy great privilege, but unlike aristocratic privilege, it is fragile, and was particularly fragile in the nineteenth century. Many a member of the comfortable rentier class lost a fortune overnight, because of a bad investment. More recently, Lloyds names have found their fortunes could disappear overnight and leave them in debt. The middle class are a people who have a lot to gain and a lot to lose, and they want greater security than the economic system they espouse can guarantee them. This has been bad for colonial peoples and it has been bad for the working class. Threatening them when you have no power and no organisation could be construed as an act of irresponsibility.

During the seventies I was once in a pub with three or four

2 Karl Marx and Frederick Engels, *The Communist Manifesto* (London: Verso, 1998), p. 33.

comrades (a term I disliked because it was never comradely in tone), and one said, "Trotsky says that the high bourgeoisie should be shipped off to an island and left to their own devices," (I don't know if this was an accurate summary) "but I think that's being too soft on them." Others agreed, and someone suggested that putting them against a wall and shooting them might be a safer approach. I have a bad habit of being in a minority of one when I join an organisation, but in this case I don't think I was. I suggested to these enlightened individuals that if the rich had been expropriated, they would have been punished enough and should be left in peace. The comrades ignored me – no doubt they had placed me in the category for "unsound petty-bourgeois elements". My sitting at their table was concession enough. Did they become leading lights in New Labour or economics reporters for the *Financial Times*? Very possibly.

I perceive the rich as victims of their own system. There is no end to the desire for profit. There are exceptions, such as Warren Buffet who spends his time giving his huge wealth away, and exhorting governments to increase taxes on the rich. He is very probably one of the happiest rich men. There are reasons why most rich people are so compulsive. Firstly, they pride themselves on their ability to make money. Obviously the more money you make, the better you must be at doing it. They want to make a point, and now there are lists of the richest people in the world, so they have to compete for billions. Secondly, a rich man's greatest fear is losing his wealth. This is greater than his fear of death, which probably does trouble the rich more than the poor, who are busy with survival. The best way to protect your billions or millions is to keep making more of them. Thirdly, rich people have to sacrifice part of their humanity to become rich, and that is a high price to pay. Epictetus provides us with an elegant thought on this point. If you see a blind man trying to cross the road, you naturally come to his assistance. But if you see someone whose behaviour reveals moral blindness, you criticise him and give him no assistance. But moral blindness is infinitely worse than visual blindness, and should also be pitied and given assistance. The very rich are mostly morally blind. They have more money than they could spend if they lived as long as Methuselah and hired the whole of the Ritz Hotel every night of their life. They hoard things that are useful when they're singular but useless when they're plural, such as houses and cars and horses. They buy things that are not that useful even when they're singular, such as castles and yachts. They attempt to buy intangible things that cannot be bought, such as friendship and love. They buy intangible things that can be bought, such as political influence and the degree of celebrity status they are most comfortable with. At least those who hoard artworks do some good, because they can bequeath them to the nation or city council when they die. And many of the rich cannot enjoy any of these wonders, because their assets are simply too many and because they are too busy making more money to increase their capital or to buy things they cannot enjoy. Do you condemn an alcoholic? Do you want to put an unhappy drug addict up against a wall and shoot him? Why would you want to harm these people? They are not in control of their own lives, any more than the sad gambler down at the casino.

The radical Catholic priest, Don Milani, perhaps meant this when he distinguished himself from the communists – that no one should be in the business of punishing anybody else. He said that communism was "a doctrine without love", unaware perhaps that Che Guevara said, "At the risk of seeming ridiculous, let me say that a true revolutionary is guided by a great feeling of love. It is impossible to think of a genuine revolutionary lacking this quality."[3] That he felt he had to qualify his statement with that "risk of seeming ridiculous" demonstrates the times, the machismo of the left and his courage at challenging it. Milani also said that he was more classist than the communists, and he might have been right about that. He was also being unfair to the Communist Party, which had not been a revolutionary party for some time when Milani was writing, and it was a communist paper that would publish him when it came to the quote below, which is taken from an open letter, "Obedience Is Not a Virtue", sent to all Italian newspapers in February 1965. He was addressing the military chaplains who had signed a press release denouncing conscientious objectors.

I'm not going to discuss the idea of fatherland here. I don't like such divisions.

If you're entitled to divide the world into Italians and foreigners, then I tell you that, in the meaning you attribute to it, I have no country and claim my right to divide the world into the dispossessed and the oppressed on the one hand and the privileged and the oppressors on the other. The former are my country and the latter my foreigners. And if you have the right, without being censured by the Curia, to teach that Italians and foreigners can lawfully and indeed heroically tear each other apart, then I claim the right to say that the poor have a right to fight against the rich. At least in the choice of methods I am better than you: the arms you approve of are horrible machines for killing, mutilating, destroying and making orphans and widows. The only arms I approve of are noble and non-violent ones: strikes and votes.[4]

3 *The Che Reader* (Melbourne: Ocean Press, 2005).
4 Lorenzo Milani, *Pensieri e parole* (Turin: Paoline, 2007), p.22.

Don Milani was forthright in his defence of the strike as a means for working people to improve their lot. I could not agree with him more. He is worth quoting in this context for two reasons. He has an intriguing and eccentric approach to things, mostly in his language. He says elsewhere, "The word 'strike' is sacred to the poor, the only weapon they have against their overlords."[5] We would not call it a "sacred right" but a social or positive one, or a fundamental freedom. And he brings up the important question of non-violence, which is a key element in what I'm trying to argue, but I am not putting as much emphasis on it as it deserves, because it has been well argued by others for a long time. We could add here that this is not a time for violent revolution, but for non-violent action particularly against the increasing use of armed force and state intrusion in international and domestic politics. In the eighties, my belief in revolutionary politics started to fade, but my belief in the long-term aims of socialism has remained undiminished. Our history since the eighties has deepened that conviction: one of the most important factors was the collapse of the Soviet Union. The irresponsible actions of America and the West in using Yeltsin to push through a revolution in reverse, showed that the East-West conflict was never about human rights. The most striking thing about that event was that the huge sacrifices made by the Russians to achieve that state all came to nothing without thier being consulted. The last thing they needed was another upheaval on the same scale as the forced collectivisation, but that is what they got. The Soviet state had to be undermined so that redistribution of wealth could be reversed. It was all a matter of class.

The Berlusconi Bonus, my satirical novel which was published

---

5 *Pensieri e parole* ..., p. 48.

by Luath in 2005, contained the following line: "Perhaps a society that ensured that everyone was above a certain threshold of poverty and below a certain threshold of wealth would not be such a bad idea after all," which was the most radical thing in the whole book. In spite of the complete absence of evidence, this line was enough for me to be accused of being a communist and even an apologist for Uncle Joe. I was "against shopping" (I heard a lot of that), and perversely denying that the right had won all the economic arguments. Strangely enough they were not wholly wrong. I am not an apologist for Stalin and I am not against shopping. I am a communist and I do question whether consumerism leads to a good life and a good society. I'm a communist in that I believe that certain things should be owned communally, particularly land, which should be treated no differently from the air and the waterways. This was a belief in many European societies until relatively recent historical times, for instance in Ireland and the Highlands of Scotland. Corporations should be state-owned, but there could be competition between them, and they should be under the control of those who work in them. Monopolies – railways, ports, airports, electricity, water, health services, education, prisons (which should only be for serious crimes), pharmaceuticals and restricted substances (drugs that are legalised but controlled) – should be nationalised and run jointly by the workforce and those who use them or are affected by them. Small capital should be allowed, because it can be innovative and some people enjoy its risks. A good society is an equal society, but absolute equality cannot be imposed, and to go that last distance would involve an unacceptable bureaucratisation of society. In any case, there are too many factors that simply cannot be measured. How, for instance, would you deal with the inequality between those who live in a beautiful city and those who live in an ugly city? What is an ugly city? And so on. Does this make me a communist? I don't know. It's a label, and I'm not scared of it.

Enough. I cannot write a constitution for a distant future, and I'm not very qualified to do so. The central point of this essay is that class is at the heart everything and concerns our relationship with property. Every class can be subdivided into a myriad different professions and trades, often very different from each other. Each trade is quite distinct, unlike the classes, which don't have clearly defined borders. Butcher, baker, candlestick-maker. Is that a candlestick you're making? Yes. Then clearly that's what you are.

The London tube, that wonderful institution for mixing and squeezing together people who are in a rush to be elsewhere, provided me with an instructive encounter. I sat opposite a very elderly Indian man whose wiry body was only now beginning to lose its strength. His face was intelligent and his expression intense. His clothes were old, threadbare and fading. He had an old briefcase of the kind used by electricians, and brown, packing-case tape held it together. He was writing copious notes on a piece of paper that had some kind of diagram at the top of the page. My curiosity, by now, was fighting with my timid desire not to reveal it. I took the opportunity of a particularly intense spurt of note-scribbling to lean over and read the letter-head. I only caught the word "Associates", but it was enough. This was work. This was work either for or on behalf of **** Associates. I had no idea what kind of company it was. He stopped writing and opened his case, from which he withdrew a video-box he had recycled as a crayon box. He then opened the box and a quantity of crayons spilt out over the chair beside him. He then spent a couple of minutes methodically returning them to their container with the exception of a few select ones. These he used to colour parts of his diagram slowly and painstakingly, perhaps almost lovingly – as someone would if they care about every aspect of their work. When he came to his station, he gathered his things together and then surveyed the seats carefully to check for forgotten items in the manner of a man only too aware of his ability to forget things. And then he was gone. He left me with a happily unsatisfied curiosity. Why was a man clearly the master of some unknown technical know-how and an obvious passion for his work so badly dressed? I like to think that it was because he cared little for material possessions and was driven solely by his love of knowledge. He spent his money on his grandchildren whom he indulged beyond belief because it cost him nothing in his unworldliness. On the other hand, he may have been half mad and designed complex, brilliant but ultimately impractical projects and inventions for **** Associates, who wearily and politely filed them away and paid him a meagre sum in order not to offend a man whose eccentric brilliance evoked fondness, respect and a degree of friendly laughter once he had left the office. Equally, he might have been entirely mad. **** Associates might have been his own imagined company and his technical drawings merely daft and meaningless lines on paper; his only life an inner life of fantasy and invented dialogue (like the equally mad novelist).

Everyone else's profession is a wonderful and absurd mystery. The Indian inventor, although an entirely truthful memory, is an excellent metaphor for the way in which we perceive professions we have never practised and can therefore never fully understand. The predictable behaviour of doctors, teacher, judges, electricians, builders and all the others we cannot avoid are often equally incomprehensible. We all rely on a wide variety of professions in our private lives but also in our own professional ones. A writer requires a publisher, and a publisher requires printers, editors, typesetters, cover designers, marketing experts, salespeople, bookshops and so on. A publisher does not have to know how to do these things, but must have some idea of their possibilities and limitations. The writer only needs to know how to write. "Only" in its singularity and not to underestimate the difficulties and varieties encompassed by that one activity. Most people take other professions for granted. They consider them to be simple and, of course, inferior to their own. If a builder fails to do a proper job, his customers are incensed, even though they may do much simpler and less responsible tasks in their own profession and work less conscientiously. We are trained in this society to believe in the sanctity of the financial transaction. "The customer is always right" and therefore can scream and shout. Failure to deliver the goods is a serious matter. But the price is decided by the market or a nomenklatura, and not the complexity of work involved. Many practised consumers take for granted and, unlike me, don't seem to be impressed by this enormous array of professions and skills that are sealed off from us, but are so useful and often essential.

There was a highly respected mathematician, who worked in a very specialist field. He was an elderly man and kept himself fit by going each morning to his university on a bicycle, whose saddle had become loose. This made the journey uncomfortable, and my neighbour offered to assist. He produced a spanner and within a few seconds had tightened the nut and entirely resolved the difficult problem. The old man was bowled over by the wonder of it, and shook his head at the cleverness of the man with the spanner. I would not be amazed by a spanner tightening a nut, but then I do not have the intelligence or knowledge to deal with the complex mathematics that stole this man's enviable brain and energies. But I am enough of an obsessive to understand how someone even more obsessive might end up with this mindset. I am amazed by the number of professions and specialitisations within professions, and that each one has a unique culture, a unique vocabulary and a unique way of thinking or perceiving the world.

Work is one of the most powerful identities, and as an identity it is the least destructive. It is not based on any mythology, but the day-to-day business of living. It concerns the very essence that we have created for ourselves, particularly now that we are less likely to follow in our fathers' professional footsteps. It is where we spend most of our waking life and, if we are lucky, it is the object of our passions and even creativity. A person who if they belonged to a profession other than your own would be boring can become the most fascinating individual simply because they are in the same line of work. You can understand what they're talking about, because of your shared expertise. That shared expertise can also be a source of rivalry or genuine disagreement. This can rankle, so we're drawn to our fellow practitioners and we're repulsed. We admire their methods or reject them. We consider them to be under or overvalued. But we do things in a completely different way to the non-practitioners, which is not to say that the non-practitioners' views are less valid: is an actor's acting to be judged better by another actor, who might, it's true, see all those little professional tricks and know which are easy and which are difficult? It is an actor's task to convince the public, not his or her peers. In other professions, it is the peers who matter. Would we want doctors and mechanics to be judged by those who aren't? Most of us have no idea whether a doctor has given us the right pill or a mechanic has fitted the right carburettor on our car. If we have a doubt, we go to someone who does know. But always we perceive professions differently according to whether we practise them or not. These are very clearly defined identities. They are cultures.

Professions and trades unite beyond all borders and boundaries. I knew an inshore fisherman. Wherever he went, he was drawn to the coast and the ports. He would wander and look at how the boats were made and how they were powered. Nets seem to have been a particular point of interest. Sometimes he would meet another fisherman and, although they had no common language, they would communicate, sometimes by actually doing something. He would point out a tear in a net, and the other fisherman would show him how he mended it. My friend would grab the net and start to show him how he mended it. The fisherman might nod with a bemused and unconvinced smile to show his indulgence for less skilled methods, or become alert as though he were about to learn something. And yet this real identity is not that strong. People of different languages, races, nations, religions, classes, ideologies and empires go to war with each other, but you don't get the butchers going to war with the bakers. Professions and trades are important to human relationships, in a way that the larger abstractions of class, religion and nation are not. Professions and trades can lead to corruption, just as family and kinship can lead to nepotism, but they are down at the most essential human level.

When Napoleon's army descended into Italy in 1797, they opened the ghettos and made all subjects citizens, which meant that they could all join the armed forces. In 1799, the Ave Maria rebellions temporarily wrested power back for the *Anciens Régimes* and this led to a series of pogroms. A band of soldiers in Orvieto, in the Papal States set out for Pitigliano in southern Tuscany to loot the Jewish community. They were not used to meeting resistance. Unknown to them, the little town perched on a natural fortress of tufo rock was well used to the Napoleonic reforms. Grand Duke Leopold I of Tuscany was possibly the only real enlightened despot of the Enlightenment period, although it was easier to introduce reforms in a small state, as he would discover when he briefly became Emperor Leopold II of Austria at the end of his life. During his long rule, he steadily introduced a series of significant reforms. On 30 November 1786, Tuscany became the first modern state to abolish the death penalty, although it had been de facto abolished there since 1769. He also opened the ghettos and introduced citizenship, and this drew in refugees from other states. The Jewish community was built up in this period, and there was intermarriage across the religious divide, often within the same trade. The band of bravos from Orvieto encountered resistance from a united population, and one of the soldiers was cut down as he entered the first house. The rest took their horses and rode back to Orvieto. The skirmish was given grandiose titles: "La notte degli Orvietani" or even "La notte della rivoluzione". The historical account I read suggested that removal of the interdiction on trades and the ensuing intermarriage explains the event. In other words the personal identities of family and trade are intermingled and are what you might call positive identities that can override the more abstract and dangerous ones.

Professions and trades go on strike, but that is class activity. Sometimes it is a very specific group on strike, like signalmen or train drivers, but more generally it's a sector, like railway workers. It is strife between employee and employer. It is not about the essence of being a signalman; it is about the essence of the relationship between the person who sells their labour and the person who buys it.

Perhaps class identification with work is greatest amongst those who are most alienated from their work – those for whom work is primarily a means for earning a salary and their working days are governed by the clock that ticks too slowly. Perhaps only those who enjoy their work identify with it personally and are defined by it, although work always defines everyone to some extent. Primo Levi was surprised that when he became famous in America he was introduced as a Jew and Holocaust-survivor. "He was puzzled that Americans had made such a song and dance of his Jewishness. He was a chemist as well as a writer; Judaism was just one of the many things that interested him."[6] This was not primarily a cultural difference between Italy and America; it was an expression of how much he enjoyed and identified with both of his professions. For a person who enjoys their work, work is not a burden; it is their life. When they're cutting their nails or having a shower, they're still thinking about it. It is their constant companion, and perhaps isn't even work as it is often perceived.

You may think that I'm writing about the creative industries. Not at all. Such people can be found in many walks of life. Business people, mechanics, technicians, scientists, academics, you name it – where there's a skill, then there are those who live off those skills, as though they were as important as the blood in their veins. Equally there are people in those professions who are just coasting along, and have either lost their passion for it or never had it. There may be good reason for having lost it. The world is not as amenable as we would like it, by which I mean not that everything should be easy – that would take the pleasure away – but that hierarchies and bureaucracies kill off autonomy. The work should be difficult, but the working environment should be on your side. So often it isn't, and in the end the individual gives up trying, because their ideas are going to be rejected anyway, or the management demands that work is done so quickly that it cannot be done well, or for a host of other reasons why work becomes a place in which the employee is just an object that is programmed and set going. Surely this is a greater political problem than the ones of productivity and GDP that are constantly reiterated in every news bulletin here, like the Soviet five-year plan

---

6 Ian Thomson, *Primo Levi* (London: Vintage, 2003), p. 475.

that was satirised in the West. The waste of human talent is now mainly caused by the insane drive for productivity.

The only way this problem can be overcome is by involving people in the decisions that affect their work. It is important to give people control over what they do and to trust them to do a good job; then they can start to enjoy their work. Not everyone has an obsessive nature. Some people enjoy their work, but at the end of the day they want to leave it behind and perhaps even forget about it. This probably means that they're well-balanced people. They too will enjoy their work more if they are given more autonomy.

Capitalism has spent the last thirty or so years introducing legislation to protect the consumer; this is also a way of pushing small businesses out of the way because they cannot sustain the extra costs, while the very large companies pass on the percentage to be paid by those of us who don't spend our lives walking in and out of shops demanding our statutory rights. I was at the cash desk in a shoe shop when a man walked in with a pair of shoes he wished to return. He had a loud voice – received pronunciation – and he claimed without any evidence that he had bought the shoes there and they were letting water in. This was not surprising because it looked as though he had walked across several mountain ranges in them, and they weren't walking boots. Of course, the shopkeepers sent him packing and perhaps he wandered off to another shoe shop, but the interesting thing is that he thought he was in with a chance. Where is the legislation to protect the producer? What little there is is being torn up. Now we have zero-hours contracts, a return to some of the worst forms of wage slavery. The producer gets the rod, and the consumer is constantly offered the carrot – all kinds of weird carrots, such as loyalty points and special promotions. Buy a newspaper and they offer you a bottle of water or a bar of chocolate. Leave me alone, you want to say, the newspaper is expensive enough. They seem very motivated to persuade you, and you wonder at the oppressiveness of it all. Where are the human relationships? Shopping isn't the problem; it's that every tuppence-ha'penny transaction becomes a complex speculation. Buying a train ticket is like entering the commodity market; their prices go up and down on the internet like stocks and shares. People don't even talk about the weather and football so much. "Did you enjoy your meal?" "Is everything as you would wish it, Sir?" There was a time when you went to the shop for the crack as well as the pint of milk, which is still possible at the corner shop, but forget it in the retail chains: now we're talking earnestly about chocolate bars and bottles of mineral water. Am I alone in objecting to having my mind invaded by this rubbish? Am I alone in rejecting the Have-a-good-day culture? Am I alone in longing for the garrulous shopkeeper and the cantankerous waitress – a world populated by real people with problems they don't have to hide? But most of all I count myself lucky that I don't have to do these things. Those who cannot beam on demand and ask insincere standard questions must be very stressed by these new demands on the workforce. Industrialisation started with the standardisation of products, and that brought some undoubted benefits. Now it has passed on to the standardisation of us – and of our relationships. We should not exaggerate: human beings are very wilful when it comes to being human and resisting those who want to turn them into machines. But then again, the more sophisticated methods of modern advertising and propaganda programme people and persuade them at the same time that they are free. Consider the yearly migration of young consumers to Ibiza for the expensive misery of a week's sun-kissed, hard-work hedonism. If we lose variety, we lose the ability to enjoy the external world. We should consume less, and when we do, we should draw on the uniqueness of its little pleasures. At work, we should regain the essentiality of important human relationships by being ourselves and doing things differently. I think of those wonderful teachers and university lecturers who taught me and would now be considered eccentric at best. They would be sacked within a month. One glance from the inspectors and they'd be off. Each generation has its own reason for self-medicating with alcohol.

A good society not only has to provide work for its citizens – not too much and not too little – but has to create the right conditions for its citizens to go about their work and enjoy it. The idea goes back at least as far as Plato, but the idea that everyone has the perfect job suited to their nature is as questionable as the idea that everyone has a perfect partner – an idea also found in Plato.[7] People grow to like their work, if they are allowed to; ideally it is a relationship in which they change the work and the work changes them, but how a person gets to a certain occupation will always be dependent on a degree of happenchance.

Plato also asserted that both affluence and poverty are detrimental to work and to craftsmanship.[8] An idea that we can surely embrace. He also argued that the guardians should live a life of poverty.[9] They were not representatives – far from it – but the idea that those who rule should not be highly remunerated is a good one. Marx said that representatives should only get a worker's average wage, as no one who is rich could understand most people's lives. That is still true, and the professionalisation of politicians is in fact

7 Plato, *The Symposium* (London: Penguin, 1951), trans. by W. Hamilton, pp59-65 (1906-193e) Plato has Aristophanes argue that Zeus split the original arrogant, four-legged humans in two, and so love became a search for the other half.
8 Plato, *Republic* (Oxford: OUP, 1993), p. 125 (421d-e).
9 Plato, *Republic* ..., pp. 121-24 (416c-421-a)

the antithesis of democracy. The Westminster Compound is busy with whatever it has to do, but there is absolutely no awareness of what is going on in the rest of the country. This is perhaps the most startling aspect of the current referendum campaign on Scottish independence. No politicians and very few London journalists have bothered to find out what it's about. Belatedly someone has notified them that it's about social rights, and this has been reinterpreted as moral superiority on the part of Scots, and Labour in Scotland, which up until yesterday was complaining about the "something-for-nothing society", is wanting to project itself as the defender of those who need something because they have nothing, after thirty years of "neo-liberalism". If they earned an average wage, they would never have been so deaf to the people they were supposed to represent.

Politics, then, is about class. That's been said before and long ago. Each class is a conglomerate of economic activities we call work. We are defined by both class and work, but class defines our political interests, even if we are unaware of it or wish to disregard them, and work defines our own natures. The longer we do a certain kind of work, the more we become imbued with it and the more difficult it is to break free of it, if we dislike it – and sadly some people do. Work is where we can be creative if we're lucky enough to have the right conditions. These three things – class, work and politics – are all closely interrelated. Work is where real democratic politics starts, and it was there that the first determined campaign for universal manhood suffrage was launched (sadly, it was only manhood suffrage at that stage). The various stages of the Chartist movement had all run their course long before every worker got the vote, at the same time as women did, but with a bizarre difference in the age qualification for women, which as far as I know was never introduced anywhere else.

Only in Britain! The middle class was the beneficiary, but it displayed no gratitude.

A couple of years ago I heard a young old Etonian, whose qualification to advise the country through the microphones of the BBC seemed unclear. He was arguing that there should be a return to the property qualification for electors, because people had to be educated enough to vote (an interesting category shift here). This issue, once considered ancient history, will be revived again. He scorned the term "working class", but that was what he meant: the working class should have its vote taken away. Once I laughed at the idiot ideas of the right, now I am fearful. They have a bad habit of passing into law a decade or so later. I take some encouragement from the fact that the current ideas of the right were once believed back in the late nineteenth century, and when I was in my teens, those ideas were considered something laughable that belonged permanently to the past. If that was the case for the right, then we can also come back from the dead and start to create a more equal society. And this time we will hopefully do it better. We will do it with good manners, with understanding. We will do it slowly, with sensitivity to the losers of the present as well as correcting the harm done to the losers of the past. We will not do it from central command, but through debate and involvement at local level. We will do it not for our own affluence, but for our children and our environment, by investing in education and in preventing pollution. And we will do it for our creative satisfaction by starting with how we work and why we work. As I have said, every kind of work is opaque to the outsider, even when the outsider thinks there isn't much to it, so none of us can dictate how this should happen. Each profession and trade will have to make its own decisions.

Lastly we should speak up for the irreducibly lazy, for whom I personally have great affection. On this I am genuinely on my own. I could probably read all the ancients and never find one to support my belief, never mind all the busy people who came after. Sometimes I happen upon a beautifully lazy person, who has perhaps secured some gentle sinecure that has gone unnoticed by the accountants and time-and-motion people, possibly in one of our more remote villages or islands. They usually drive a crippled van and roll their own. Typically they roll a cigarette slowly, enjoying every movement, and then only start talking when they place the skinny roll-up in their mouth. This is a tricky business and the sentences are fragmented, which only makes them more interesting. They look out to sea and focus on a distant headland and say things like, "Aye, he's only working his way through life, like the rest of us," or "There's no need for all this rush, you know." They rarely read or do the crossword puzzle, and never go on cross-country runs, but have their own reliable thoughts, occasionally assisted by illegal or legal substances. They never harm anyone, and often do a good turn. When I look at them, exchange a few words and observe how snugly they fit into this world, I don't feel envy but relief that they exist. I don't envy them, because I wouldn't want to live like them. I, like most of my fellow human beings, have been cursed with restlessness and this need to do things – very possibly things that don't need to be done, but seem inexplicably important because they fill in time – the double enemy that both eats away at life and yet weighs upon us if we don't get busy.

I am sick of hearing Labour and Conservative politicians talking about helping "hardworking families", even as they prepare another blow to the living standards of those families, and pay large amounts of money to ATOS to interview disabled people. Surely a country that can afford to subsidise house buyers to keep the inflated house prices in their inflated state can afford to carry the very few individuals who don't want to work or who cannot work. There are many ways to contribute to society, and many of them cannot be detected by accountants, economists, moralists, politicians, intellectuals and other grand people who know what's what and what we should do.[10] "Hardworking families" is a cheap propaganda trick to shift blame to some vague category which presumably could be defined as "work-shy families". If they exist, and they probably do in very small numbers, they are not the problem.

---

10 Some will say that I'm in this group, and they would be right: I have already admitted that the intellectual and the writer require arrogance for their uncertain metiers.

On Essays

A good essay examines the arguments for and against, and requires a degree of balance not found in the polemic. The essay is not better or worse than the polemic, but it is more suited to certain writers and, more interestingly, to certain times. When the left is more influential, the polemic is important because it can make a difference. Writers in such times write because they want something to happen, and that is a responsibility (even if they do not realise it). The irresponsibility of writers often consists in their desire to demonstrate their own worthiness and commitment to the temporarily popular cause.

When the left is weak, polemic is generally more muted, although the evils to be denounced are more common and more outrageous. This is a time for the essay, which examines questions more deeply precisely because there is little hope of immediate action to address them.

I won't say much about writers of the right here, mainly because their behaviour is not a mirror image of the left's. The right's ideas go with the grain of the hierarchies, and their authors find it easy to publish whether or not the right is on the rise. There are notable exceptions, such as Nietzsche and Ortega y Gasset. The former was an outcast throughout his active life, and the latter was, at the very least, a maverick. More common are talentless writers like Gabriele d'Annunzio whose real talents lay in the self-promotion and bombast that left a miserable legacy for Italian letters. The courtier intellectuals of the right allow themselves crass errors that writers of the left would not be excused.

The freedom the essay offers the writer of the left is the opportunity to put ideology aside and investigate even those unpalatable truths that undermine our belief in a better and more equal society. The word "essay" derives from the same root as "assay", the Latin *exagium* which means "weighing" – hence the title of this collection of essays.

The essay is a literary form precisely because it does not have to have the last word. An essay is generally short: it should be easily digestible, but also satisfying – if not a good meal, at least a hearty snack.[1] But this is not what defines it. The essay does not instruct the reader; it provides material for an already thoughtful reader to chew on. This makes it ideal for fragmented reading, such as short train journeys or for keeping on the bedside table. You plough on with a novel but, as I say, each essay has to be digested before you move on to the next, because the important thing is where it takes *your thoughts*.

An essay can have fun. It can be perverse. It can occasionally set out to rile people, but too much of that would be tiresome. Its tone should appear conversational, but only appear. That conversationality is artifice, and good artifice is never apparent. Essayists can talk about themselves, but never lament. The best ones are usually self-deprecating, and this apparent intimacy has been around since Montaigne, who sometimes took it too far, but then his original readers were probably known to him. The important thing – and Montaigne understood this, I think – is that the "I" in an essay must be an observer and not a protagonist.

The essay borders with the article – on the one side with the journalistic article and on the other with the academic article. The former must entertain as well as inform, whereas the latter often appears to suggest that entertainment is beneath

---

1 If I were you, I would now protest that some of these essays, this one included, are mere nibbles. Your money will not be refunded.

its dignity.[2] I occasionally look over my unpublished works – an unpleasant task on the whole – and I retrieved one essay for this collection, "Nations and Nationalism".[3] When I wrote it – some time ago – I still wrote like an academic. I seemed concerned with demonstrating that I had done the necessary background reading, and assuming that anyone would care a damn about some of the writers mentioned. I was more concerned with disproving what had been said than with saying what might be new and interesting. There was less recklessness and there was a fear of being misunderstood. These are constraints that should never concern an essayist.

Now I'm a hack – not a successful one, but a hack no less. "Hack" is a good word, and it is one of those derogatory words that don't really offend. It is a better word than the Italian one, *poligrafo*, which is a pompous term but also a very precise definition: someone who writes on all manner of subjects and, the implication is, with little knowledge. Generally speaking hacks and *poligrafi* write because they need to earn some money, but they may write because they are graphomaniacs. What's this? you ask. It's a word I have just coined – or rather just calqued on the Italian, *grafomane* – someone with a mania for writing. Essayists are generally hacks and graphomaniacs, and happy to be so. Note, please, that English has some great words, but it also lacks some.

Surely the greatest essayist of twentieth-century English

---

2 Journalists' articles quite often are pure essays in the literary sense, and only journalistic in that they're published in a newspaper or magazine. Obviously some academics write beautiful articles, which are published in collections and earn a wider readership, possibly earning the opprobrium of other academics who accuse the writer of "popularising" their subject. These are not clear distinctions.
3 The justification for its inclusion was that it contains arguments putting the case for small-nation nationalism, which is often confused with the more self-important great-nation nationalism. It was a wordy piece, and I have cut it back considerably.

literature was George Orwell. No doubt some would challenge this. Certainly I think he was a greater essayist than novelist, but his novels are more prominent, because they project him into an almost exclusively anti-communist stance, and he was an anti-communist with good reason, following his Spanish experience. He was also once a communist fellow traveller in his own opinion and in that of MI5. He had the attributes of a good essayist, as I have listed them, and when he described, for instance, how he shot an elephant, he observed his own experience to explain an important point about the relationship between the oppressor and the oppressed, while showing himself in a negative light. No one could argue with him, because he was the perpetrator. That he may have been overly harsh on himself is not the point, or rather it is: that's what makes the essay so effective.

Orwell's masterpiece is *Homage to Catalonia*, a mix of long essay and reportage. This hybrid genre would become the stock-in-trade of Kapuściński, who was more whimsical, literary and possibly even more brilliant. Orwell, on the other hand, had something more specific to say: he was a socialist at a time when socialism was a force, and even though he became very pessimistic about humanity's future in the light of what had happened in Russia or, from his personal experience, in Spain, he remained a socialist. This is something many people forget. When politicians and the press discuss Orwell, they make constant references to his Englishness, as though there were something strange or even unnatural in there being an English socialist, in spite of England having been home to most of the pre-Marxist socialist ideas. English socialists are reviled in their lifetimes and then beatified on death along with a sigh of relief. Tony Benn is only the most recent example. Benn, an agreeable soul, did not have the stature of Orwell, who was a great man for two reasons: his combat in Spain with his invaluable record of it, and his essays. His novels are important, but they need to be viewed within the context of his whole work.

Kapuściński did write a short collection of essays,[4] but they didn't match the reportage essays. We remember from school the sometimes bizarre essay titles we were set for homework. These were both enjoyable and useful, because they were merely a trigger – because it is difficult to write when there is complete freedom. Some authors, like Kapuściński and Chatwin, need to travel in order to write, and this does not detract from the brilliance of their writing. It enhances it.

An aphorism is a few bold lines on a page, and the boldness prompts the viewer to develop it further. The depth is in what is not shown – not said. The essay is a detailed sketch and has a greater range and versatility. It too is a limited form empowered by its limitations. But the most important thing with an essay is to know when to stop...

---

4 Ryszard Kapuściński, *The Other* (London, Verso, 2009).

A Sceptic's Defence of Religion

Ortega y Gasset argued that the ideas of intellectuals become the ideological currency of the streets three or four generations later. There is a distastefully elitist truth in what he wrote, although his own subtleties have never become common currency.

In the second half of the nineteenth century, atheism, which in my opinion was always present in ancient, medieval and early modern societies, suddenly became an intellectual force and spread widely amongst thinkers of all kinds and in all classes, even amongst those like George Eliot who had a certain religiosity. This was in many ways a positive force as it challenged the decadence of religion, its remoteness and, to be frank, its barminess. It was not until my generation reached adulthood that atheism and agnosticism became the majority credo of our societies. As a child, I witnessed adults drift a little reluctantly off to church dragging us along with them. Many were simply conforming, and the signs of the various churches' doubtful futures were there for all to see. Perhaps we children had a clearer idea. Marx, Nietzsche and Darwin had filtered out into every corner of society, albeit in a very anodyne form.

I was an atheist from the moment I was capable of forming a view on the question, probably when I was seven or eight. The usual arguments occurred. How could an all-powerful God allow such terrible injustices to take place? If there are many religions in this world, why should we think that our religion is the right one? I found the paraphernalia of church services unconvincing and even distasteful. I didn't mind the sermons, although I rarely agreed with them. Christian ethics remained an influence.

I therefore approached the question of religion as a tolerant non-believer and sceptic, and that approach has not really changed, although I now believe that God probably does exist, whereas life after death remains for me an unlikely possibility. This change in thinking was not the product of any religious experience or revelation. It was principally a reaction against the thoughtlessness with which modern Europeans reject God – a mirror image of the thoughtlessness of those who accept God and even personalise Him and turn Him into a father figure. Partly the change arose from reading medieval and early modern writers, and finding that their views were very distant from the caricature of religion presented to me by believers and unbelievers alike.

I am distrustful of modern Christian phraseology: "Jesus loves me" and the less egotistical but still non-sensical "God loves you" are meaningless statements, as they confuse categories. Human beings can love, and that emotion, which is peculiarly ours and embraces – in common parlance at least – a spectrum of emotions, must surely have evolved from another perhaps cruder emotion known to our animal forbears. The statement "God is love" is, on the other hand, entirely comprehensible. I do not say that it is true, because I am aware that this is something I want to believe – an act of faith, if you like, or an opinion, and therefore not of interest to anyone but myself. Besides, it is only one of the many definitions of God that I occasionally entertain in my mind, without coming to any meaningful conclusion.

With the process of secularisation that commenced at the end of the wars of religion in the seventeenth century, religion was increasingly abandoned to extremists and literalists. The voices of people like Erasmus and Servetus[1]

1 I have long been obsessed with Servetus, because I have read much about him and he seems to represent an alternative liberal Reformation. His terrible death at Calvin's hands was a crime at the time, and Voltaire justly took up the

had all but disappeared. Later other religions appear to have been affected in a similar manner, while the problem for Christianity had probably started a little earlier at the beginning of the modern era, in the wake of the changes brought about by the printing press and the Reformation. New ideas had to be staunched with rigid and often quite bizarre certainties. Transubstantiation – an outlandish belief in the physical powers of the Eucharist – had been circulating in the Middle Ages but only in the 1560s did it become official Catholic dogma that every Catholic had to believe in unquestioningly. In the 1860s the Catholic Church introduced Papal Infallibility, which would have perplexed the medieval mind as much as it does ours.

Of course the Protestants were not be outdone in their craziness: they believed in the literal truth of the Bible, something that even a cursory reading, such as mine, demonstrates to be impossible as it is full of inconsistencies and contradictory assertions. It is more literature than philosophy, full of myth and opaque allegory. God Himself appears to behave differently in different books of the Bible.

Protestants also ran off with the Augustinian concept of predestination, a possible contribution from the cult of Isis, which reflected the huge burden of their contempt for humanity and ran counter to humanism and a belief in man's potential. Scientifically and philosophically there are

---

posthumous cause. For this book I have read parts of the recent English translation his *Christianismi Restitutio*: Michael Servetus, *The Restoration of Christianity* (Lewiston, Queenston and Lampeter: Edwin Mellen Press, 2007). It has an explanation of the circulation of blood, which was overlooked for a long time and had to be rediscovered by William Harvey in the seventeenth century, but it sounded disappointingly like so many works of the time – covered with the biblical references of the mad proselytiser who today stands on a box near a shopping centre, quoting Isaiah, berating the public about their consumerist rituals and proselytising no one. When you read Servetus, noble in his own way, you realise the uniqueness of Erasmus amongst all the other religious voices.

good arguments in favour of necessity – the secular version of predestination – but the existential void it creates undermines ethics.

It is however with my atheist friends that I most wish to engage in argument. They claim to be rationalists, and sometimes are, but as with other faithful believers there are areas of discussion that are taboo and make them feel uncomfortable. They suffer from the irrationalism of rationalism, which is an almost religious belief in the knowability of everything and, worse, the idea that a human being is a naturally rational animal and therefore, if released from want, capable of living in a rationally organised society. This was the act of faith that motivated the great socialist and communist societies of the twentieth century, to which I still harbour a profound allegiance. At this stage in the argument, I am probably confusing you, just as I'm unsettling myself, in spite of the many times I have rehearsed this in my head. Here I will restrict myself to this assertion: one of the great failings of those deeply flawed societies was precisely their desire to interfere with areas of people's private lives that were not a concern of the state, the most important of which was the area of religious belief (those societies were not alone in this). The justification for this policy on religion was that religion is irrational, superstitious and divisive, and thus undermines the proper functions of society. If leading figures in those societies had read Zamyatin's *We*, instead of banning it and persecuting its author, a long-time Bolshevik who abandoned the Bolshevik Party soon after the Revolution, they would have learnt an important lesson: the good society must be tolerant of the bad and the irrational; it has to leave space for the profound differences in human nature, for the good of everyone including the good, whoever they may be.

Lenin wrote an essay on religion, in which he very liberally accepted that believers should be able to join the party, adding with the irritating superiority of those who have worked it all out that such people would have to live with the "contradiction" between their beliefs and their membership. I pity the person who does not carry a few contradictions around.

Religious tolerance is the product of the conflicts resulting from the fragmentation of Christianity in the sixteenth and seventeenth centuries, as well as the more rationalist thinking of the Enlightenment in the late seventeenth and eighteenth centuries, and of the French Revolution and the Napoleonic Wars, and that tolerance is quite simply a social good in itself – one that we must defend whatever the good or bad effects of religion. But I will argue here that the prejudice against other people's religions is still with us, particularly in Western Europe, and religion may have as many benefits as drawbacks. Atheists often suffer from smugness and intellectual rigidity, which resemble the religious dogmatism they despise. It is true that some religions are dogmatic and quixotic in the rejection of truths that science has discovered, forcing impossible and unnecessary dilemmas on their followers, but that is not the principal subject of this essay and has been adequately covered elsewhere. Readers of this essay will probably take that as a given anyway.

Some of the positivist intellectuals in the second half of the nineteenth century worried about how ethics would be maintained, if God and His revelations were abandoned. This did not undermine their atheism, but merely posed a problem for the good order of the societies they lived in. There was, however, no discernible loss of morality amongst atheists – quite the opposite: socialists who often disseminated such ideas were clearly motivated by a well-defined morality, whereas those who claimed religious orthodoxy often appeared to lack one. Much later Sartre claimed to have solved this problem in his fascinating but not wholly relevant essay, *Existentialism is a Humanism*. That no immediate change was detectable should not surprise us, as people were still growing up with religious education, and churchgoing, which was already much lower than expected in late-Victorian Britain, was only declining slowly. My generation was probably the last in which religion was generally taught and in which we became familiar with religious concepts and stories. They were little more than an ethical language or shorthand. The miracles were not believed, but the ethos rested somewhere at the back of our brains, muddled in with our youthful ambitions, desires and curiosities.

I find that atheists under fifty are unlike atheists of my age (ten years above that line and on the way out), because they have no understanding of what religion is. They only see a caricature. They have lost the perception of our moral interdependence, which can be retained at the same time as rejecting religion with all its impossible claims. The positivists' ideas have completed their course, and the loneliness Nietzsche predicted is here but undetected in an orgy of material consumption. There are several reasons for my qualified defence of religion, as will become clear, but one of the principal ones is that without religions being practised somewhere, many people will not come into contact with the useful consciousness they can engender. That philosophy can do this so much better is not the point; philosophy is currently an elitist pastime. In a better society with better universal education, philosophy may be able to fill the gap, but that moment is still far off (and probably never would be for everyone).

Religions are about the principal areas of human doubt, but they claim to provide some certainties that supposedly resolve the problem. In the case of Christianity, I have never thought that it does. This religion, which I was born into, only starts to make sense if Jesus was a man and not just "God in disguise", to use John Cowper Jones's expression. If Jesus was a man and not God on holiday to see how the other half live, then Christianity can provide me with a series of complex intuitions about the humanity to which he belonged. And his death, so like many other deaths suffered by the innocent and guilty alike, becomes a symbol of our tragic but also heroic existences. That he died for suggesting a series of divine ideas such as loving your enemy deepens that symbol with further meanings that are all the more intense for being a little vague. Vagueness lies at the heart of religion, but churches and other organised religions marshal that vagueness into an unnatural orderliness.

For the first millennium of Christianity, heretics were constantly rebelling against the idea that God can be a man, and a man a god. Only in antiquity and modernity has this impossibility appeared to present no problems. The Virgin Birth is another impossibility, and Christianity attempts to prove it by evading all sensible argument. But religions are not just these assaults on human reason; they are institutions and they have many functions. It would be useful to list them, though the list is probably not exhaustive:

1. Religions provide off-the-peg philosophies for those who have other things to do in life.
2. Religions provide a set of ethical commands, which have to be obeyed simply because they were supposedly laid down by God. It is better to educate people to formulate their own morality, but as a system it does at least set a minimum about which most of us can agree, although some of the Ten Commandments have remained more relevant than others. Christianity has the merit, in theory if not in Church practice, of emphasising that

morality is about our own behaviour and we should not judge others.

3. Religions require people to gather together regularly and meditate in public on things beyond their own personal interests. This is a mental and spiritual exercise, and can have a profound influence on how individuals perceive themselves.

4. Religions require people to gather together for what is at one level a purely social occasion. In societies where everyone belongs to the same religion (organic societies), this has the function of inclusiveness, and often such religions are reasonably tolerant as long as their adherents don't challenge fundamental beliefs too publicly; in societies where religion is fragmented, the fragments can split over minute questions of dogma, and tolerance is often very limited, but given the fragmentation, a space is created for the irreligious to avoid oppressive religious conformism.

5. Religions provide a collection of parables and moral dictums that become an ethical language for that religious community. In fact, nearly all religious ideas are included in each religion, but they are expressed in the ethical language of a particular religion. Quakers may resemble Sufis in some ways, but Sufis pray to saints and in that they resemble Catholics, but all Christians, dogmatic or liberal, draw on the same biblical stories, just as all Muslims, dogmatic or liberal, draw on the same Koranic ones. The ethical language changes but more or less the same range of religious ideas are represented.

6. Religions organise rites of passage. Sometimes these are obscure or even dangerous, but more generally they're innocuous and reassuring for the religious community.

7. Religions that are functional place limits on the powerful, such as the restrictions on usury that were once in force in Christianity and still are in Islam. It took Christianity a very long time to eradicate slavery within Christian

society, although once Christianity had become a state religion, free Christians could not be enslaved. Islam had a very similar approach, and slave traders adhering to both religions had to go in search of pagans to enslave. Religions therefore have a mildly egalitarian element, but that relative equality was restricted to members of the religion. Today most Christian Churches place little or no restrictions on the powerful, and the cult of poverty has all but disappeared.

8. Religions organise redistributive policies which resemble a rudimentary welfare state. With the birth of the modern state these functions were taken over by secular institutions, which initially were more brutal, as in the case of British workhouses. When the welfare state starts to crumble, religions become more important. That the welfare state recedes is a tragedy, but no one should criticise religions for assisting those who have been abandoned (as long as they don't attach strings).

9. Religions provide an identity, which can be sought out now in all parts of the globe. Most human beings like identities, although some of us are distrustful of them. If identities bring people pleasure, why should they matter, as long as the identities don't spill over into intolerance and violence? In this, religions are no different from secular organisations such as political parties, clubs and aficionados of particular kinds of music, dance or leisure activity.

10. Religions provide succour to those who have suffered terrible losses or are in fear for their lives or for other people's lives. In early modern literature there is the often repeated example of the ship in a storm: as soon as it hits the ship all the passengers rush off to pray to their God, who could be Christian, Islamic or Jewish or any of the varieties within those religions. They pray fervently throughout the storm, promising their God all manner

of penances, but if they don't go down to a watery death and survive the storm, they immediately return to their former nonchalance and forget the divinity they promised never to forget. Is there anyone with a seriously ill child who has not been tempted, however atheistic their beliefs? Is it right to condemn such behaviour? It seems to me that it is entirely understandable. I knew of a woman who suffered the death of her only child and then of her husband a few months later. Previously uninterested in religion, she turned to it for the only small relief she could get. Isn't that understandable, and is that a worse way to be treated than to be handed a packet of pills? An interventionist God is more likely to be believed in by the downtrodden and the afflicted, because they are in more need of Him. Should any comfortable Western intellectual snort with disapproval at such things? It's true that this very human need leaves the way open for religions to abuse their influence in order to assist the powerful. Not all religions do, and not all clerics do, but this is another temptation. This leads to the final point.

11. As organised religions are preoccupied with ensuring their continuance, they are tempted to buttress existing political hierarchies in order to receive their support in return. Almost all religions are guilty of this, and the exceptions are small religions that live on the margins of society, often suffering discrimination. Religion as an instrument of government has been known about probably since the earliest states were formed in agricultural societies. Whether or not people were conscious of it, it must have been there. *Instrumentum regni* is the Latin term still current in Italy and probably other countries. Supposedly eternal truths are used for the contingent interests of a political clique or more simply as social order. As religions often have a fair range of eternal

truths, different ones can be used in different circumstances. I have said that modernity has in many ways
damaged religion and made it barmier than it was before.
This was not always the case: both Christianity and
Islam were the voice of rationalism and whatever limited scientific activity was taking place during the middle
period of the Middle Ages (thus from the very beginning
in the case of Islam). However modernity has brought
one advantage for religion: it has secularised society and
cast religion free from the chains of power – or rather it
has pretended to have done this, but only partially implemented it. It has opened the way for religion to change
its tone, accept the discoveries science has placed before
us and is placing before us at such an increasingly hectic
speed we struggle to keep up with, and take on a more
subversive role in society that puts humanity as a whole
at the centre of its thinking. Many religious people have
been doing this for a very long time, but the principal
institutions have proved to be much more rigid.

Freud writes, "The religions of mankind too must be
described as examples of mass delusion." In part, he is right.
I find it very difficult to understand how people can believe
in the Immaculate Conception, the Eucharist, the divinity of
Christ, the Resurrection and all the miracles. But the scriptures were written in a different time, when historiography
as we know it simply didn't exist. The Greeks might have
come close to it, but theirs was an exceptional society. People
engaged in the laborious task of making written records for
their own ideological reasons, and to some extent, little has
changed if we examine the great majority of writing today,
including journalism.[2] When they did get round to recording

---

religious accounts, it was long after the event, and was based on oral records. We need therefore to treat these extravagant claims with a little more subtlety. Religions can still contain wisdom, even if we reject the literal truth of their narratives.

Besides, do we believe that all followers of religion believe in these things throughout their entire lives? Only a fanatic could do that. Nearly everyone has their doubts, although they may not reveal them publicly. Religions are not alone in this: political organisations also demand unity of their members, who are required to change their positions in line with the changing positions of their leaderships. And for the most part they do.

Freud also believes that religion is means to overcoming unhappiness, albeit an unreliable one. In fact he interprets human behaviour as a constant search for happiness, which in turn is a method for resolving our inability to satisfy our drives. Religion is one of a few strategies we deploy, none of them very successful, according to him. This is not all that religions do, and this function of placating the troubled psyche really only concerns the idea of life after death and of a perfect one at that. If you remove this delusion, religions are not left with nothing. Religious believers don't cling any less to life than do non-believers, and it therefore seems logical to conclude that they don't believe that much, and yet continue to practise their religions.

Freud's analysis of civilisation ignores entirely the wretched conditions of the working class at the time he was writing. In that class, the wretchedness suffered by individuals in Freud's analysis would not have appeared to be much of a problem. Freud was charting the alienation that arises from the market economy and particularly affects isolated egos of the middle class, in which so much more is expected of life. Surely some

are only a tiny part of the output, because we clearly have a greater facility to reproduce the written word.

of the most terrible blows we suffer in life are not the ones that affect us directly but the ones that affect people who are close to us. It is in our human relationships that we find happiness, because they take us out of ourselves, but they also make us vulnerable. If the people we love are taken away from us or suffer disabling conditions, we are bereft. It is that vulnerability that Freud appears to find so intolerable. He is right to mention the risk, but the vulnerability is more tolerable if we learn to approach it with greater passivity, and religions can help us to do that. That part of religion is not a delusion. Philosophy might achieve the same without delusions or with far fewer of them, but it may be a harder road.

Leaving aside whether there's life after death, believing in life after death is harmful to the psyche and to a good life. It leads to an obsession that interferes with our ability to live a meaningful life in human society, something that is a concrete possibility, though not always easy to achieve. The next life is used by organised religions to impose hierarchies and discipline. It may get people to carry out "good acts", but they are carried out for the wrong reasons, and more importantly, religions end up claiming that they at least have a hand in opening the way to a blissful afterlife and thus entrance to the next world is governed not by justice or divinity but by powerful men and committees.

Whether or not God exists, belief in philosophical materialism leads not immediately, but within a generation or two, to consumerist materialism, or it is at least a contributing factor. If you believe not only that this life is all you have, but also that your life is not part of some spiritual ecology that nurtures your own life and is to some infinitely small degree influenced by your own life, then you are drawn towards a mindset where everything is justifiable in order to obtain the maximum pleasure for yourself out of this brief, unconnected worldly existence and in so doing you're turning the pleasant greenness of our human world into a moral desert. Of course, many – probably most – atheists live moral lives. We are never consistent with our ideas. The pious are often the most "sinful", if I can borrow a term they use. But the intellectual core of materialism is, I believe, affecting the way we relate to each other, and this is also true of many of those who claim to be religious in our societies. Capitalism likes materialism, because it is consistent with its unsubtle, linear, common-sense approach to life. In Europe this is the direction of travel. In North America and possibly in both the Americas, capitalism follows an extreme faith-based assertion of the self, which is often in direct contradiction of the religion it is supposed to represent. Both these extremes lead towards solipsism and an isolation of the self, which is damaging to the individual's psychological health.

If we can divide how we live from how we behave, then we should perhaps live as atheists and behave as believers in God. Or put more simply, we can forget about the afterlife, which is whatever it is, like all other natural phenomena, and we can at least entertain the possibility of God, understood as some kind of interconnection between all humanity or, as many argue, between all animal life, all organic things or even all things without exception. I have no idea, but by inclination or prejudice, I prefer the interconnection between all humanity, but I realise that modern science – particularly the discovery of DNA – suggests that humanity is not so unique. One thing is certain: our ideas on this subject are going to develop dramatically, and religions will inevitably have to adapt to these changes if they are to survive. In any case, we can no longer conceive humanity outside its dependency on its restricted environment.

I don't want to convert any atheists to religion – heaven forbid! – and I don't want to convert any religious person to agnosticism. While I defend religion, I have little time for proselytising, an acceptable activity but one I always perceive as a form of bad manners. What I would like is more tolerance and less caricature, although some religious people do lend themselves to caricature, such as the UKIP official who claimed the floods in England resulted from God's anger at the law introducing gay marriage. Once such idiocies only provoked mild jollity, but not now the threat of the various fundamentalisms appears to be more real.

Tolerance does however have to be tolerant of history and tradition to some extent. I would not support a law banning Holocaust-denial except in Germany and Austria where such laws are entirely justifiable and in fact necessary. Irving initiated a court case in England and the process only served to reveal his dishonest methodology. The legal balance was correct for England, but that doesn't mean that this balance should be respected everywhere. So it is with religious tolerance: the French republican tradition in public institutions may be acceptable, but only if it is applied to all religions with the same rigour. The problem is that categorising forms of dress as religious symbols is questionable. Consistency is essential in state tolerance, but the individual should apply a greater and more nuanced tolerance, adapting to situations and complexities. If someone commits an act of bigotry in a public institution, it cannot be tolerated, but in private encounters even in public places, greater tolerance is usually the best way to deal with it, and intolerance of that intolerance may be counterproductive. In any event, we should not equate religion with religious fundamentalism.

I am not a particularly religious person, and whatever religiosity I have is personal and suited only to me. I am not a particularly selfless person, and am not therefore close to God. I have, though, a certain experience of this world and feel that I have encountered people close to God who are recognisable by their detachment from the self, and some of them have been members of a religion, some have been clergy (very few), some have been agnostics and some atheists. Labels, as ever, are not indicative of precise realities – not even the labels we apply to ourselves with a degree of self-knowledge. I am interested in religions perhaps for the same reason that I am even more interested in languages. They have been around me in their diversity, particularly during my childhood. I observe with horror the complete misrepresentation of the Islamic world, which has replaced communism as America's favourite bête noire – communism apparently being no more.

How then should I summarise my defence of religion? I think that my defence is not just to be found in this essay, but in all these essays. I argue against the idea that all things – politics, sport, culture and you name it – are forms of religions, which is a passing fashion amongst academics who illogically infer that similar social phenomena produced by religious and political organisations prove that religions and political movements are the same. All it proves is that they are both produced in human society. Political movements and religions are very different, and religions, which are concerned with eternity and eternal truths even though they are constantly changing them, are much more resilient than political movements. Is there a political movement that has survived two millennia like the Catholic Church? Religions survive principally because, while they are busying with eternity, it is often unclear what they are doing about the present, so they are less likely to be held to account and they claim to be above or outside politics. I also argue that in spite of themselves, politics and religion do permeate each other to some extent, and the influence of one on the other is more cultural than anything else. I argue in these essays for the primacy of politics – in particular class politics, but religion is important to politics and also to itself – that is to say that it has its own aims, and some of which affect us while others don't. There are signs that as the crisis starts to bite, the major religions are going to play a more significant but still secondary role in affecting political developments, and this may assist in increasing social responsibility, which would be helpful for the left. The shift is from pronouncements on matters of personal morality as interpreted by the churches to ones on public morality. Leading clerics are usually wise enough to restrict the number of times they join in public debate, and their influence is often exaggerated. So the private religious functions of religions are precisely that, and are not the business of anyone else. Their public ones, which they have a right to exercise anyway, are probably going to tend towards the "progressive" in the near future, if I may use an irritatingly vague adjective, but public religious pronouncements usually are a little vague. Religions are not the threat they once were – from the religious wars of the sixteenth century through to the mass religious bigotry of the first half of the twentieth century, and much bigotry along the way. There is the nightmare of the so-called clash of civilisations between the incredibly similar religions of Christianity and Islam. This is not however an interference of religion in politics, but an interference of politics in religion.

We still have a margin of freedom in our conformist Western societies. I don't say that these are wholly free societies: there is no absolute rule of law, there is corruption, there is surveillance and there is abuse of power, particularly against minorities and most particularly against black people. I know from my experience as a shop steward in the seventies that private companies used to issue death threats against trade unionists, and I would be surprised if things have improved since then. But there is also a lot of space for invention that simply isn't being made use of. Partly this is because our regime seems very secure to us, the powerless, while the powerful, quite aware of the instability in the system, are intent on reducing our powers before they carry through structural changes that will undo everything we have gained over the last hundred years. Partly this is because we are wedded to the consumer society and feel we could not survive without its tasteless, anodyne, sometimes quite unnecessary and, more rarely, toxic bounty. Partly this is because we have finally allowed a wholly materialist philosophy, invented over a century ago with some very positive initial effects, to implant itself so deeply in our consciousness that we have become not so much atheists or humanists, as pagans – not the distant pagans of hunter-gatherer societies, who may or may not have been noble savages, but the near pagans of early classical times: the religion of success, fame, celebrity and above all the sacralised self – what we might call the "because-I'm-worth-it" society. And worth, here, is most definitely a monetary quantity.

We are not living in the Soviet Union under Stalin or the United States under McCarthyism, which was a much more widespread repression than is generally admitted. If people in those societies could continue to write and challenge their regimes in various ways, we have no excuse for remaining silent, and many do not. But too many are living like automatons, driven by financial needs – not always necessary ones – and a consumerist culture that judges people on their ability to consume. I am not saying everyone should rush out to the church, mosque or synagogue.

I am not saying that to act independently and challenge the status quo, you have to be religious. What I am saying is that for many people, religion is a useful way to get out of that sense of being powerless and trapped in a self whose desires can never be fulfilled. About a decade ago, Caspar Melville, the editor of *The New Humanist* and therefore no friend of religion, interviewed a group of black converts to Islam and found that religion gave them a sense of belonging and being in control of their own lives. But quite often conversions can lead to fanaticism; I'm suggesting something even gentler: an awareness of something beyond ourselves, which does not have to be dressed up in religion, but if that makes it easier, then there should be no objection. Equally, if people wish to believe that this will store up a place in heaven, then there may be no harm to the public good in that either. A sensitivity to the world beyond the self, which we might define as a belief in God, is something that brings a reward in this life. It makes it easier to engage politically, socially, emotionally, creatively and perhaps spiritually with the world around us. It takes us back to Martin Buber, I think.

To my mind, education is more important than religious sensitivity, but that is much less controversial. Perhaps religion is also now less controversial than it was when Richard Dawkins and Christopher Hitchens wrote their fierce attacks on it,[3] and that is why this is a much less ambitious work than the one I originally planned at the time.

One of the most potent arguments used by such critics of religion is that religion leads to bitter inter-communal strife, and this cannot be denied, although often perpetrators of

---

3 Richard Dawkins, *The God Delusion* (London: Black Swan, 2006), and Christopher Hitchens, *God Is Not Great* (London: Atlantic Books, 2007) Hitchens' title is purposely insulting to Islam, which is unmannerly and obtuse.

such violence are not particularly religious. In many ways, it is no different from the conflicts between language communities, ethnic groups, and all the other identities some people cling to. There is however another division, more subtle and less catastrophic than the inter-communal one, but damaging to the individual nonetheless.

Religion can lead to separation from society. The pious wish to keep away from the "sinners", and this is often found amongst the founders of religions and religious organisations. George Fox, the founder of the Religious Society of Friends (or Quakers), went to the tavern with a cousin and some others to have a drink. But one round did not suffice, and they called for more, saying that whoever did not drink would have to pay for them all. Fox was shocked by this behaviour, so he paid and left, resolving to leave his family and never to be familiar or friendly with young or old. While he was overreacting, the Lord spoke to him, "Thou seest how young people go together into vanity and old people into the earth; and thou must forsake all, both young and old, and keep out of all, and be as a stranger unto all."[4] To my mind, he should have got back down to the tavern, where life was. As a young man, he wouldn't learn anything from the constant companionship of himself and his piety. And I don't think that God speaks to anyone. Apart from the assumptions this makes about the nature of God, who through the two-way dialogue becomes a personal protector of the elected person, the very contradictory orders that God is supposed to have given betray a voice that is surely generated in the mind of the listener.

As I think that the Quakers' religion is one of the best, this episode says more about founders than adherents. I would like to balance that quote with another, which in my

---

4 *Quaker Faith and Practice*, 19.01.

opinion shows great wisdom. It is William Penn on the unity of all religions:

> The humble, meek, merciful, just, pious and devout souls are everywhere of one religion; and when death has taken off the mask they will know one another, though the divers liveries they wear here makes them strangers. This world is form; our bodies are forms; and no visible acts of devotion can be without forms. But yet the less form in the religion the better, since God is a spirit; for the more mental our worship, the more adequate to the nature of God; the more silent, the more suitable to the language of a Spirit.[5]

Perhaps he is right about form, but personally I like it. I have no interest in participating in it, but I enjoy the fact that it exists and that people get something from it. Above all, I enjoy their variety and feel that, like art, they add something to our understanding of the world. It is sad that the Yezudis, whose faith is a syncretic mix of Christianity and Islam with a strong emphasis on baptism, have been driven from their Iraqi homeland as a result of the reckless Anglo-American invasion, but it's good that many of them have found refuge in Sweden where, in the absence of a warm river like the Tigris, they have to baptise themselves in a warm bath. They put on long-flowing white robes, similar to the ones Muslims wear at the Mosque during Ramadan, and immerse themselves in the warm water while saying their prayers. There is no end to the ways that human beings can express their religious sentiments, but in the end they are all saying the same thing: there is a better way to live beyond self-interest,

---

5 *Quaker Faith and Practice*, 19.28.

and we find significance and dignity in helping one another. It is true that this shared core is surrounded by innumerable accretions, often of bizarrely minor differences, which divide people and lead to violence, such as the persecution of the Old Believers who crossed themselves with three fingers rather than two.

My arguments and my own unpleasantness are best summed up by a conversation I had with a religious zealot. I had gone to hear Professor Mona Siddiqui at a public event. She gave an interesting talk on Islam which was marred by the pres- ence of Christian zealots who had packed the meeting with the express purpose of verbally attacking the speaker and her religion. Not that Siddiqi seemed particularly bothered. Perhaps she had encountered such people before. I hadn't, but they did vaguely remind me of the American Sparticist League.[6] Afterwards a fierce woman marched towards me, and I could feel her anger even before she spoke. I must have said something in defence of Islam, and this had caused great hurt.

"Are you a Christian," she asked.

I knew this to be an awkward question. I was certainly not a Christian as she was, but clearly a negative answer was going to trigger an avalanche of moralistic opprobrium.

"Yes," I said.

"A born-again Christian?"

"No," I replied emphatically.

"How very clever of you! How did you manage that?" She made no attempt to disguise her sarcasm, lest I had any doubt.

---

6 I won't waste our time explaining this reference, which you can probably guess at. Those who have had the misfortune to encounter this embodiment of certainty and proselytising zeal will shudder and dislike me for stirring up an unpleasant memory that should have been left alone.

"By having Christian parents. Not very devout ones, it's true, but they considered themselves to be Christians."

"And that's all you need to be a Christian?"

"No, you can also convert. But if my parents had been Muslims, I would have been a Muslim too. That's generally how it works. You can reject a religion, but its cultural imprint remains."

There followed a heated dialogue of the deaf. She was so angry that I found it easy to appear calm, even though her ignorance and bigotry riled me. Eventually I said, "Well, I don't want us all to be of the same religion."

"And I do!"

"That, I'm afraid, is the road that leads to Auschwitz."

There was something wrong in my reply, although it held an undoubted truth. The road leads somewhere, but it is not always followed the whole way. She looked hurt and left like scalded cat. I doubt that what I said dented her certainties, so it was foolish to engage in that conversation, and I was sorry to have offended her.

If, however, I lived in the United States, where atheists are a discriminated minority, this essay would have been called "A Defence of Atheism", and that conversation would have appeared at the beginning, not the end. All these religions and all these philosophies (including atheism) have their share of truth and their patent untruths. If they are treated in a measured fashion, they can be a useful part of our cultures. But I live in Europe, and most people I meet are atheists. Occasionally we argue on this point, and they are much politer than the zealot was but no less prejudiced. Their reaction is one of surprise and you can see them quietly placing you in the religious nutter category as soon as you fail to agree with their simple narrative. If they have any doubts, they would never express them, because the associations are so deeply entrenched.

Can we deny with absolute certainty that the decline of religion has not damaged some of the core values that hold society together? We cannot assert it with absolute certainty either, but we should at least admit to the possibility. I wrote a novel that was a modern reversal of Apuleius's *The Golden Ass* principally because I thought that the post-Christian West may be returning to classical paganism. Apuleius was a rich and powerful patron of gladiatorial games, and his book was an ancient literary precursor of the video nasty. His morality was stark and nasty too: failure is contagious, so no one should help anybody who has fallen on hard times, even if they were once a close friend; the important thing is not to be found out, and if you aren't, what you did is of no importance; finally it is necessary to project an image of success onto society (by, for instance, organising gladiatorial games) and this helps you to increase your success. This looked remarkably familiar in the late eighties when I wrote the book, and still does.

The reason might have had nothing to do with religion, particularly as Christians were often the ones most affected by these changing attitudes, which were typified by Thatcher, Reagan and Blair, all supposedly believers. It might have been the failure of the "secular god" of socialism. Socialists and communists have a clear morality, but no one is so deprived of morality as socialists and communists who cease to be socialists and communists, with the usual proviso on notable exceptions.

I conclude this summary with my principal argument, and one that I assert with unusual confidence: religion is a private matter that the state should not interfere with, and equally it is not a matter that should divide anyone – not even atheist and believer. There is only one division that is fundamental to our lives, and that was one I examined in the previous essay.

What Was Wrong with the Left?

Essay titles that start with a question threaten to be didactic, and my choice was influenced by the typical approach of the left when it goes in for a little self-criticism, which generally turns out to be self-justification. For instance, *What Is Left?* by Nick Cohen, whom I first read as a combative, investigative journalist for the *New Statesman* endowed with a good sense of humour, suggests the game is over and all that's left is a shared past, a cultural museum. The book was published before the economic crisis, and it was generally thought that capitalism had more or less solved the problem of human want and the only remaining problem was a group of intransigent Islamists who were intent upon dragging this new paradise back into the Middle Ages or the Middle Ages as they are currently conceived. Of course, this belief required not only prejudice but also a rank ignorance of what Mike Davis has called a "planet of slums" and of "deprivation" much closer to home. During the nineties, an interviewer in the *New Statesman* stated that his interviewee, Perry Anderson, was not one of those stupid leftists who don't accept that the right has won all the economic arguments. At the other extreme, a few people feel that nothing was wrong with the left in the past, and all they had to do was shout their message even louder than before.

It has seemed to me throughout this crisis of the left, which now goes back a long time, that there was something fundamentally wrong with the left but it was about how we did things and not about policy. I cannot and probably should not provide a detailed solution to these problems. That is because I don't have the knowledge and political experience to do so, but if I identify the problems, others perhaps could think about the solutions – which on the whole should emerge from some kind of collective experience. The important question is how much these are problems inherent to the left and how much these were cultural features of twentieth-century society as a whole. Some social phenomena, particularly in the thirties, were common to left-wing, right-wing and "democratic" societies. Equally the problems I list below are problems that concern all sections of the left or supposed left, although paradoxically they particularly affect Leninist parties and the new parties of the reformed left, such as New Labour and the Democratic Party in Italy, which I would define as right-of-centre parties. Both have their reasons for not listening to their membership and in particular for not listening to reality.

The first significant problem is that the left has always identified itself with modernity. There were many reasons for this, not least that history appeared to be on its side. The ethos of the left had filtered out into many circles where its presence would have been unthinkable before the Second World War. The resulting self-confidence meant that the left felt it could compete with capitalism on productivity. It is true that left-wing policies regenerated the capitalist economies after the War and the more social-democratic they were, the quicker the recovery. The Liberal ministers who ran the Italian economy after the War allowed Mattei to maintain the small state corporations set up under Fascism, because they considered them to be an irrelevance, but these organisations grew into monstrous industrial complexes with activities in a great number of sectors. The times were on their side.

However, regional contingent factors should not lead us to ignore some basic problems for the left. If the left means anything, it has to mean the protection and advancement of the less well-off sections of society. It therefore can never have the flexibility of an extreme free-market economy, which can happily close down factories and possibly transfer them elsewhere, even if the savings on the whole operation are minuscule. I recently heard an interesting dictum, which has no doubt been doing the rounds of business schools and think tanks for a long time: "Turnover is vanity; profit is sanity." This must be true for an individual company within a capitalist society, but it is not sanity for a whole economy, even a capitalist one. Profit is what ensures the survival of the company, but the turnover, particularly if there's a large workforce, is what keeps that economy functioning and creates demand so that other companies can also survive. This is a fundamental weakness in capitalist society, but why should socialist societies emulate them?

When Mao Zedong came up with his insane idea of getting peasants to produce steel, he was trying to compete with capitalist societies without considering the effects on those peasants. He accepted the capitalist idea that high productivity is the greatest social good, even though it usually turns work into misery, and he forgot about why people wanted a socialist society in the first place. He applied the same ruthlessness of the corporation when it came to moving "human resources" around and putting them to work. In other words, he treated humans as a means, with little certainty over what the end was, other than a powerful desire to overtake the capitalist competitors and overtake them quickly. He didn't intend to starve the peasants to death, but neither did he give much consideration to them, their needs and indeed their opinions. He moved them around as a general deploys his troops.

The time has come for the left to think about whether GDP or any other measure of productivity should be guiding political decision-making. Not all goods, products and outcomes are equally necessary. Food, housing, education, health, leisure, safe working conditions and fulfilling work are all necessities. Great mountains of ugly and rarely used plastic toys in every house with a child are not. In a polluted world, society has to think about its resources and its priorities. Soviet economies may have been overly centralised, but some degree of central planning is required, and is in fact in place in our societies, where it works in the interests of capital and not people.

The second problem is how we impose discipline. The left is about equality and the right about hierarchy, so the right has no inner conflict in establishing a chain of command. It is often the case that in setting out to do something, we end up doing exactly the opposite, sometimes without ever realising it. It is not surprising that militants after the world wars voluntarily subjected themselves to rigid discipline within a long chain of command all in the name of ending war and class divisions. They were horrified by the wars they had been forced to participate in, but those wars had also taught them to accept harsh discipline. They transferred some of the behavioural patterns of the imperialist war they detested to their war against empire and war. There was something heroic in this. Victor Serge's novels show how people realised that there was something wrong in Soviet society, but they felt that their generation had to make a huge sacrifice for future generations. In such chains of command, it is by no means the best and the most talented who rise to the top, and the men who control authoritarian power of the left start to behave like those who in other regimes control authoritarian power of the right, just as authoritarian power of the right adopts the mass language of authoritarian power of the left. In the bitter struggle of mutual hatred, everyone starts to resemble the other side, although some important differences remain. The equivalence of all authoritarian regimes was invented in the post-war period to smear the left which enjoyed a degree of cultural influence even in capitalist countries. This influence took several decades to dissipate.

Both Stalin and Blair detested the rank and file of their own organisations. This has made some people believe that Stalin must have been a police spy who, following the collapse of the regime he supposedly worked for, found himself in a position of authority within an organisation dedicated to a cause with which he had an ambiguous relationship. If he had been a spy, he would have been a man used to intrigue and playing his cards close to his chest in a position of total isolation, and he would therefore have been well placed to take over the reins of power, which come most easily to those who are utterly ruthless. This might also explain his strange obsession with Bulgakov's *The White Guard*. And I might even find this argument a little convincing, if it were not for the fact that so many other Stalins followed in his wake. No sane person would believe that Mao had been a police spy, but the behavioural patterns were very similar. It is much more likely that the combination of a powerful political position and an absolute belief in human reason, which so easily translates into an absolute belief in one's own reasoning, leads to a psychosis whereby the revolution and the self become entirely identified the one with the other, not only in mass propaganda but in the dictator's own mind.

The third problem is that political movements in general are intolerant of dissent. Lenin started a particularly restrictive tradition when he forced the break between the Bolsheviks and the Mensheviks. This is the stuff of politics and goes much further back than the existence of the left. There are two reasons why the left should be particularly careful about proper internal democracy. Firstly they claim to want a more democratic society with the involvement of as many people as possible. Secondly good decisions come out of open debate. A question of values and a question of practicalities. I was a member of a small Trotskyist organisation in the seventies – it doesn't matter which. The guru for this group was Ernest Mandel, a stern, humourless, besuited man who sat on podiums and moulded the truth like a blacksmith hammers hot iron. You're not quite sure what point he's trying to make so emphatically but eventually some kind of shape does appear. But is it of any use? We were summoned to a cadre school, which was actually a kind of rally. He was sitting up there with some other important individuals and they were denouncing Pabloism, because someone had decided that we had to be informed about this particular heresy and guarded against its dangerous allurements. For me this was like going to the dentist, because they had omitted to tell us what Pabloism was. It was assumed that everyone knew, but why then did we have to discuss it? Mandel gave us the whole watertight case against poor old Pablo. Then other people came up on the platform to briefly add their outrage at his unspeakable behaviour. But what had he done? I was probably stupider than your average Trotskyist, but I was still not grasping the point. Then something exciting happened. An old man with an American accent clambered up onto the stage. He mumbled that he wanted more than the statutory two minutes (this was a tactical mistake on his part). He said that the other side of the story needed to be heard. Now the panel looked quite alarmed. Then he did it. He announced that he was a Pabloite! Mayhem ensued. He was manhandled off the stage very quickly and where he went and what happened to him I do not know. Some of us at the back shouted, "Let him speak!" The crowed turned – this was worrying too – they were angry and they told us to be quiet. I sensed the sturdiness of the crowd, and you knew that nothing could be done. I felt helpless and a few months later I left the organisation. I looked around for another organisation before I did, but I was to discover that it was no different and stayed a very short time. There was an inherent problem, and we need to ask why.

People in left-wing organisations often make considerable sacrifices and so it's quite difficult for them to accept that they have been making sacrifices for a flawed organisation. Maybe. Or perhaps it is just the crowd – any crowd.

> There was an old man of Whitehaven
> Who danced a quadrille with a raven;
> They said, "How absurd
> To encourage the bird,"
> So they smashed the old man of Whitehaven.

I don't know who was responsible for that particular limerick which was quoted by an English teacher at school and stuck fast in my brain. It explains the phenomenon quite well. The history of the left (and the right, for that matter) is studded with the excesses of moralistic verve, which are very similar to acts by Christian crowds and invaders. The Cultural Revolution was an example on a terrifyingly large scale. One of the BBC's greatest series was *People's Century*, and there was a chilling interview with a by then middle-aged woman, who explained the terrible humiliations she and her fellow college students heaped upon their headmaster. The interviewer asked if he was a particularly oppressive man, and she replied in surprise, Oh no, he was a lovely man. He was always at the gates in the morning to welcome us in. It was just that everyone was doing this at the time.

The left has to admit that it has a problem if it is going to avoid repeating it in the future, and we're not just talking about the revolutionary left here. Decades later I was to see a similar incident at a Labour Party conference, when Wolfgang, a lifelong party member and keen supporter of CND was heckling Jack Straw. Two stewards manhandled him out of the conference hall in front of the BBC cameras, and the news editor that night correctly decided to run this episode as the first item. When I saw it on TV, I recognised the incident, although it was slightly different. A party that cannot have an open and well-ordered debate is not worthy of support, however bitter and significant the differences may be.

I don't want anyone as ignorant as I was to be left in a state of suspense, so I will explain Pabloism as it was explained to me many years later. Having been involved in the Algerian national liberation movement, he became a minister in the first Algerian government with the FLN, a coalition of "bourgeois parties". It doesn't seem that bad. In fact it sounds the sort of pragmatic act we should approve of. Purism! Purism and the need to be purer than everyone else is a probable cause of this intolerance.

Ernest Mandel wrote a book called rather optimistically, *Late Capitalism*. He also said that Russia could never revert to capitalism. Revolutions in reverse are a historical impossibility. He laughed at the absurdity of it, but lived long enough to see that he was wrong. The left attracts too many people who think they have a handle on history. They believe in political predestination.

Fourthly, my generation was alone in developing a tendency on the left towards what can only be called bad manners. This was not so much the politics of equality as a holiday from reality in which anyone who interfered with the fantasy was shouted at. Everybody wanted to prove that they were actually more left-wing than everyone else, and moral outrage was the de rigueur fashion accessory of the time. This unmannerly left was not the whole left in the seventies; it belonged to the youthful left, and particularly the youthful, middle-class left (Bradbury's *History Man* comes to mind). The right suffered from ill-mannered youth in the eighties, but we're not talking about the right here, and if this unmannerliness were simply a feature of the seventies and no more, it would be of little importance. The problem is that the phenomenon has left its trace in the left – a kind of seediness, a lack of moral direction. We must be careful about this word, "moral"; it is central to any political debate, but slips so easily into the "moralistic".

There is still a tendency on the left (no more than that) to consider the act of belonging to the left to confer such moral rectitude that left-wingers rise above morality and have no need to apply it to themselves. Strangely, New Labour, which is a fundamentalist Thatcherite credo, is the part of the "left" that is most imbued with this thinking – one of the few aspects of the seventies left that they have clung to. After them comes the "revolutionary" left, which still contains the good, the bad and the mad, which it probably always has done since Bolshevik times, though the proportions might differ. The trouble is that the organised left between those extremes seems to be very thin on the ground, although I believe it to be a huge constituency out there in the electorate, but one no politician wishes to tap – or represent.

The roots of this phenomenon are in the hedonism of the late sixties and early seventies. The revolution of the ego against the super-ego. There is the wonderful scene of a group of "revolutionaries" holed up in a requisitioned hotel in the centre of Paris, which now lies at their feet. The chief of police rings them and asks for instructions. The president is packing his bags and preparing to leave the country. The deposed powers haven't yet realised that the "revolutionaries" have no plans. This is not so much "the ends justify the means" as "the means are all the fun we need".

This was a social revolution that had the rhetoric of a political revolution.

There were in fact two revolutions, a youth social revolution and a working-class political revolution. This was much more evident in Italy, where the latter was dominant and continued for a decade, bringing enormous political and economic changes, and considerable political instability, while never actually changing the government. There was a tacit agreement that the Americans wouldn't allow it.

It was not that the social revolution was bad and the political revolution good. It was more complicated than that. The tiny group I joined in Italy belonged primarily to the social revolution, but both trends were there and the age gap coincided with that division. The older members had been in the Italian Communist Party, as had been entryists like the Militant Group in the Labour Party. They were in effect still communists. The organisation came out of the Communist Party too late, because it had been so snug inside, and the independent thinkers had already left to set up another organisation which became huge and eventually published a daily paper. I was with the rump. And I was in the rump because I just happened to end up living in a group of flats mainly populated by students and drifters, all of whom belonged to this rump organisation. I made no considered choice, and fell in with the crowd. My neighbours were the young ones and new recruits who had never been in the Communist Party. In my dopiness, I never sensed the depth of the rift between the youngsters and the oldies. After I went back to Britain, they split: the oldies continued to meet every month and predict that inevitable collapse of capitalism and the youngsters went off to have fun. They opened a literary restaurant called Stazione di Zima, after the long poem by Yevtushenko, and for a time it became a hub for cultural activities. The rift was total, but I liked both sides for different reasons – as human beings and for their political ideals – but both were out of touch with reality. That was how I got into the British sister organisation, and had to listen to Ernest Mandel, whose name had never been mentioned in Italy, even though he was the head of the same umbrella organisation, which very probably still exists. The movement seemed saner in Italy, perhaps because the whole society was affected one way or another, although the movement would soon disappear as quickly as it had emerged. Something we have seen elsewhere, most recently in Egypt and sadly over an even shorter period.

Fifthly we have sectarianism, which is largely the result of the previous four points, but is a problem of its own, and the smaller the organisation, the greater the problem. In many ways, the relationship between the Moscow-based communist movement and the various sects that either split from it or grew up around it is similar to the one between the Catholic Church and the Protestant sects. I have already stressed that religion is not politics, in spite of some remarkable parallels.[1] However, you cannot pass by this analogy, which is particularly striking given that the Churches are by definition organisations that hand down unchallengeable truths, because these were apparently laid down by God, while political parties are supposed to create their policy decisions through internal debate. Surely such organisations could never resemble each other? Of course, the divine truths were not actually written by God, who tends to be wilfully reticent on these matters, so they were actually hammered out by clerics in the Councils, Conclaves, Presbyteries, Assemblies, Synods and all manner of other committees. The scientific truths of Marxist parties were also hammered out in small committees and ratified under the old threat, "Don't let our enemies think that we're divided."

The large organisation is more stable, partly because the

1 See Emilio Gentile, *Politics as Religion* (Princeton and Oxford: PUP 2006), trans. by George Staunton

idea of starting again from scratch is off-putting to dissidents, however much they are hounded, and partly because large organisations know that they have to live with a degree of dissidence and it is more a matter of keeping it under control. None of these restraints apply to the sect or groupuscule, once they have struck out into the wilderness, and some of them are so small, they're little more than large families. The Catholic Church is still a political power, particularly in Italy, but it is not the power it once was, and so it is more tolerant than it used to be (although there are small cycles; it was more tolerant under John XXIII and Paul VI than under John Paul II and Benedict XVI). It disapproved of radical priests such as Don Milani and Padre Balducci, but it did not expel them. When such people die, the Church waits to see if there there's going to be a cult, and if there is, they fight it for a period. If the cult proves to be stubborn, then they suddenly accept it and co-opt it. You can learn a lot in two thousand years. The Soviet Union changed a great deal over its brief history, but it never developed a very mature attitude to dissidence, even in its most tolerant periods. There's a lack of conviction behind incessant self-promotion, which the Americans also suffer from, and thus have to get their children to swear allegiance to their flag every morning. Time is one of the factors in legitimacy, and youthful states need to work harder.

The question that arises from these two cases is this: is the large organisation responsible for the fragmentation of the smaller ones? I think it probably is: take the Second International as another example. It had no centre, and each country developed its own social-democratic or socialist party, and they joined the international. There was no centre like Moscow or Rome, and they were autonomous. They did travel in more or less the same direction, but they were not coerced, and most importantly they did not fragment as much as the communist parties linked to the

Communist International would do. In fact, the Second International, although diminished by the arrival of the Communist one, remained reasonably stable. I look on the collapse of the Soviet Union as a disaster for Russia and a disaster for humanity, although this was not my opinion at the time. One benefit it may have brought could be an end to the fragmentation of the left. But at the moment the left is so weak in the West, it is impossible to judge.

Sectarianism often arises from the fanciful idea that organisations should have a "position" on every damn thing, even if they're tiny. Political sects fall out over the most obscure points of dogma. If politics is the art of the possible, members of small political groups are not in politics in the strict sense of the term; they're in a kind of sport and the important thing is to win the argument. As there is no sports body to judge who has won and who hasn't, all the sects decide that they have won, and the other ones are irrelevant.

The intensity of the dislikes between sects is quite over-powering, particularly between the two halves of a sect that has just split. These newly created and depleted groupuscules hate each other more than they hate capitalism or anything else they're supposed to hate. In Italy, a group divided over-night and in the morning its members were confused about which part of the party they were in. Adding to their confusion was the fact that both sides produced their weekly newspaper and both were denouncing the other in more or less the same language. Which was the proper Communist Party of Italy (Marxist-Leninist)? They showed a little maturity by agreeing to put a red line on one masthead and a black one on the other.

All this is an intolerable waste of time and energy. Every party must have different ideas within its membership, if the membership is made up of human beings and not automa-tons. Or perhaps not. Perhaps the natural way of doing poli-tics is a series of shifting alliances in which the allies pretend to agree on all things for the duration of each alliance. More complex than robots, human beings are not ideal for rational organisation. Another question we might ask is, is this something peculiarly male? Would women do a better job? I cannot answer any of these questions.

I will, however, end with one answer I do have ready. I have said that the only distinction that should divide us is the one of class and redistribution. It follows then that the left needs only one party. People can have erudite conversations about degenerated workers' states and state capitalism, although my life is too short for them. They can disagree over priorities and the whys and wherefores. They can even disagree over gradual and revolutionary change, traditionally an important distinction within the left. Revolutionaries are not people who want to blow up the houses of parliament; they are people who believe that when the "objective conditions exist" (that's a blast from the past) and the forces are arrayed against each, they're on the side of change and ultimately change can only come about through violent overthrow. Those objective conditions are unlikely to occur, particularly in the West. *Sine die*. Let's not fall out over what isn't going to happen. We are up against a technological state that has only two forces that can breach its absolute power: non-violence and mass movement (in that order). We can forget the storming of the Winter Palace.

Whether or not justifications existed for the Leninist model (and we could have another erudite conversation on that), they no longer do. The left never had to change its long-term aims (*pace* Tony Blair and his kind); what we need to do is change the way we do politics, and organise around the defence of our social rights. The rest will follow, and its exact direction is unpredictable.

Conclusion

I have said that in one of my dialogues, the three principal participants were Socialist Voice, Liberal Voice and Cynical Voice. These were and to some extent still are the three voices in my head or, in more rationalist terminology, what I call the three irresolvables. The first irresolvable is one that is well known to the Italian left, which experienced the first fascist regime for a twenty-year period. It is the conflict between justice and freedom and was reflected in the movements that adhered to Liberal-Socialism. This is the most pressing thing we have to resolve, but as something that can never be resolved; it has to be resolved anew in every generation through some kind of ad hoc compromise. I would push the balance quite far in favour of justice: the state should insist that everyone work in an unskilled working-class job for at least a year. I do not mean something akin to *servizio civile*, a replacement for national service in Italy whereby conscientious objectors could work in charities assisting the low-paid and destitute. I mean living the life of the low-paid and destitute. This is a restriction on people's liberty, I admit. It is perhaps a regrettable one, but it is the only way to genuinely educate people about the life of the poorest in society and the ever-present threat of unemployment which drives their behaviour. However, many of those who will be outraged at my authoritarianism would not bat an eyelid at the idea of national service or conscription to force young men into senseless drudgery designed to kill humanity in each of them and train them to kill others when ordered to. It is my own experience of life that the middle classes cannot understand the injustices, humiliations and occasional violence that are inflicted on working people unless they experience them for themselves or at least witness them up close from a different viewpoint. In this manner people would learn that the only truly bourgeois freedom – the freedom to control human beings through financial inducement – is wage slavery and therefore an infringement on the freedom of others. This economic freedom therefore has to be either abolished or severely restricted. After a generation or two, this practice of enforced unskilled labour might pervade social attitudes so deeply that it would no longer be necessary.

The second irresolvable is the one between cynicism and freedom. Cynicism says that freedom is always simply the right of individuals and classes to do what they wish, and their wishes are only enforced where those individuals, classes or imagined "ethnicities" have the power to enforce them. Cynicism says that freedom does not exist, only power. The Israelis say that they have a right to use the land they live on because it was given to them by God (secular Israelis have more complex and Byzantine justifications), while the Palestinians say they have a right to use the land because it belonged to their parents, grandparents and many generations before them. In fact, the Israelis have freedom to use the land because they have the tanks, jet fighters, artillery, munitions, propaganda machinery, lobbies, alliances and atom bombs to enforce that freedom. Cynicism takes yet another tack, and says that there is in any case no free will. We are all simply driven by the chemistry of our bodies and brains. Ultimately we need to enjoy life and accept the world as it is. We need to take as much as we can get, and you cannot change the course of history. Freedom argues back that freedom has to be achieved consciously and, in any case, only exists in consciousness, where it brings its own spiritual pleasures. Freedom allies itself with justice to counterbalance the dangers of cynicism, and together these bring more peace than the insatiable pleasures of greed and desire.

By engaging with society in the name of justice, an individual can create an inner freedom, which is almost unassailable – almost, because with physical and psychological torture you can destroy freedom even in the strongest person. In fact, we are all called to freedom, but some of us defend it with more vigour than others. The thing that weakens our resolve most is not our DNA, our diet, our gods, our stars or our destinies; it is the failure to believe in our own moral capabilities. We are social animals and, perhaps uniquely, we are moral animals. Cynicism undermines that with the potent arguments of common sense. Hannah Arendt rightly spoke of the banality of evil, but it might have been better to speak of the evil of banality. However, cynicism's acceptance of the complexity and limitations of human society is a voice that to some extent has to be listened to, although the destructiveness of its world-weary nagging often grates and feels overly predictable. You can redress the balance by recalling the repulsive piety of those who think they embody justice and the arrogance of those who talk of absolute freedom. Cynicism accuses the other two of oversimplification and to some degree it is right. As freedom involves interaction between the individual and ideas, freedom ultimately is strengthened by education, because education frees the individual not only from the self but also from the strictures of the society in which that individual lives.

The third irresolvable, between cynicism and justice resembles the second irresolvable in many of the arguments, because cynicism also adds a touch of realism to what justice can and cannot achieve. However, cynicism has an even more negative role in its relationship with justice, which is an intrinsically social good, and thus creates a slight circular movement around the three irresolvables (freedom is more undermined by justice than it is by cynicism, justice more by cynicism than by freedom and cynicism more by freedom than by justice). Because cynicism encourages inaction and acceptance of the status quo, a society in which cynicism is pervasive is a society adrift – much as ours is at the moment. Widespread social acceptance of the world as it is does not restrict the freedom of the mind to speculate. In fact, power feels so secure during a period of pervasive cynicism that it is often less authoritarian. Lone voices are allowed to go about their business – not encouraged but ignored, because suppression might only draw attention to them. But pervasive cynicism cripples a society and takes away its ability to evolve consciously through some kind of political process. This seesaw relationship between cynicism and justice explains the dramatic shifts between generations within the same culture. It is the reason why countries feel like different countries as the decades slip by. Marx was ignored during most of his lifetime, but later those who espoused his ideas would face repression, including those in "liberal" Britain. Our triangle of irresolvables comes alive in history.

I have said that there is a slight circular motion around the three irresolvables, because although there are currents running in both directions, the current in one direction is slightly stronger than the other one.

The cynical voice is the most dangerous, but we should not be deaf to it. You want to believe in humanity and to hope. This makes life sweeter and is therefore of benefit to you, but at the same time that persistent voice of cynicism says, "How can you? Did you not see what A did to B last week, and how the pompous idiot C bragged about what he had done? Do you really believe that this humanity is capable of making the changes it needs to make?" And in the name of justice and freedom you wilfully suppress that hideous voice, while accepting its element of truth. People do this all the time: they force themselves to take a more positive view of the society around them. Is that not a semi-religious moment, whatever your religious views? The word "religion" derives from the Latin verb, *religo*, to bind fast, to hold fast and perhaps originally to bind again or reconnect. In Italian, this meaning of binding society together remains, but in a hierarchical sense: so the expression, "There's no longer any religion" is not about Church attendance or indeed religion as we understand it; it means that "There's no longer any respect for those who deserve it."[1] This is the binding together of a hierarchy. Religion can have that function, and that is why it is quite reasonably distrusted on the left. But distrust should not lead to intolerance. The infinitive *religare* immediately suggests the Italian *rilegare*, which means to bind in the sense of binding a book. Book-binding and religion having the same etymology in a language is a good start to this argument. But how do we want to be bound together? This is the fundamental difference between right and left. Do we want to be bound together in deference and within a chain of command, or do we want to be bound together in a dialogue with each other as equals? Equality should not be the equality of the football stadium, where everyone is a spectator passively bound to all the others while an elite plays the game, which is how real existing socialism often worked. Equality that liberates is equality that binds together while retaining individuality. Often I have found that this idea receives opposition on the left, which derives from a strange idea that the mass really is a mass and the working class potentially can think in the same way, if only false consciousness could be removed. No just and free society could ever be uniform. Equality concerns distribution of wealth, not what people do with their lives. A good society cannot be created without education and tolerance, and it cannot

---

1 The Italian original: "Non c'è più religione."

survive without the understanding that a permanently good society has to be reargued and refined incessantly and never quite achieves its aims. Within that good society, conflicts and tensions will and must remain.

Perhaps at the risk of pushing this model too far, we could argue that the right kind of *religare* would occur in an ideal state of freedom and justice. In any case, where there's a proper balance between *religare* and cynicism, you have scepticism, but I wouldn't know where that balance is, and it is right that everyone finds their own. Each generation finds its own balance, and each generation rebels against the imbalance of the previous generation, creating a new and often opposite imbalance. The human condition is that we are pushed and shoved by these forces, and different ones predominate in different periods of our lives. There is also a tendency for different forces to predominate in society during particular periods. Cynicism, always there, predominated in the nineties and continued until the financial crisis. It brings a stultifying conformism and senseless, ruthless competition. On the other hand, periods of insane moral outrage bind people together in terrifying social hysteria: the *parabolani* of Alexandria, the iconoclasts of Byzantium, the nicely termed *piagnoni* of Savonarola's Florence,[2] and the Red Guards of the Cultural Revolution are extreme examples. These were all people with such a tin ear for that cynical voice that they invented a conformism more terrifying than that of cynicism. Not all forms of equality are good. Fortunately such periods are relatively short, but their passing usually ushers in extreme cynicism and social amnesia, as though society's entire stock of utopian vision had been consumed in a short but crazed festival of finger-pointing.

---

2 i piagnoni: the whingers.

One concept that is particularly dangerous is the perfectibility of humanity, which is associated with the less questionable concept of progress. Freud spoke of "human ideals, the notion, formed by human beings, of the possible perfection of the individual person, the nation and humanity as a whole".[3] It could be said that this was the road that led to the Gulag (Freud did not necessarily agree, as he was only listing the features generally associated with civilisation, as they were perceived in the late twenties, and he summarised positivist thinking very well while adding some healthy scepticism – an old man's work and a great extended essay). Progress, if it exists, does not perfect society or individuals, who are and must remain mixed. Religions have a better understanding of this: they accept the world as it is, and some might say they are too accepting. Political movements are in a hurry, and that is understandable, given the magnitude of human misery, but you cannot perfect people and you can only change their behaviour rapidly through terror. Even then it is arguable that you can change them in the direction you want or that any changes made will be permanent. The best we can ask is better education that will liberate minds and allow future generations to make better decisions, but we cannot know what they will be like.

The arguments for and against progress are finely balanced. It appears that progress, like happiness, occurs when people are busy with other things. Progress, if it exists, concerns the ability of societies to organise themselves more efficiently and more equitably, often as a result of improving technology. We live in a period of increasing disorder and lawlessness, in which there is very little long-term planning and educational standards are slipping. That we consume more is meaningless, if these levels of consumption are not

3 Sigmund Freud, *Civilisation and Its Discontents* (London: Penguin, 2002), trans. by David McLintock, p. 31.

sustainable. Progress, when it occurs in the short term, creates new problems that could not have been predicted, but when such sudden progress starts to unravel, the negative features of progress remain in place. Even a statist like me, who wants to see renationalisation, an end to private education and the exclusion of private companies from the health service, is concerned by the constant state encroachment on our freedoms. All regimes, whether of the left or the right, have overseen increasing interference of the state in the private lives of its citizens. In the West, armies of officials – often not state officials but officials working for private corporations to which the state has delegated its powers – are poking around in people's lives, making judgements on scarce information and handing down quasi-judicial sentences. Recent revelations demonstrate that the American and British governments are spying on their citizens to a level that the Stasi could only have dreamt of.

I have asserted that there is a soul, but my definition is, I admit, a little vague. Reason suggests there isn't, but experience suggests that there is. If we're hit by a falling brick and survive with a damaged brain, we are no longer the same person. Logically, it appears that we are, as Dr. Swaab said, no more than our brains. Nietzsche crumpled while embracing a horse that was being beaten, his brain destroyed by work and illness. Walter Kaufmann provides us with a dramatic portrayal of his working day, as his brilliance fought with everything: his isolation, his manic ideas, his failing eyesight and his failing health. Then all these things were gone. He was a shell, an object that could be manoeuvred by others, and emptied of intellect and integrity. He became an object wholly owned by his hellish sister.[4] The will was gone,

---

4 Walter Kaufmann is also good on the sister; see W. Kaufmann, *Nietzsche* (Princeton: PUP, 1968, 1950[1]).

but what a will! That will, now broken, was highlighted by its absence. The body lived on, but the soul had died. Or the bit we didn't understand had died. The animal husk was there, and in its tragic state was much more comprehensible. Which attracts our admiration more, the husk or the will? Clearly it is that indefinable will – the soul. How can we then say that it does not exist? That we cannot pinpoint it, does not mean that it doesn't exist (it doesn't mean that it does either). There is no reason to believe that the soul is immortal, just because this has been the dominant belief for millennia. But the mortal soul is something we should be looking for in others. It is the element that makes human relationships significant.

If I were to sum up my disjointed thoughts as they emerge from these assorted essays, I would say that they concern the quality of human relationships, as suggested by the thinking of Martin Buber. Those relationships are caught up in the triad of freedom, justice and cynicism. Cynicism is in our minds, freedom is both in our minds and in society, and justice is in society. The circular movement of the triad also concerns the relationship between ideas and society, and at the centre of that is the will which makes things happen, but we have to take into account the enormous constraints on what we can achieve. Cynicism is that brake on free will, a note of realism, but it should be no more than a thin voice, or it becomes something that debilitates us.

By the Metre

The Mystic

I died and having died
could no more feel the touch of life
but lived, and living, moved
within a shell, which hollowed out,
contains a wealth of emptied thoughts
that settle, like dried leaves, lining
the bottom of my soul, sediment
of a life that's passed away.

My brother fights with hatred in his heart.
Because he fights, he lives and hopes.
Because he hopes, he builds
a future in this head.
Because he builds, he feels his body
move within a world to which he still belongs.

The foreign soldiers came and fought
a folly of a war.
They knew how to be killed and killed
in turn. They shone in our sun
and smelt of milk and acrid tears.
The fears they brought never left with them,
but clung like mist to hills and mountain roads,
and dampened our dry hearts
and dulled the brightness of our songs
the students later took.

And took for good; their rigid rules –
some vain hope of order where war
decreed the chaos of our lives.
The order clashed with other orders
better ordered, better armed and
driven by some rapacious force.

Then there was the wedding feast;
a column of our cars was snaking through
the hamlets, orchards, arid tracts
of this, our Afghan land.
And yes, the joy, the smiling crowds,
the waving wedding guests, gleeful
on the back of trucks, their open hearts,
their loving talk, the child's excited chatter,
enveloped in a thin, translucent cloud of dust.

Fierce, so fierce, the horror came,
the airplane stumbled in our skies
and cast its bombs like seeds of death,
and swooped and swung like the groom's mother
who moving in a trance does dance and show
her bitter jubilation.
Something starts and something ends.
Something changes now forever.

And so did I. I died when the moment died,
and quickly such a crop of bloodied bodies
stretched in the thicker dust of wailing sorrow.
Life died in me, but my hollow corpse
moves on, or stills itself in huddled form
beside the pleasant river.
Long hours I spend in empty thought,
while all around they argue, scream
and laugh again, bold builders
of their future selves. They mix
with foreign lords and my brother's
band of fighters – each the image of their foe.

Like a diseased tree whose healthy bark
conceals its vacant trunk that stays erect
and dismal waits the blessed wind that'll fell it,
I cross-legged sit and nothing stirs
the desiccated leaves of thought.
They call me mad for looking on
the madness of their world in silence.

Life's a Bitch

(or The Deist's God Goes Walking in a Back Lane)

The father, silent in his thoughts, guided
the pushchair down the darkened lane.
The child, placid in its existence seemed –
unprovoked did scream an anguished scream
that parted from the heart, the centre
of his being. Red eyes, red face, red hair:
red fury scolded sky and all
the hapless clutter of that narrow lane,
where human life was only known
by it detritus. Father continued
unconcerned, unseeing of the fragile load
that life unloaded on his eternal tread.
He judged but did not intervene.

The Poverty of Wealth

"How poor you are, my gilded friend,"
I said and watched his wrinkled face.
"I?" he laughed and heaved his chest
with grandeur suited to his sharpened state.
"I have a corporation listed on the bourse,
a yacht whose cabinets are filled with drink
to keep my retinue tight within the joyless joy
the sycophant encounters while securing
comfort for his future days living in my shadow.
I have a house so large, I cannot know
the number of its rooms, the meanders
of its patronage to souls deflated by my power.
I am a king whose subjects do not know my name;
I little care for vassalage from those so low
they cannot see the strings I pull to make them move
their hollow carcasses across their broken dreams.
You call me poor, you ragged man who beckons
with the arrogance of thought. Clear my path
or I shall crush you like the worm you are."
"A sorry state is yours indeed," I sympathised
with all my heart. "What you call carcasses
are full of hope and gentle kindness
that lives forever in the human soul.
A carcass passive like a fallen leaf told one
such as you to cast away his riches
and then to follow. They crushed him
as the worm they reckoned him to be,
and then their children made him king of kings,
who pronounces on all their hidden wants
and justifies their power. His real children

are the poor, who hold eternal riches
in their sagging arms. His real children
are the abused whose names are dragged
through streams of mud. His real children
are the dispossessed whose voices
are not heard. And yet what riches
they encounter on their heavy trudge
through life: their loves, their likes, their losses
all come carrying them to the greenness of their death,
unlike yours, that lonely thing that divides you
from the barren fertility of wealth."
"Away you madman. I'll not touch the contagion
of your thought. I'll not whip the fool, though
you deserve it well," he seethed.
"I am a shadow of your own fear," I answered him again,
"and similar fools will come as the sunlight
plays on each green budding leaf. I am each second
of your corroded brain. Each second that cries
for freedom from the stuff that in making stuff is fecund."

Where the Beauty, Where the Hope

A young man walked his dog,
and his bravado too.
Behind, modern builds of square and Lego look
grouped their sadness in a lot
of awkward silence
at their lifeless dress.
He swung the stick that held a ball,
well-chewed no doubt, and off it went,
the dog in chase. Predictable
as the starting of that sullen day.

The parkland's paths he held within his head,
and well he knew that none
could lead him from the drudge his life'd become.

Beyond, what else would be there but strangers
staring in disbelief at the ilk of conformity
he'd take with him? More dull hillocks,
shocks of weeds, and rivers running dark
and loaded with the discards of consumer life.

Where the beauty, where the hope?

Scientific Progress

The words that are not said,
but shouted from the roofs
are hollowed out, and stripped
of sense and sound that carries
doubt and complex quirks of knowing not
the whys and wherefores of the beauties
of this world...

The sea loch's vast, and paints a mottled blue
before my eyes. Beyond, a strip of brownish flatland
catches a patch of brightness
the clouds have failed to grasp.
Below, near to the rocks, a man –
a darkened silhouette – busies in the wind,
as does his jacket – blue, I think.
The purpose of his rushing back and forth
eludes me, as do many things.

The kitchen clock is running late
but beats the rhythm of our time
no less. A half hour passes and still
he's running left and right. He has a rope!
I've grown my knowledge base! And then,
he's gone and took those busied moments
he'd displayed. In the stillness of the quiet field below
a grey goose waddles slow and sure
about the business of eating grass.

The empty washing line jerks rhythmic,
pointless, endless in the breeze. The clouds
closed off the light illumining
the drab thread of a Highland town.
All has darkened, and in that dull light,
my not knowing lifts my heart,
excites my sense of living
in this most intoxicating point in space.

Time and my Wife

I have wasted many things
and many things have taught me why
I wasted all these years. Life!
Ambition too came sneaking through the grass;
pleasure thickened lazy days
and busy times dried out the human humours
of my heart. I spoke and held too keenly
to my thoughts. I loved not women real
in heart and mind, but constructs of what
I wanted them to be. I gave, but wanted back
my gift with interest on account.
I studied, foolish in my wish to be the best at something
no one values any more.

And then you came and held me strong;
led me out and took me to the vantage
of my faults. The pleasure is in the act itself:
the giving, loving, feeling, seeing the tight
compactness of this lonely, cluttered world
in which a perfect sun does rise on Cox's Beach
and wintry blasts do scour the Artic wastes.
Every life is a journey between the one and the other.
At the beach, you dug your hands deep and laughed apace
with all the brightness of your soul, and sand like snow
weeping fell and carried in the wind.

Riflusso[1]

All of the words the day had sprung
The night has buried now.
Now do the hopes we cherished then
Seem dark and shameful to our weaker sort
And those who took the ride.

From high upon our greatest chance,
The structures of our hierarking chiefs,
Whose loyalty to equal lives was largely
Founded on their grand usage of the state
And the comfort of their over-equal fate,
Made war and weapons quite grotesque
And not inclined to free mankind –
But to destroy it.

---

1 *Riflusso*: a return to conservative thinking; disengagement with politics – another word we don't have in English.

On Seeing a Photo of Victims' Skulls from the Cambodian Genocide

The grinning teeth and vacant stares, they have no purpose,
nor do their daily cares sift and shake the fibre of their bones.
Which was the slender lad whose passions stalked a female
frame
he could not banish from this thoughts? Where is the girl
who sang so sweet, her feelings echoed in her schoolmates'
heads?
The brooding teacher vanquished by the failure of her
years,
the greedy trader whose mind just counts the movements
of his wealth, the sullen housewife once instructed in French
and foreign ways, the brawny warehouse worker who
seldom sought
to cause offence or darken others' days, they all vacated
what was theirs
and hastened off or were. They left these shells,
indictments of a crime so foul,
it weighs upon the human mind and questions who we are.

I see these skulls so neatly ordered on their shelves like
books or pans
or useful things – they're not. Read them if you can, I
cannot find
the syntax of their hollow laugh; they have one letter, that
is all,
and look alike: ghastly fruits grown in the garden of our
most gruesome thoughts.

To stare at their staring orbs is to intrude on others' holy grief
and to turn away is turning from what should never be forgot,
into oblivion's unfeeling want of nothing but the comfort of
the self,
blinder than these dear blinded and hurted discards of souls
whose silence is their loudest roar.

This

Conscience and its failures.

To *this* and all the sadness of this world
I write these words of happy oblivion
desired and almost gained! I felt
and feared that at some future date
I would feel no more.
No more hear the cries of pain that sear the night
and invade my dreams. But then I felt and always feared
that I would never cease to feel those pointless wounds
that never brought a balm to those who scream
and doubtless suffer out of sight.

Memory and the struggle to retain it. We live in history but cannot see it. Our will is feeble but essential in its feebleness

This is a struggle to retain – to re-evoke those moments
of the past that could slip away like leaves scattered by
a gust
or simply rotting where they lie, losing all the colours
they displayed
on the branch or brightened and nuanced during early
stages
of their desiccation.
Memories take on bright golds, yellows and reddish browns
burnished by their retelling. And then they too rot or
carry
far off in rushing time so they can come back blasting
into our brains heavy with new meanings. These joys
and bitter blows lift or shatter hopes and tell us truths
of what *this* is – the crazy thing that we all know well
and yet cannot define.

I try to recall what I witnessed standing safely at a
                              hotel window,
while the smallest cogs of history turned and ground
                              another people's
hopes to dust, as they always do. I saws the crowd of
                              sans-culottes,
then full of faces but faceless now the image fades – a
                              crowd of Bengalis
in their lungis and singlets marching by the million to
                              the racetrack,
hemmed in on every side by soldiers wielding batons
                              lethargically,
beating without passion, without zest, because they
                              had to.
And these same soldiers, Bengalis too, some months
                              from then
would fight and die for a nation they would never see,
forgotten in history's unforgiving flood.

The image fades but not what I have learnt: there are
few wholly good or evil men, only individuals swept
                              along
and now and then resisting – vainly – all the vicious
                              power
of that amorphous flood.

This is to feel with all our senses sharpened by the will
                              to be –
to be in the moment and forget
for once the weight of years to come or drawn behind
that drags us down or will.
This moment sweet – to lie within another's arms and
                              feel
the smoothness of her skin, the involucre of her warm

*We live
through the
experience of
our senses*

and naked soul. This moment when the wind comes in
and bites the cheeks with unrelenting force – the force
of nature
that cohabits still this manufactured land. This lunch
when food plays long and vibrant on our budding nerves
and slips forgotten into the abyss of our unending needs.
And how we shout and turn upon each other with our
cares,
our thoughts, our strong beliefs of all the things we
cannot know
with any certitude. We fret and manipulate our words,
wanting to win – but what? And will they understand
those words
in a century, in a decade's time or even in ten days
from now?
We have the now. We stand in it and declare our truths.

And now those vinous moments of the now are in the
past
and mainly inhabit my memories of Italy, a land where
they know how to talk and did. The flasks of wine, the
grated cheese
that smelt, the oil so new it stings upon the tongue, all
those heady,
heady words that melt within the brain and touch
those nerves
that, for too long, have not had anything to feel or grasp.

Inferno here
on earth.
Suffering
teaches but
also destroys.

This hell, this hole: how many times do we return to the
darkness
of the past? This earthly hell is surely not followed by
unearthly one.

This feeling trapped within the self, a bag of nerves
                                        that jangle
not just with our own pain, but also with compassion.
Our own pain, if it does not break us, makes us strong
                                        and therefore
serves a purpose. If ever you foolishly dwell on the
                        your pains of the past,
then take a look at the pompous prick who pampered
                                        all his life
now smugly observes from his position of great or petty
                                        power
his secure kingdom of unappreciated delights and
                        honours granted
for his acceptance of hierarchy's chain into which he
                        so snugly fits.
Such people at the slightest slight react with anger or
                        self-pity.
They do not know, success locks the cell
in which the self is caught
and makes a prison of a tight abode.

This is also made of raptures, those moments of escape
when mind pinpoints one thing and distils its pleasure
from some problematic of a kind our passions can
                        delight in.
A sport, a broke-down car, a mountain face, a place
                        unknown,
a book, a canvass stabbed with paint, these all suppress
                        the self,
throw wide the cell door and reveal a limitless plain of
                        ways
and ways of doing, seeing, moving, searching, calling,
                        expressing

*Where my
arts council
grant? I need
to express
myself – my
inner message
surely
everyone
must want to
hear.*

to others and to oneself the permutations of how we
                                                 can consume
this, this elusive thing we never notice until it is at risk.

The artist measured up his work with steady eyes and
                                                 critically
calculated all those marks of paint: the colours,
                                 contrast, composition
brushwork, pose, poise, expression of the hurt, pathos
of the suffering saint – a noose loosely fitted round his
                                         scraggy neck.
Then he leapt, large brush in hand heavy with black
                                     paint. And how
he laboured with that destructive arm, which spread a
                                       night across
the surface of his work. No dawn would resurrect the
                                   fearsome portrayal
of a martyred end. But still he paints a lonely figure
whose afflicted corpse-to-be stands free of ground, of
                                 time, of pain perhaps,
levitated by the energy of sacrifice. The hooded
                             hangman's noose is gone,
so has the crowd that gleeful jostled and stretched
                             forward to enjoy the show.
The light of the heavens triumphant has been dulled,
                                 so loneliness remains.

Microcosm and macrocosm *This* contains those civic moments
by which we measure out the passing years:
birth, pair-bonding of some kind, birth of children,
the repeating cycle of their *this*, and then death.
This, rather grandly, also posits such events within

the timeline history dictates: "two years before the
war",
"just after the recession", "when they landed on the
moon".
This is how the micro- and the macrocosm
should relate: their unequal trajectories are not
mechanic things – the individual can rebel and should.
This belongs beyond oneself and beyond the triteness
of one's age and its conformist certitudes.

This is this little thing that seems so big, this life we
share
this tangle of shattered nerves, this string of thoughts
that lonely twist and turn, fly up into the airless light
where ideas are born and the gods sing, or sink into
the deep,
depressing water that presses on our lungs
and cruel clears away all hope,
where drags us down the leaden weight
of that elusive thing we call the real.
Like all small things, this life's capable of endless
variegations, and the stack of stuff
of which it's made can be shuffled in so many ways.
In one backyard behind a block of flats,
a history of lives can be played out,
and more happens in one small child's brain
than in several light-years of space.
This is a divine gift we have to please ourselves,
to please others and to waste,
and of course regret.

*What this is.
You haven't
guessed?*

When life's end comes, it's a book that's writ and left unread.
No chance to correct and polish here –
the pages turning yellow. It's a story
randomly told and what it lacks and incoheres
is made up for
in tragicomic commerce of traducements
and prodigal human passions.